KURT WARNER

And the last shall be first

By Rich Wolfe and Bob Margeas

Cover Design by Jack W. Davis

Edited by Kim Heusel

Interior Design by Kim Heusel

DEDICATION

To Josh McDowell, who wrote the most important book
I've ever read,
and
to Tom Shrader, who gave it to me.

ACKNOWLEDGMENTS

The people who helped me put this book together could be sorted into three groups, probably. I don't know what the three groups are or why I would want to sort them, but since everything else in this book is sorted into groups, I thought this would be an appropriate place to start. I'm sure I could figure out the three groups if I had to.

This book was the idea of Bob Margeas in Des Moines, Iowa. His infectious smile and enthusiasm is wonderful to behold. On the other hand, if anything in this book bothers you, be sure to go directly to Doctor Bob with your complaint.

Sincere thanks to Rick Smith of the St. Louis Rams, Matt Fernandes and Mike Smith of the *St. Louis Post-Dispatch*, Tom Alex and Janeane Lynch in Des Moines, Mr. Walter B. Planner in Davenport, Iowa, the excellent baseball historian Bill James of Lawrence, Kansas, Cory Laslocky and the gang at NFL Films, Robert Anderson and Heather Woody in Cedar Falls and Ben Settles and all the "Ring-Tailed Tooters" in St. Louis.

The best part was the help, encouragement, and shared laughter with old friends in Cedar Rapids and the excitement of meeting new ones in St. Louis.

I am personally responsible for all errors, misstatements, inaccuracies, omissions, commissions, comminglings, communisms, fallacies.... If it's wrong and it's in this book, it's my fault. But thanks anyway to Kim Heusel, Holly Kondras, and Jack Davis for production help.

My thanks to Special K for everything, and especially, to Ellen Brewer, the most beautiful, talented and nicest woman in Edmond, Oklahoma, if not the entire state, and clearly the best typist any Sooner has seen since Troy Aikman of Henryetta (OK) High School won the state high school boys' typing championship in 1983.

CHAT ROOMS

PREFACE

In August of 1999, I was more likely to be struck by lightning while honeymooning with Miss America than Kurt Warner was to become the NFL's MVP. You were more likely to see a left-handed female golfer than to ever see Kurt Warner become MVP of the Super Bowl.

At least I knew who he was. Like Warner, I'm a native Iowan. Iowans tend to have tremendous pride in their state and if any native son reaches the big time, almost all Iowans – no matter their current residence – root hard for that person to make good.

Thus, during Kurt and Brenda's Excellent Adventure in the Rams' magical carpet Super Bowl season, even though I was in Pittsburgh doing signings for a book on Mike Ditka, I was well aware that he became the Rams' starting quarterback in late preseason, and true to every Hawkeye sports fan, his stats were the first ones checked on Monday morning.

On my way back home to Arizona at the start of the millennium, I stopped in Des Moines to see my dentist, Bob Margeas. Bob looks and acts like Andre Agassi except he has more money, less hair, dates prettier girls, and gives better advice like, "Always wear brown ties. They go better with your yellow teeth!"

While scanning the Ditka book, *Da Coach*, Dr. Bob said, "Why don't you do a book on Kurt Warner?" After saying "No" almost immediately, there was ample time to rethink that answer when Bob took a lengthy call from a patient...Kurt Warner...a real "rags-to-riches" story...A role model...an Iowa guy...A good guy...A great fund-raiser for his school...the Rams have an outside shot at going to the Super Bowl....Do a book on a Rams player and I could spend time in St. Louis in the spring where I could watch "my" baseball Cardinals....Hmmmm.

After all, I had grown up 56 miles east of where Warner was raised – about three bottles of tabasco sauce sooner – near the mean streets of Lost Nation, Iowa, where I had avidly read every Horatio Alger-style book of John R. Tunis. Remember *The Kid from Left Field*, Clair Bee's Chip Hilton series, all of the Frank Merriwell and The Ozark Ike comic strips? All preached the virtues of hard work, perseverance, obedience, and sportsmanship where, sooner or later, one way or another, some forlorn underweight, underdog would succeed beyond his wildest dreams in the sports arena.

But Kurt Warner was better than Horatio Alger. He was real life. He was more natural than Roy Hobbs. He was a Rudy with talent, a John Daly who doesn't drink. He was "manna from Heaven" to the NFL and every other beleaguered professional sports league: The Washington Redskins had just sold for 800 million dollars although several other teams may have had a higher street value. More and more players were widowers by choice, Wilt Chamberlain boasted of having slept with 20,000 women (I'm not sure that I've even peed that many times), NFL general managers were hoping that bail money didn't count against the salary cap, Cowboys fans didn't know whether to root for the defense or the prosecution, and O.J. was down to about six commandments. And along comes Kurt Warner, just as if Johnny Unitas had been cryogenically frozen for forty years from a simpler time when Elvis was the King, Little Richard was the Queen, and Bruce Springsteen wasn't in middle management yet; when no NFL game could start after four in the afternoon because Commissioner Pete Rozelle wanted every kid to be able to see the game in its entirety before bedtime.

By the time Dr. Bob got off the phone, I was so excited about the possibilities of a Kurt Warner book that I almost told him to keep drilling "'cause I felt lucky."

From the age of ten, I've been a serious collector of sports books. During that time – for the sake of argument, let's call it thirty years – my favorite book style is the "eavesdropping" type where the subject talks in his own words without the "then he said" or "the air was so thick you could cut it with a butter knife" waste of verbiage that makes it harder to get to the meat of the matter. Books like Lawrence Ritter's *The Glory of Their Times*, Donald Honig's *Baseball When the Grass was Real*, or any of my friend Pete Golenbock's books like *Fenway* or *Wrigleyville*. I'm a sports fan, first and foremost. I don't care what the publisher, editors, or critics think, I'm only interested in the sports fan reader having an enjoyable time.

Plus, it's an excellent way to cover up the fact that my stories ramble – Hey, I'm Irish so it's not only legal, it's expected. Interesting and sometimes hilarious stories were cut from the Ditka book that didn't deal directly with Ditka, but, nevertheless, sports fans would have loved reading. So if you feel like there is too much material in this book about Arena football or Steve "Sudden Death" Sabol, don't complain to the publisher, just jot your criticisms down on the back of a twenty dollar bill and send them to me.

I gotta go now. The phone is ringing. Maybe it's Phyllis George. Hey, it could happen. Just ask Kurt Warner if there's an expiration date on dreams.

Rich Wolfe
Springfield/Branson, Missouri

PREVIOUS BOOKS BY RICH WOLFE

Sports Fans Who Made Headlines

I Remember Harry Caray

Da Coach (Mike Ditka)

Fandemonium

Dick Vermeil, former head coach, St. Louis Rams

FOREWORD

I think I can evaluate what it takes to be a player at most posi tions and especially at quarterback. I just thought there was something special about Kurt Warner, and I just didn't know how long it was going to take me to find out or give him the oppor- tunity to do so. In fact, the other night he was here for dinner, and he said, "Coach, do you remember what you told me when I made the squad a year ago?" I said, "No, I remember talking to you and all that stuff." He said, "You told me I had a chance to be some- thing special." And as I thought about that, and now I can recall part of that conversation as saying that, and I don't say that just to make fun. There were certain things he could do which startled you. But your reservation is you've never seen it done in live, in- tense NFL competition before and eventually he got his turn. And we already had a young quarterback here they drafted in the second round the year before who had started the whole year, Tony Banks. Then we had a veteran backup who was here, Steve Bono, and signed before we ever saw Kurt throw the ball on our practice field. We had seen Kurt in the World League.

I think John Becker mentioned his name to me because Al Luginbill had spoken so highly of him and Charley Armey was the guy really responsible for getting him signed for the World League. I watched all the games he played in World League. I thought he just seemed to be able to do all the intrinsic things well, other than the discipline things. Just the little things like you get back in the pocket, slide in the right direction, throw the ball accurately to the right guy. And all these little differences – scramble out and, Boom, throw the ball downfield complete, handle the pressure of a comeback, and all those things.

First of all, it starts with his ability to throw the ball accurately with a wide variety of throws and then, the other thing is, how does he throw it when he's not just playing catch – "he's under pressure." And if you look at both the big plays in the last two games of the year, the play that beat Tampa Bay. He got smacked on a safety blitz. He throws a touchdown. On the play that beat Tennessee in the Super Bowl, he got knocked on his butt. He has uncanny ability to maintain focus on his throw under extreme pressure and while getting hit.

We had given Will Furrer the opportunity the year before, and I still thought Will could play, but Kurt had not been given the same opportunity. In my opinion, Kurt had a more natural throw, and was a more naturally accurate passer. Will was a very disciplined, very hard-working brilliant kid that worked hard to throw the ball accurately. Kurt could, I think, get out of the shower, walk out into the street, and throw strikes.

In the second to the last game of the '98 season, I had him prepared to play against Carolina and I was thinking about it on the sideline, but when you're leading, like we were leading at the time, we just had a small lead with just two and a half minutes to go, it's pretty hard to change quarterbacks at that time.

Kurt Warner had never been given a good enough opportunity. Well he earned that opportunity he had in St. Louis. I stuck my neck out on him and I believed that he would do a fine job. What's funny is one year before Kurt took over as our starting quarterback, Trent Green, who was in Washington at the time, had only thrown one regular-season NFL pass where Kurt had thrown eleven passes and completed four for us in the fall of '98.

The reason we left Kurt unprotected in the expansion draft to the Cleveland Browns was we thought there was no risk, that it wasn't even a gamble. That's why we did it. The Browns were in a position where they could almost not do it because they had so many other needs. We knew they were going to take a quarterback with their first-round pick and they already had another quarterback there. It made sense for them to take an experienced quarterback in the draft. The Browns just didn't need another quarterback that they didn't know anything about who was almost twenty-eight years old. The day we put together our expansion list, I called Kurt into the office and told him the reason behind the move – why we were leaving him unprotected. He understood. The Browns had nothing to go on; there was no reason for them to draft him. If I were the Browns, I wouldn't have taken him either.

When Trent Green went down with injury in the '99 preseason, Kurt knew I believed in him. I didn't think Kurt would be Trent Green right away but I hoped he would do what Trent Green did when he got his first opportunity a year before – that's all I was asking and, Boy, was I surprised! Well you know, first off I think I did it in front of the whole squad. It was a very emotional meeting. We were talking about losing our quarterback and everything else, and this is what I'm gonna do. I pointed right to Kurt, and said, "Kurt you're gonna be our starting quarterback and I expect you to play well enough for us to win." In front of the whole squad. And I was really emotional you know as I get. It was a very, very intense meeting.

When we went with Kurt as our starting quarterback at the start of the season, the only thing I could lose was my job if it didn't work out, and at sixty-three years old, you're not too concerned about that.

Well, I was really pleased when he started in the Detroit preseason game, the fourth game of the preseason, his first start. He played very well. Then I thought he did an excellent job in the first game of the season. Then again the next week in the big game against Atlanta, a lot of pressure; they're a returning Super Bowl team and I thought he did some spectacular things. Then we go to Cincinnati and play and he did a good job. Then we played the 49ers and we get 21 points on the board and he threw two touchdown passes in that ballgame – early in the game. We had run those patterns a number of times in practice and never thrown the ball to the guy that caught the touchdown pass. He just had a natural flair for where that ball was gonna go based on the coverage. Some guys you could drill them for hours on it and they still wouldn't do it right. In that game, we realized Kurt could be the best in the league.

The other thing about Kurt is, he cares. He's concerned about other teammates. A lot of superstars can really deal with the other top players on the team. He had the compassion for the guy playing backup position and it helps add depth to the whole morale of the football team. I can think of a situation where we had a player who went through an emotional breakdown and we sent him to Meninger Clinic in Topeka, Kansas, for a month. Kurt sent him a Christmas present – he's just a very, very thoughtful guy.

When Trent Green went down, Kurt was very concerned about him. His basic instinct is to care for others. We have London Fletcher, a middle linebacker, he's a great story, a great story, but he's a linebacker and it's his first year as starter and they're not as spectacular but he played the position about as well as Kurt played quarterback.

Kurt's qualities are so innate and instinctive that it's gonna be tough to screw him up. He's not a bluff; he'll get better. Believe me, this is no fluke, he's for real. But Kurt's not a fairy tale. It's real life. He's an example of what we'd all like to be on and off the field. What else can you write? He's a book. He's a movie. This guy is unbelievable.

When Kurt and I hugged after the Super Bowl game and were talking, I said, "I love you." and he said, "I love you." That's not unusual in the relationships I have with my players. There are a number of them who have expressed those thoughts.

I don't think it's gonna go to his head. He'll change a little bit but not enough for you to notice a difference.

The Super Bowl parade in St. Louis was just awesome, unbelievable; the emotion, from the people living on welfare to the top executives. They were all deeply involved in that parade and in welcoming us home, and it was a big thing. I spent a day and half thinking about what I ought to do with the rest of my life and I made the decision to walk away from coaching. I haven't had any second thoughts. I may somewhere down the road.

I was glad to be a part of it.

Coach Dick Vermeil
St. Louis, Missouri

KURT WARNER

And the last shall be first

Chapter 1

Sue Warner

Barb Kruth

Cindy Glynn

Special K – Too Good to be True

The Warner brothers had time.

SHE WAS A GOOD MOM...NO JOAN CRAWFORD, THOUGH
SUE WARNER

Sue Warner is Kurt's mother. If Kurt Warner is Most Valuable Player of the National Football League, Sue Warner should be the Most Valuable Mother in the United States. Divorced from her husband, Gene, when Kurt and her other son, Matthew, were young boys, she raised her children as a single mother. She still lives and works in Cedar Rapids.

It's crazy; there are so many feelings. The main thing, as a parent you always want your kids to be happy and realize their dreams and Kurt's realizing his. Even though his dream was way out in "lala" land, he's still managed with his perseverance to get there. So you're overwhelmed and you're awed, and mainly you're just tickled pink that Kurt's doing this. He just truly loves playing football. He's my younger son. He just has always liked playing ball and he just always loved doing that. When he was in fourth grade, I signed him up for flag football through the "Y" when we moved to another part of town through Jane Boyd Community House, which caters to the less affluent people. He played flag football and went from there to playing grade-school football and on to high school, and that's the rest of the story. He's always loved sports; he played sports year-round. To me, as his mother, he always looked a little better than the other kids. Everybody's kids probably look a little better to their mothers.

It was after he got into high school that I personally could see that he had an edge. He does have a God-given talent, there's no doubt about that, but it was also that he's so focused and he wasn't going to do anything that would hinder his playing his sport. He wasn't going to break any rules, he wasn't going to sass the coaches, he wasn't going to miss practice. I think that's one of the reasons his coaches enjoyed Kurt so is because he was a model athlete to coach.

Faith was a big part of our family. He was raised a Catholic and we attended church every Sunday, first at St. Joe's in Marion, Iowa; then we went to All Saints in Cedar Rapids. We praised the Lord. We thanked the Lord for what we got. Kurtis attended Catholic grade and high schools.

I didn't handle disrespect; I didn't handle insolence – not that I had to. I just think that maybe somewhere along the line the kids knew that I wasn't going to put up with that. I demanded their respect and it started with their grandparents, and it started with me and with their teachers, and I think a lot of that was helped by going to the parochial schools because in the public schools the teachers' hands are tied a lot. In parochial schools, my kids had to learn to respect their teachers or they would be out on their tush. Maybe I put the fear of God into them, I don't really know. Being a single mother, and my boys are both big boys, they could have chosen to walk over me anytime

Being a single mother, and my boys are both big boys, they could have chosen to walk over me anytime they wanted to, but they didn't do that.

they wanted to, but they didn't do that. We were close, and maybe they never wanted to do that; we were always..we had a lot of fun. We hung out together. Tough love, that was hard. I had to be the disciplinarian and the mom before I could be the fun person. There wasn't always time in my day to do both and I always...it was hard to be

Kurt, left, at 18 months; Matt, nearly 3 years

tough love, but not that hard, but you had to do that. If you let them go once, then you're beat. If he hadn't made the NFL, through his perseverance, he truly enjoyed his years in Arena Football. And even though he sat on the bench for four years at the University of Northern Iowa he enjoyed that senior year tremendously.

I am very proud of both Kurt and his brother Matt and they couldn't have turned out any better if I had had a script. I truly love the men they have grown into and they're the men that I wanted them to grow into. I think God gave me good kids. I got into sports when Kurt got into sports and I was a bleacher mom. I've had people say, "Did you have to go to every game?" I say, "No, I didn't have to go to any game; I wanted to be there." I wanted to support my son. My kids were my life. And it wasn't just Kurt and his sports. My other son was into music and other things and I was there, too. It wasn't just doing what Kurt did and even though Kurt did more and so I probably did more of Kurt's things, I did everything with my older son, too. And Kurt had to do for Matt what Matt did for Kurt. It couldn't just be Kurt. Even though Kurt wasn't interested in what Matt was doing...Hey, Matt was at all Kurt's games so "Kurtis you get your little tush over there, and you're gonna support your brother" and it was just kind of the way it was. My kids knew that whatever they undertook they would have me behind them as long as it was in their best interest.

He was pretty much always the best player. His Dad played football in high school but he wasn't the star. Probably the fathers of all the boys had played and were vicariously trying to achieve their dreams for their sons. I didn't care about that and didn't have any athletic aspirations but I encouraged the sport because being a single mother, I'm not home a lot, and especially in the summer I wanted my kids to have a diversion from just hanging out and running around and getting into trouble. Kurt turned out to be such a devoted athlete that I knew he was out there swinging the bat, and throwing the ball and dunking the basketball and he wasn't out looking for trouble. They did have fun. Matt was right along with Kurt. He was never the star athlete like Kurt was—he didn't have the talent, but he was right there with him. I wouldn't have pushed my kids. Kurt got signed up for these things because that's what he truly wanted to do. Like I said, there was an ulterior motive on my part to keep them out of trouble but I wouldn't have forced them to do that if that wasn't their thing. I just would not have done that. That's no fun.

His first love was basketball and it was hard for him to decide to go with football because that gets approached before the basketball season is even over. And that being his first love, he kind of wanted to hold out to see if maybe he could play basketball in college but we knew he wasn't tall enough to do that. It would have had to be a small, small college, which wouldn't have mattered to Kurt, either.

But he decided to go with the sure thing and that's the rest of the story. I attended every game at Northern, even drove seven hours to attend the out-of-town games on the premise that maybe he might get in the game for a minute or two. I didn't want to miss that and not only that like my son Matt, when this season started and he began to go to the out-of-town games, said, "Mom, when Kurt loses, he needs someone to be there." That's just how it is. I wasn't supporting my son because he was a star. I love my son; football wasn't my love.

Last summer was busy and I loved having him come home and spend a couple of days and I would go down to St. Louis and visit. When he gave a speech at the Regis Hall of Fame, I was very proud. He's so giving and remembers people who helped him along the way. This season has been weird for a mom.

> More U.S. kids today play soccer than any organized sport including youth football. The reason so many kids play soccer is so they don't have to watch it.

We were there at the second-to-last preseason game at the Trans World Dome last August when Trent Green got hurt and it was odd because I had taken some friends with me down to St. Louis to the game. We knew Kurt would get to play in the preseason and then probably not play the rest of the season. Then Trent Green went down, and it was an awful feeling. They put Kurt in, he threw one pass, and they immediately took him out. One play! They didn't want him to get hurt, too. My friends looked at me and said, "Is that it? We came all the way down here for one pass." I said, "Well." They said, "One pass, this is all we're ever gonna see this kid do." He completed the pass, and it was a beautiful pass. It was the third preseason game, two weeks before the season started. We were just sitting there stunned – the crowd, the whole stadium, everybody just stunned.

> **We knew Kurt would get to play in the preseason and then probably not play the rest of the season. Then Trent Green went down, and it was an awful feeling.**

It wasn't until we went home, we had spent the night with Kurt and were expecting to have this fun time 'cause we had gotten to see him play and the season's getting ready to start. He was so devastated – for Trent. Then you had all these comments on the radio about, "Now what are they going to do, all our hopes are dashed." I was sitting there thinking, "You've got my son." And Kurt was thinking, "They've got me. I don't understand this. This is what a backup is supposed to do." The headlines the next morning were, "Rams Hopes Dashed" and I'm thinking, "You have my son!" There was a lot of controversy and it wasn't until Monday night Brenda, Kurt's wife, called to say they decided to go with Kurt. It was very difficult because he didn't know if they were going to bring somebody else in ahead of him again and bump him down to No. 3 or whatever. Then next year what would they do? They wouldn't need all these quarterbacks. We're thinking, "Boy, what..."Kurt's biggest fear was for Trent. He called him right away when he got home, and Trent was so supportive. He said, "Kurt, this is your chance – go for it." Of course we didn't know if they were going to give him the green light or not but they did, and the rest is history.

I went to every Rams game this year except two. It was too emotional. I've spent all these months going down there, and I don't get to see my kid and I come home feeling a little empty because I didn't get to bond. So if I know I'm not going to get to see him, and I know there's no possibility, then I'm better mentally. It's very hard to go up to my child after they lose a ballgame. So I watched the game at a local bar because I don't have the NFL TV package. Throughout the season we all met at the bar to see it – Paddy O'Rourkes in Cedar Rapids. They were very sweet there; we had our own little "Ram Room." Then the Sunday when the big game against Tampa Bay for the right to go to the Super Bowl came. Of course, we went to the bar because we'd gone there all season; it was awesome.

During the playoff games, Fox would show the women in the stands and John Madden would identify them as Brenda, Kurt's wife, and the other one as Kurt's mom. But I was watching at a bar in Cedar Rapids. Brenda's sister, Kim Hawley, was the lady sitting by her that was introduced on television as Kurt's mom. My only claim to fame and they screw it up.

Kurt says he is a born-again Christian now, but he was raised a Catholic. To me that may mean someone who maybe had religion but never had Christ, or who has now recently dedicated their life to Christ. When Kurt and I talked about that, too, he said Christ has always been important in his life. When he switched from the "building of the Catholic Church" I think maybe it was the influence of his wife. Brenda wasn't real comfortable in the Catholic Church and it was very important to both of them that they raise their children in a common faith – not have Daddy go here and Mommy go there. God's God and Jesus is Jesus – doesn't matter what building and that's the rest of the story. Now that he's gotten to his current church, he likes the openness and the praising and the worship – the head to the toe thing – the rocking and having a good time, which is not part of the Catholic Church for the most part. I go to church with Kurt and Brenda when I go down there, and they haven't been home yet so I don't know what they'll do when they come up here. They go to what's called The Family Church. I think it's just a nondenominational church in St. Louis. They found this particular church; they're in love with the pastor. They thought, "Hey this is God's plan because Kurt can't get there on Sunday." So they go Friday nights. So this is a plan – a big plan God's got going. Lots of people had doubts about Deion Sanders, and I suppose there is a fine line or I suppose maybe people want to get the point across so well they come across

> One out of 40 high school basketball players
> play college basketball.
> One out of 15 play football.

fakey. Kurt's not there yet. Kurt's just Kurt, so what comes out of Kurt's mouth just comes out of Kurt's mouth. It doesn't come out of Kurt's head; it comes out of his heart. When all this started to go – bing, bing, bing, bing, bing – you can't help but know that there's a plan from up above for Kurtis here.

Did Kurt ever get in trouble? No big stuff; he was never even grounded.

Kurt must have been about three. When he was little he loved to eat so he goes to the refrigerator and gets this two-quart pitcher of red Kool Aid. He thinks he is going to do it himself. He takes it into the living room and spills it on my two-week-old brand-new sofa. I was so mad I killed him and now he is a reincarnation. No, he stood in the corner and I have pictures of him standing there in that corner.

Once when he was a toddler he threw light bulbs into the clothes dryer with his diapers. I had to vacuum each diaper one by one to get the little pieces of glass. I said if there's any glass still in there and it cuts his butt, it's his own fault since he did it. He was in diapers so he must have been younger than two.

Recently my older son was being interviewed. I think they were trying to figure out if there was anything they ever did wrong. He said, yeah, we used to sneak out the window when mom was in bed and go out and play with the neighbors. I probably made my kids go to bed about 7 – no not quite.

When you're a single mother by yourself, what choice do you have? You're by yourself, you have two kids so you don't have a choice. You don't tell kids the sacrifices you made, we just did them.

For Kurtis, it is a dream come true. With me, it is – I guess maybe dream world's not exactly right – it's surreal, it's wonderful, it's overwhelming. I'm just so gosh darn happy with Kurt. Kurt's the one living in the dream world. We're living somewhat removed from it as far as we don't see it all the time. Sometimes we're kind of like everyone else. We read about this, too, and say, "Oh, that's my son."

If somebody is looking at somebody and not being touched by that person, I think that goes back to who God has a handle on. I think God's got a handle on Kurt and so he's going to have positive influence because he's truly walking the walk.

FOR FEAR IT MIGHT GO ON HIS PERMANENT RECORD
BARB KRUTH

Barb Kruth was Kurt Warner's third- and fourth-grade teacher at All Saints grade school in Cedar Rapids, Iowa.

Kurt was in my third- and fourth-grade classes. He was one of those kids who did what he was told and was a really good little boy. His mom raised him and his brother Matt, and she was really strict with them. I think if those boys had screwed up she probably would have killed them. The only thing that I really remember about that whole group of boys – and Kurt was one of them – they played football all the time at recess. They were just like animals at recess, playing football all the time. Because of safety rules, we would only let them play touch football. But what I do remember is, you'd ring the bell, it was time to come in, and Kurt would probably throw another pass. You know that's really the only naughty thing he ever did – just wanted to get one more play in before they had to come in. But he really was just a good kid – did what he was told, just a good kid. It's a wonderful story.

He's such a role model for the kids we have now. Kurt was just another kid and when these boys are eight and nine years old, I have never had one kid that hasn't said, "I want to be an NFL player when I grow up." All little boys say that and the fact that he made it has just given these little boys just this dream that, "Oh my God, I can really do it." He's just such an inspiration playing in the NFL, and they know he went here. They are really, really excited to know that somebody who actually walked the halls here actually made it.

I'm a major Vikings fan but I would like to have the Rams win because of him. I was really torn when they played each other in the playoffs.

> The Minnesota Vikings have not been
> in the Super Bowl since the Lou and Bud Grant era.

HE MADE STRAIGHT A's, BUT HIS B's WERE A LITTLE CROOKED
CINDY GLYNN

Cindy Glynn was his teacher in middle school at All Saints in Cedar Rapids, Iowa.

He was an excellent student. I had him in fifth, sixth, and eighth grades because I moved up his eighth-grade year. He was a quiet, excellent student a real good friend to the other kids and just a good, wholesome, all-around kid. I can't recall him ever getting into any big-time trouble; he was just a good kid. He was very much into sports. During recess he always had a ball in his hand. He played football, kickball, whatever was going on at the time at that age. We had a junior high sports team and he was involved in that. He won one of the awards, I think the Jack Ogden Award that was given at the end of the year to an eighth-grade student.

I followed him and all our former students at Regis High School because my husband taught there. When Kurt was in school it was Kitty Breitbach, the wife of one of the coaches, who had to teach me about football. I had not been to many football games and did not know much about the game. As Dick was coaching all the time, she would explain the rules and what was going on to me. I enjoyed the sports when I knew the kids who were playing and followed all the football games and all the basketball games up there; softball, baseball, big follower of all the kids. Now if it's televised, my husband and I watch it.

I think he has been a real wholesome hero for kids to look up to and it's honest. It's not fake. Knowing him both in grade school and high school, it's honest, it's very sincere. We've talked a lot in our religion classes of heroes and a lot of times there's not a lot of modern-day ones that you want the children to model after because many times they are heroes on the court or field but they are not in real life. But this time the two go hand in hand.

Chapter 2

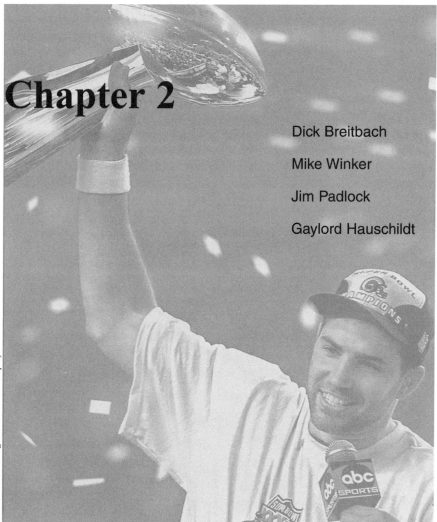

Dick Breitbach

Mike Winker

Jim Padlock

Gaylord Hauschildt

Kurt's So Good

Mike Winker

Gaylord Haushildt

THE DUKE OF DUBUQUE
DICK BREITBACH

Dick Breitbach is a native of Dubuque, Iowa, where he starred in athletics at Loras Academy. After graduation, he attended Notre Dame for one year before returning home and graduating from Loras College. He then became an almost legendary teacher and coach in Cedar Rapids at Regis High School. In the spring of 1999 he retired from a 40-year career in education. At his retirement dinner, Kurt Warner stood up and said, "There is one other goal I always had every time I played a football game in high school, and it went on to college, and it goes on now. That was to impress this man right here....I didn't ever want to let this guy down."

The first time I saw Kurt, I was down visiting an eighth-grader from All Saints Grade School at the Universityof Iowa Hospital and Kurt was also there visiting. He was a classmate of the kid. At that time he just looked like an athlete, he was kinda rangy even at that time. In eighth grade he was probably 5'11" or 6'. Then he came to Regis High School. We don't see or hear much about grade-school kids other than you know they've done well, and we knew he had done well in grade school. But when he came to Regis as a ninth-grader, just everything he did spoke a lot about himself – very classy, very mature for a young man. You don't always expect that of eighth-graders.

I was offensive and defensive back coach for the varsity football team his junior and senior years and was his head coach in basketball. It was just like he was doing now only on a high school level. He was the main man. You could count on him – the person who was the leader out on the field or on the basketball floor and just did a great job. He ended up being an all-stater in both football and basketball. He led us both his junior and senior years in rebounding and scoring. He didn't get any offers from Division I basketball, mainly due to his size. He was more of a wing player and he would post up for us but in high school he was posting up against a kid that would be his size so he was tough. But in college, he probably would have had to be a number 2 man and I don't think that was his forte. He got some offers; a lot of teams wanted him in Division III for basketball. He just played football at the University of Northern Iowa.

He was a good kid. I don't remember him ever getting in trouble. His freshman year, I was the associate principal and was meeting with his mother, Sue, at conferences. She was very adamant – she called him Kurtis – that Kurtis was going to make sure he did as well as he should do based on his ability in academics or he wouldn't be playing any athletics. Those kind of people you appreciate because you know the kid is going to listen to her and he is going to be a top-notch kid. The parents divorced when he was four or five years old. His mother still lives in Cedar Rapids. Gene, his father, lives just outside of Cedar Rapids, so I see both of them. He lives in Solon, Iowa, and works in Cedar Rapids. Sue didn't go to the playoff game; she stayed here in Cedar Rapids and watched it with some friends. The person always shown on television during the games was not his mother.

You would never have dreamed this would happen to him. You knew he was a great high school player but look at how many players there are that never get a shot. And he never did really get a good shot at the University of Northern Iowa until his fifth year, his senior year. He was red-shirted his freshman year and he never did get to play much. He played as a fifth-year senior and all of a sudden he sets records in the Gateway Conference. The starting quarterback was a kid named Johnson who was also a pretty good quarterback. But you listen to Kurt talk now and he was a little disappointed because he thought he should have been given some opportunities. I think sometimes coaches...they had been winning a decent amount of time so they just didn't make a change.

I retired this past year from school and had been in Catholic education for 40 years. Kurt came up in May and talked at my retirement party and afterward I got to talk to him quite a bit. Also, we inducted him into the Regis Hall of Fame last February and so I got a chance to talk to him a couple of times. Then I went to the wedding of another of my players last May and Kurt was best man, so in the space of about three months I got to talk to him quite a bit.

> The word "varsity" is the British short form
> of the word "university."

Kurt Warner, 1989 Regis High School graduate

He said he thought he would be second team – didn't think he would get to play a whole lot because they had just signed Trent Green for about 16 million and he was a St. Louis native, but he said, "As long as Vermeil stays as coach, I'll be here. Vermeil likes me, knows that I'll be ready if the time ever comes, but I'm not gonna be demanding he play me or trade me and stuff like that." Kurt was pretty loyal that way. He says, "Now make sure if you want to come down and see a game give me a call." Well after the first few games he was so inundated, I don't even call him. I send word via his mother or his brother. They don't even get a chance, his parents say, when they go down there. They get a visit with him for a few minutes because the media is after him all the time. If they go down on Saturday, he is focusing on the game the next day. He's listening to you but he really doesn't hear you because his mind's on the game. Then after the game, it's two and a half or three hours before he even gets out of the stadium because everybody is all over him. So I think they'll be glad when this season is over and they get a chance to sit down and talk to him a little bit.

Right now in the town of Cedar Rapids, Kurt is all you hear, all they talk about. When they know you coached him or knew him that's all they ask about. It's some story. They ask if I knew he was gonna be a pro quarterback and we knew he was a pretty good quarterback in high school, but no, you really didn't. It's hard to imagine. I'd never known anybody from Cedar Rapids who had ever made it "this big like this" in pro sports. He is very much family oriented; is really first class all the way. So many pro players don't understand the game because they don't take the time to watch and listen and learn – they really don't. It's funny because when Kurt was back for his induction into the Hall of Fame, the first thing they wanted to know was if I could get the keys so they could go in and play basketball the next morning – he and his buddies. Very down to earth.

Here in Cedar Rapids, there's a story every day in the news; usually big color pictures of Kurt. When Tim Dwight was playing high school ball in Iowa City, 35 miles away, then when he went to Iowa, then to the Atlanta Falcons, there would be some things on him, too, in our paper because it was unusual to have someone making it in professional football. But when someone has made it so big, there's 20 times more publicity. And every time, in every story, it's mentioned that he's a former Regis and University of Northern Iowa quarterback. So there's a lot of notoriety for Regis. We have our grade school football games at Xavier on Sunday and the

We have our grade school football games at Xavier on Sunday and the first thing the announcer would do every Sunday was give an update on what Kurt was doing.

first thing the announcer would do every Sunday was give an update on what Kurt was doing. One day was especially remarkable, when he threw the five touchdown passes against San Francisco in October and everybody just wanted to know how he was doing and what was going on.

Reporters wanted to know anything about Kurt. Did he play tough practical jokes on people? He really didn't. He was serious, had fun and enjoyed it, but was a guy who was just down to earth and he respected people. His best friend, Tom Petsche, was a guy whose wedding I went to where Kurt was best man. He lives in Solon, also the place where Gene Warner lives. I think they hung around, played cards in somebody's house, maybe watched some videos. They didn't do things to get in trouble and that kind of thing.

A COACH IS A TEACHER
WITH A DEATH WISH
MIKE WINKER

Mike Winker was an assistant freshman football coach during Kurt Warner's freshman year at Regis High School in Cedar Rapids, Iowa. He continued coaching football at Regis and eventually became the varsity coach and the athletic director. Now he is the athletic director at Xavier High School, the school that replaced Regis. Winker also coached girls basketball and some baseball but never had the opportunity to coach Kurt Warner after the freshman year.

Kurt Warner is just an outstanding person. I had the opportunity to be his assistant freshman football coach at Regis. In fact, it was my second year of coaching. I was a junior in college, and I was only a volunteer coach. I was young and inexperienced. He was such a good quarterback I thought coaching was easy. It was only my second year and I was pretty naïve; I thought I was a pretty good coach and it turns out 15 or 18 or so years after that that he was the best one I ever coached.

He was mature for his age both in his physical ability and, especially, in his mind-set – just very mature very poised. Pressure never got to him. It seemed if he had pressure it was on the inside and you could never see it on the outside so that's a pretty great quality to have to be a quarterback or any type of athlete. He was very good, but I never would have dreamed he would be in the NFL. I remember when he was a senior being disappointed that he wasn't recruited by a Division I school. When you're in high school, you don't necessarily think of the NFL, you're thinking of college. And I was just disappointed that Iowa or an Iowa State didn't go after him. But he ended up being recruited at the University of Northern Iowa, which was nice, but I just felt he could have been a Division I football player and he's proven that now.

There is one game I really remember. Linn Mar was a big rival of ours and I don't know if it was the last game of the season or not. We went 8 and 0 when he was a freshman. I just remember being up 7 – nothing with a few minutes left in the second quarter and we had been messing around with a two-minute drill. Not too many varsity high school teams are too adept at doing that let alone freshman teams. We ran our two-minute drill and he took us down and we scored right before half to put us up two touchdowns and that momentum and score pretty much ensured that we were gonna win the game. I just remember, again, probably being a kinda cocky young coach thinking how great our offense was but when I look back, I didn't have anybody that could run a two-minute offense at the freshman or sophomore varsity level like he could as a freshman.

This was on a freshman team. At Regis we had a freshman team, sophomore team, and then juniors and seniors were on the varsity. He was the only player I've had who was able to run a two-minute drill like that. He was like the old cliché: being another coach on the field. He was very quiet, very mature, had self-confidence – not cocky but confident. No nonsense when it came to athletics. I don't ever remember him being in trouble in school or screwing around. I know he

> **He was very quiet, very mature, had self-confidence – not cocky but confident.**

was like any other teenager who does screw around a little bit but nothing where you thought anything but that he was a great kid. Almost, if anything, too good to be true. Never a smart aleck, the thing I really liked about him. I can remember I was just an average athlete and stuff but I can remember, sometimes not demeaning, but maybe putting down a kid in conversation sometimes. Kurtis never did any of that. He bent over backwards to make everybody feel important and he did the same thing with teachers, too. He made teachers feel good and how he helped them. I remember a couple of the teachers who were a little older, near retirement. Sometimes you can get away with things with teachers like that. He just bent over backwards to make sure classes were being conducted the way they should – that other kids weren't screwing around. He wasn't afraid to be a leader. There's a lot of good kids, but a lot of them are afraid. They don't want to be a "goody two shoes" or whatever but he wasn't afraid to be a leader – just a very quiet leader.

> Former Iowa State and current Chicago Bulls
> Coach Tim Floyd was once a New Orleans Saints ball boy.

I've never known anyone personally who has played at the professional level like this – either major-league baseball, NBA, NFL, so it's exciting to know someone, first of all. The thing that makes it fun and so much fun to root for him is that he's such a good person. I don't think there are people who are jealous of him or that hope deep down that he doesn't do well because he was a jerk or didn't treat them right. It's neat that everybody in Cedar Rapids is rooting for him because he's such a good person. You know sometimes I think high school coaches will have a great athlete who goes on to be a great college star – maybe not play or maybe play in professional sports but is kind of a jerk or cocky. You root for him publicly, but, privately, you might think, "I hope he gets it handed to him sometime just to keep him somewhat humble."

> **It's neat that everybody in Cedar Rapids is rooting for him because he's such a good person.**

But with Kurt, you hope everything goes well every step of the way – hoping he'd be in the Pro Bowl, hoping he'd be in the playoffs – MVP. You just keep rooting and rooting. Dick Vermeil obviously likes him and I remember when I talked to Kurt a little bit when he was back in town. He had mentioned that he thought Dick Vermeil really was behind him so I know he was hoping that Vermeil was gonna stay around. You know they had had two losing seasons the last two years so I was just hoping that the Rams and Vermeil had a good year so Kurt would still be on the team. That's what I was hoping. I had no idea he'd eventually become the starter. Of course, he did through injury, I realize, at the beginning. I was just hoping he could keep his spot on the roster as the backup and that Vermeil would keep his job so Kurt would get a nice living in the NFL for three or four years. I watched him play in a game at the University of Northern Iowa. I remember going up to watch him play. He had a great game. I was proud of him. Didn't get to talk to him afterward.

About the fifth game of the '99 season, I was getting four or five calls of people wanting to get in touch with him or wanting things, and I think his high school coaches and people back in Cedar Rapids just bent over backwards not to give Kurt's number out. It's changed so many times I don't even know what it is now. Dick Breitbach had access to some of that stuff and we just kinda bent over backwards to not bother him.

The students here, since the two schools merged, might have been more excited if Regis had still been up and running. They are excited but that tie is lost with Regis closing two years ago. The students know that I am here and other people who have had contact with him or coached him and know who he is. Last year, when we brought him back and inducted him into the Hall of Fame, they kinda sat up a little bit when we said this guy is in the NFL. We've invited him back and I hope he will come back after the season. He'll just be swamped by everyone else. That would have been the neatest story because Regis never had one person who played in the NFL, and now one does play and Regis is closed.

In order to host the Pro Bowl from 1994-1998,
the state of Hawaii had to donate
the use of the stadium rent-free and guarantee
the NFL one million dollars income each year.

Rice is the smallest Division I
football school with 2600 students.

COACH, EXPLAIN THAT RUSSIAN ROULETTE DRILL AGAIN
JIM PADLOCK

If anyone can lay claim to making Kurt Warner a quarterback, it would be his freshman coach in high school, Jim Padlock. If anyone can lay claim to training Kurt Warner to stand in the pocket, it would be Jim Padlock. Padlock is a native of Kenosha, Wisconsin, who played football at Coe College in Cedar Rapids, Iowa, and upon graduation joined the faculty and coaching staff of Regis High School. Today he still lives in his native Wisconsin where he is the athletic director and Dean of Students at Wilmot High School.

The thing I miss about Cedar Rapids is the emphasis on high school sports. I was the high school head wrestling coach there and got to do some other real enjoyable things and I just love the emphasis on high school sports in Cedar Rapids.

Kurt Warner was my quarterback as a freshman at Regis High School – that was my second year there as a teacher. I never dreamed I was coaching a future NFL MVP! I guess we looked at him as a quarterback at the time because of his size. He was 5'10" – 5'11" at that time – a big kid. We weren't tempted to move him to the line because he wasn't built – he wasn't thick. He wanted to be a wide receiver, maybe a tight end, and wanted to play defense for us. When we wanted him to play quarterback, he really wasn't interested in the pressure of being a quarterback; kinda just wanted to be out there as a receiver and catch the football. Now he seems to thrive on the pressure.

I think it's fantastic. The fact that's not surprising is that he's continued to work at it and work to achieve his goals. I've always thought he's that kind of a kid. You don't know about athletic skills to that level when a kid's in the ninth grade, but I'm not surprised that he's continued to work at it.

I had not heard of Kurt before the first day of practice. We asked who wanted to be quarterback and we had a guy who was pretty small. We were a little concerned over having just one quarterback and him being very small. Not that Brian did a bad job or anything, but he was just a little guy. So we asked around and talked to them and took a look at Kurt. He was tall, so we said what do you think? "Can you throw the football?" He didn't want to play quarterback at all; he wanted to play receiver and defensive end. I said, "Why don't you try throwing the football up?" He didn't have a Brett Favre, John Elway gun kind of thing like "Oh, my gosh!" But he's a very accurate thrower. He throws very accurately. He didn't, at that time, fire and knock people's chests in or anything like that but he just got the ball where it needed to be.

It was the fall of 1985. We did a lot of three-step drop at that time. We did three and five. We didn't do a lot of deep drops. Once we got Kurt started as a quarterback and ran our offense we did a lot of three-step, throw the football. He would read the free safety. What he was doing in the first game or two, he would three-step drop, and that's right behind the line and he'd panic and take off. He's not a great runner. He'd take off running and that's not what we wanted. So we needed to get him to get in there and realize he was gonna get hit and he had to stand there and deliver the ball. So we ran a drill where he had all his receivers and he had a center and that was it. Then we put two linebackers with arm pads on the other side of the line and we would snap the ball and as soon as he'd set up the linebackers would just blitz forward. Well, he'd set up, throw the ball, complete the pass, and then the linebackers would come up with arm pads and knock him over – knock him down. He hated it. I think the linebackers and linemen named it the "Kill Kurt" drill because they all got to rotate and hit him and knock him over. It was the idea that it hurts less if you complete the pass, so sit in there and complete the pass. That was the drill we ran. About two years ago, my son and I went to Milwaukee to see him play in an Arena Football game against the Milwaukee Mustangs. After the game the first thing he said to me was, "Do you remember that stupid drill?" I said, "Drill?" And he explained it to me, and I said, "Oh, yeah, I remember it." He said, "I hated that stupid drill then but it helped me so much to be able to just sit in the pocket and throw the football." He brought it up then and he brought it

> Lost time due to injury in high school football is six days.
> Lost time due to injury to a high school cheerleader is 29 days.

up to John Madden at those playoff games. He does a very nice job of sitting in and throwing the football.

Kurt was driving for a touchdown in the first playoff game and John Madden made a comment about how, despite the things going on in the ballgame, Kurt sat in the pocket, looked down the field and threw the ball. In fact, on one play a linebacker gets flipped completely over. When they show the replay, Kurt's not even looking at it, and the linebacker has been flipped *completely over*. He looks down the field and completes a pass. John Madden brought up the fact that Kurt Warner had told him that he thought some of that had come from this drill we did which we called "Kill Kurt" drill in ninth grade. Then he brought it up and talked about it a couple of times in that playoff game. Then he talked about it the next week in the NFC Championship game. That's when I got some calls from St. Louis and my brother had called the local paper here and they did a big article on it which was after John Madden had made a couple of comments on it.

> **The one thing I always think is neat is that the Rams run that spread formation with no one in the backfield and we ran that same formation when he was a ninth-grader.**

He was a good kid, very nice, very friendly, very easy to coach. You know, one of the things that I guess at the time we took for granted. Now when I think about it, it's pretty amazing. We threw the ball about 50 percent of the time, which for a ninth-grade team was a lot. We ran a lot of different formations, probably over 20 different kinds of formations. The one thing I always think is neat is that the Rams run that spread formation with no one in the backfield and we ran that same formation when he was a ninth-grader. We would start with a fullback and motion him out of the backfield and we'd run that spread. Because we'd run against teams that would run three deep and with five guys going out for a pattern, if linebackers didn't react, people'd be wide open. We did a lot of that kind of spread formation and those kind of things when he was in ninth grade. That was the first ninth-grade team Regis had that went undefeated, and we ended the season 8–0. We saved a lot of plays for second halves; there was no scouting in ninth grades and no one would know. We'd come out and be conservative in the first half and in the second half we'd run the spread and do this and that and we scored a lot of points and played good defense.

Photo©James V. Biever

Green Bay was overrun with quarterbacks. Coach Mike Holmgren confers with Ty Detmer, Warner, Brett Favre, and Mark Brunell during a preseason game against the Los Angeles Rams. Warner was assigned number 12 because kicker Chris Jacke wore number 13.

The reason we ran such a sophisticated offense was that it was a lot of fun and did it all four years I was there. We tried to do as much as we could because when it's fun, the kids like it. If you teach kids to run in motion, they think its great. The receiver does, the quarterback clicks his heels when they go, it changes up what the defense does. When you sell the kids on the fact that, "Hey, we're going to freak out the defense, we're going to put this guy in motion", It makes the whole thing fun. That's why we did a lot of the things we did. We told the kids, we'll do as much as YOU have the ability to master. If you're gonna jump off-side, etc., we can't do it. If we can run motion and the spread, if we can come out of the offense and run the spread where there's no backs and throw the ball, we'll do it. And some years we did and some we didn't, but Kurt had the ability to do it and we had some other smart kids doing it. And I'm sure he would tell you it was a fun offense. We had a lot of fun doing what we were doing.

We were running offenses and formations, and for ninth-grade football we were running 20 different formations and were in motion all the time. I look back now and I think I can't believe we were doing all those things. That comes directly from your confidence in the ability of the person who's running the show. Obviously, we felt so good about Kurt and what he was doing and he felt so good about what he was doing and we continued to expand our offenses as the year went on.

Kurt was not a real spiritual kid at that time. He was real nice, real friendly, very mature kid, not squirrelly, handled a lot of things very well. He didn't screw around a lot, wasn't into a lot of girl stuff, that just wasn't his thing then. He was more into athletics. He was very mature for his age and was a little bigger than the other kids and I think they looked up to him and he showed more of an air of maturity.

I came back to Wisconsin and didn't see or really hear anything about him except for the fact that he had gone to Northern Iowa. I hadn't even heard about the "Gateway Player of the Year" thing. The next thing I heard was that he'd gone to Green Bay. Since I was in Wisconsin and being a big Packer fan, all of a sudden just seeing him sign up at Green Bay made me proud. I had plans to go up and watch practice. My son and I were going and the night before the day we were going, he was cut so I didn't get to go. I think they cut him a week or two earlier than I thought they would. But when you look at it, they had Mark Brunell, Kurt, Brett Favre, and Ty Detmer all in the same camp.

But when you look at it, they had Mark Brunell, Kurt, Brett Favre, and Ty Detmer all in the same camp.

I went down to St. Louis to the New Orleans game. The first half he didn't play very well and they didn't play very well. I kinda thought New Orleans had them flustered. He moved around a little more, his feet shuffled, and all that kind of stuff. Then they came out the second half and the first three plays they ran timing patterns where he set up, boom, turned and threw the football. He hit Bruce on a long out – just perfect timing patterns. Then all of a sudden it was all back and they came out and just blew them out. But the first half he was off sync a little bit. He was nervous and he got hit more than he probably felt he wanted to be and everything was off sync. They came out and were real smart about how to run the timing patterns in the second half. They were three-step drops, quick passes, boom, boom, boom, and he completed three in a row and that was it and they just blew them away.

I sometimes wonder what would have happened if we had not asked for another quarterback and Kurt had stayed at receiver or we didn't do the "Kill Kurt" drills. If we couldn't have coaxed him into playing quarterback, I wonder what he would be doing right now. A funny thing: I did do this with one other kid, but not to this extent.

The whole story of Kurt is pretty amazing – incredibly amazing. You feel like the Rudy story kind of thing. Actually it's even bigger than that when you look at it. Rudy got to play one play for Notre Dame, and here you're looking at a guy who's very much at the top. What worries me is, how do you better what you've done this year? You can't. You've got both the league and Super Bowl MVP, 41 touchdowns, all those things. Any other year compared probably won't compare. Kurt's true character will have to show when that doesn't happen down the line. If things don't happen for him consistently, we'll have to see how his character proves out. I think he's shown outstanding character to this point but the losses and being blamed for the losses are coming.

What I feel real bad about: we had a beautiful tape of him at our last game and I don't have it. I can't find it anymore. We won 26 to 6. He played great. I've watched the tape a million times but it's been at least six months since I watched it and can't find it now. I started looking for it at the beginning of this year when he was starting as quarterback and I have been looking for it and looking for it. It would just be wonderful to sit down and I'm sure a lot of people would like to look at this ballgame because we did so many different things when we were playing. We did some things. He reverse pivoted and came back, we threw the ball on the slant; some things that I guess at that time I took for granted. And he just did it very smooth and very confident and ran things with a good air of confidence about him. I thought I had it at my house, but in some cleaning, it may have gotten tossed. I don't remember if it was labeled.

When we went to see him in the Milwaukee Arena game, he was on the sideline after the game, and I yelled at him. He turned around and said, "Coach Padlock." Yeah, he remembered.

Attendance at Halls of Fame for all of the major sports has been in a downward spiral for the last several years.

NO, HIS NAME IS KURT.
HIS DAD IS POP WARNER.
GAYLORD HAUSCHILDT

Gaylord was Kurt Warner's head football coach during his junior and senior years at Regis High School in Cedar Rapids, Iowa.

I've been out of the coaching life for nine years but that's okay; it's been fun. Regis was a small Catholic high school in Cedar Rapids with about 400 students. You pretty much know everybody. As varsity football coach, you pretty much check on who the athletes are in the younger grades because you will get them as juniors and seniors. I had a chance to watch Kurt specifically as a sophomore quarterback playing on the sophomore team. He certainly showed some terrific passing ability. We had some coaches there who allowed him to throw, which was what we wanted. He seemed to be able to see the field really well and we were anxious to get him up in the varsity.

I was the sophomore basketball coach so I had a chance to coach him his sophomore year in basketball and I found him to be just an intense competitor, a levelheaded guy. He always had himself under control and poised. He was an outstanding basketball player in addition to being a football player at that level. When he got to varsity, we basically decided we would play him as a junior and deal with any mistakes he might make and allow him to really shine as a senior. As we found out, we didn't have a very successful win-loss record his junior year but he just rapidly improved and the reason for that is you could coach him; give him an instruction the first time, he'd pick up a lot of it. If he made a mistake during the course of practice or game he would correct it, and you never had to worry about that happening again. He basically consumed everything you could give him in football. Consequently, both his junior and senior years, from an individual standpoint, were outstanding and he basically really took us into the playoffs in Iowa in our class his senior year.

I thought for sure he would play major college football and I was a little bit disappointed. I was probably a little bit naïve as a coach in thinking that colleges would really seek out and find all the best players. I realized after Kurt's situation that you really have to promote your kids. Hayden Fry was at the University of Iowa and was really interested in him and it came down to the final choice between him and Paul Burmeister from Iowa City West. They had him in camp, Burmeister, and he was more their standard 6'4", 210-pound kid out of high school. They had just got done with Chuck Long, an outstanding college quarterback, and saw the physical size advantage.

Kurt was, I think, content to stay around Iowa. I don't think he wanted to travel out of state and Terry Allen was at the University of Northern Iowa, so we eventually got that worked out. I was very surprised that he was not playing more there. I never did talk to Coach Allen about it, but when Kurt would come back I would just ask how things were going and being the gentleman that he is, he just said, "Okay." He knew Jay Johnson, the starting quarterback, would graduate and he would have one more year, but Kurt's the kind of guy, I really thought would be very impatient sitting on the sidelines. But he dealt with that for four years and then he really made the most of his chance that last year.

> **I don't think you will find somebody who doesn't really like Kurt and that's what has made him difficult to really be understood by people because they just don't believe there's somebody out there like that.**

I don't think you will find somebody who doesn't really like Kurt and that's what has made him difficult to really be understood by people because they just don't believe there's somebody out there like that. We knew when he was in high school; he's no different now than he was at 15 or 16. All the characteristics you see and the positive image he portrays is a reality. That's the way he is. He was a down-to-earth guy in high school in terms of he knew what he had to do academically; he knew what he had to do from an athletic sense, and he just basically took care of his life.

Most of this is, I think, due to his close relationship with his Mom and she thinks the world of her two boys so I'm sure that influence and relationship has a lot to do with how he is now. His Dad was at athletic events but they pretty much stayed out of the way. I never had to deal with them specifically, just compliment them at banquets – that sort of stuff. Kurt had big numbers for two years. We hadn't been known as a passing school. When I became head coach I kinda liked to have basketball players playing football and Kurt was one of those basketball players. In his 18 games, I think we threw 375 times, completed 57 percent of them, had 25 TD's and were just short of 3000 yards. We threw more than 20 times per game and that's a lot for any high school around here.

I never saw him play at the University of Northern Iowa his senior year because we were busy with our season and our other sports and only got to see him play if they were on television.

It's just beyond belief to me personally. We went to Atlanta for the Super Bowl. We had an arrangement with Sportshuddle.com, a Web site in St. Louis, where they brought the two high school coaches of the starting quarterbacks down for the Super Bowl and we did some promotion stuff. The fact that we went down there and saw him in the Super Bowl is just unbelievable.

Regis has since closed and was turned into a middle school. There has been a lot of attention on the part of students around Xavier, the new high school that replaced Regis, because he's a former Catholic high school graduate. It's been tremendous for people who graduated around the same time or knew Kurt personally. Cedar Rapids had him at high school and Cedar Falls had him in college, and the Barnstormers had him in Des Moines. You take three of the big metropolitan areas of the state and now it's become an all-Iowa thing. But right now in Cedar Rapids, everybody knows Kurt from some way, somehow, and some age.

We didn't get to go to any of the Rams games. We tried to go to some but after the third or fourth one, there were no tickets available so we weren't able to go.

When retired Iowa Coach Hayden Fry was a high school teacher and coach in west Texas, one of his homeroom students was Roy Orbison.

Chapter 3

Terry Allen

Jay Johnson

Rick Hartzell

Jack Harbaugh

Rick Coleman

Is This Heaven?
No, It's Iowa.
Okay, It's the University
of Northern Iowa

Matt Warner gives toast at Kurt and Brenda's wedding in October, 1997.

Courtesy University of Kansas

THERE'S MORE TO COACHING THAN IGNORING YOUR BEST PLAYER
TERRY ALLEN

Terry Allen, the head football coach at the University of Kansas was Kurt Warner's head coach during Warner's five years at Northern Iowa. The graduate of Iowa City West (1975) spent 23 years on the UNI campus. His father, Bob Allen, was the University of Iowa swimming coach.

I grew up in Iowa City. Kurt was a former pupil, and I never would have dreamed he would be the most valuable football player in the National Football League but I thought he could get a shot at it. The first time I met Kurt was when we recruited him out of Regis High School. In Iowa, at the time, there were two senior high school quarterbacks – one was in Iowa City, Paul Burmeister, and one in Cedar Rapids, Kurt Warner. We were recruiting both of those kids, knowing we would get the other one at Northern Iowa. We were hopeful Iowa would take Burmeister, and they did, and we got Kurt, the one we wanted. In high school we saw him play and watched his tapes, and I was very instrumental in recruiting him. He was a good kid, good family situation, at the parochial school there. He was a kid who could throw – they didn't throw that much, but he showed some things. And you knew that kid had an arm.

In Cedar Falls, he didn't start till his senior year. It was bad timing. The kid in front of him was a year ahead of him. Jay Johnson, my quarterback coach right now at Kansas, was a good quarterback, son of a coach from Lakeville, Minnesota, and got ahead of him because he was a year older and didn't do anything wrong. We went to the playoffs three straight times under Jay and, in fact, Jay's senior year and Kurt's junior year we were the No. 1 team in 1-AA football so it was not that there was anything wrong with Kurt. We knew he could throw it but Jay did everything right. Kurt played in a backup capacity and got good action but obviously wasn't the starter.

Kurt's final year came and we were a little fearful early in the year. As a starter he made some mistakes and got hurt in the Wyoming game. Then Kurt came back and was the offensive player that year in our league. In 1994, one of our coaches contacted the people up at Green Bay and they got him the free agent shot and he didn't make that because of the guys they had there at that time – Brett Favre, Mark Brunell, and Ty Detmer. Kurt came back to this area and we knew he had a really strong arm and it was just a matter of getting some experience. John Gregory, a guy I coached with, a Northern Iowa grad, was head coach of the Iowa Barnstormers, and they took him down there and he got the experience he needed and, lo and behold, he made it back to the Rams.

I've touched base with Kurt briefly through the media people but am anxious to talk to him after the season. He was never any trouble. What you see is what you get there. That's not a made-up deal. That person you see and the way he handles things and people…he's been doing that since he was a 17-year-old.

Even in college you knew his arm was something special.

Even in college you knew his arm was something special. You'd go to practice and go, "Gosh, he can throw it but he just needs some experience. Can you afford to make the changes?" Obviously, we chose not to and it worked out pretty good for us. We went to the semifinals for the national championship. But you

Courtesy University of Northern Iowa

Kurt Warner in action at the University of Northern Iowa

knew Kurt had the potential to be something special. I'll never forget early in the season when we had a couple of ballgames where you could win the game by running the football and Kurt got a little antsy but turned in a couple of great games. He can really throw; obviously his accuracy is much better, but you can see he can throw it. We had pro scouts look at several people – Kenny Shedd, Bryce Paup, Dedric Ward with the Jets, James Jones with the Lions – seven maybe eight guys from Northern Iowa still on teams in the NFL. We were a pretty good 1-AA school so we had as many scouts there as we do here at a Big 12 school. Everything you see with Kurt is what you get. He's not putting on a front; he's that pure and a great person.

> The Kansas basketball coach with the worst record
> is Dr. James Naismith, the inventor of the game.

Courtesy University of Kansas

IF MY BACKUP IS THE MVP IN THE NFL, WHAT AM I DOING IN KANSAS, TOTO?
JAY JOHNSON

Jay Johnson graduated from Northern Iowa in 1993 and is currently the quarterbacks coach at the University of Kansas. Johnson grew up in Lakeville, Minnesota, and was second in the nation in passing efficiency in 1991. Kurt Warner was Johnson's backup quarterback for three years at UNI.

Good old Kurt – I'm proud of him. He's done a tremendous job and taken advantage of the opportunity and I'm looking forward to seeing him again. I was a year ahead of Kurt at Northern Iowa so I tried to be at the top of my game. We had a very successful football team, too, so I was surrounded by a lot of very talented players and we experienced a lot of success and really had some great years there. I did not start as a freshman, but I played a little bit. When Kurt came my sophomore year I knew he was good, but I was confident in my abilities and felt I could play. Any good athlete has that competitive spirit and wants the ball and wants to have the chance to compete and help their team be successful, and that's definitely how I felt. After I graduated I went to graduate school and started working on my master's degree at the University of Missouri.

We got along great. Kurt was always supportive of what I was doing. We studied the game films and helped each other out and had a great relationship – a good working relationship. He was supportive of me the whole way and of what we were doing as a football team. My last year to play was '92. His redshirt year was '93. It's hard to know what the NFL guys look for but I always thought Kurt could throw the heck out of the football; his arm strength was unbelievable, I always thought. Then, when he first got his free agent look with the Packers, from what I heard they were very impressed with him and obviously he was battling a little bit of the odds because they had three pretty good quarter-

A postgame celebration at UNI with, from left, Grandma, Aunt Sharon, Kurt, Matt, and Mom

backs stacked up already in Green Bay – Favre, Brunell, and Detmer. I didn't really know how he would do. I knew he was a very competitive person and was a winner. Really, as far as an NFL quarterback, I felt he had the arm skills to really compete at that level.

I haven't seen him much. But this summer, a couple of KU coaches and I went over to Macomb, Illinois, to the first day of training camp and he ate lunch with us and we visited with him. I wish I would have known to say, "When you're named MVP and go to the Super Bowl, would you get me a couple of tickets." But really, it was awesome to see him doing well during the season. I was happy for him.

He's persevered through a great deal and when the opportunity has arisen for him, he's taken advantage of it. You can say that about him back in his Iowa Barnstormer days, too, and when he went to NFL Europe and now with his opportunity in St. Louis. We kept trying to follow him and said, "Wow, he's on fire." Week after week after week, really, he was doing great things. When we played together you always felt you had to do your best because he was very good and was capable of getting play. He was playing sparingly but I don't remember how much. The coaching and the program we had going at UNI were successful and we were winning a lot of football games and had a good team. Kenny Shedd was on our team and was a phenomenal player. Bryce Paup was there, James Jones, so we really had some successful players.

Courtesy University of Northern Iowa

WHEN THE PANTHERS CALL, YA GOTTA ACCEPT THE CHARGES
RICK HARTZELL

A native of Klemme, Iowa, Rick became athletic director at UNI in August 1999. From 1977 – 1980, he was head baseball coach at Coe College. UNI has mass-produced a special trading card on Kurt Warner.

W hat we're trying to do with the card is honor a guy who is a quality human being and who has obviously accomplished some great things. The trading cards are a limited edition with a signed picture of him in his UNI Panthers uniform in an acrylic case. To do this project, he wanted to do something to give back to UNI so all contributions from this project are going to benefit the Kurt Warner Scholarship Endowment Fund that will go to a UNI athlete. It sells for $25, and we have had very good response. We sell them on our Web site, we sell them at our games, they're tagged in all of our advertisements; word of mouth has been really big. We have 1,000 on order. We will do a total of 1,994 because 1994 was when he graduated from UNI. We hope this will raise $50,000.

We're doing that scholarship in his name and we're gonna do a couple of other events in his name simply to establish a scholarship to try to help some kids be able to become the best they can. That's that part of it. Other than that, he's attracted a whole bunch of positive attention for UNI that we all know is a really, really good place. He's obviously a quality human being and that doesn't hurt because, I think, people look at that and think, "Gee, a guy like that comes out of UNI. It must be a good place. They're preparing the right kind of people, good solid moral folks." So that's been good, as a second thing. Thirdly, and indirectly,

By winning percentage, Indiana ranks 12th in all-time Big Ten Football standings behind the University of Chicago.

that name recognition out there has made it somewhat easier for our coaches to talk to potential recruits that are outside of Iowa. For example, our football recruiting this year has been made a little more accessible by the fact that Kurt was out there having success and people knew who he was and where he was from. Particularly in the St. Louis metropolitan area, but also, interestingly enough, in Ohio and southern Illinois and places where we've always tried to get kids. What his name recognition and our name recognition associated with him has done, I think, is make things a little easier. When you add all those things up – and our football team was eight and three, he's added to our momentum – if that makes sense. We have a guy like Bryce Paup in the NFL, who was defensive Most Valuable Player a few years ago, and we've got Kurt and James Jones and Ty Talton, Kenny Shedd, and Dedric Ward. When people start talking about that, and you've got winning programs, too, people start saying maybe these guys do, in fact, know what they're doing. It's been great to be here, and it's a fun time, and obviously what Kurt's doing well hasn't hurt.

I referee basketball in the Big Ten and in the ACC, so I had a little bit of interaction with Dr. Tom Davis, the former Iowa head basketball coach. The very first note I got at UNI after I took that job, the very first one, was from Tom Davis. To me, that was amazing. A lot of people knew I was coming, and for him to do that was wonderful. He just said, "'Congratulations' and 'great to see you've succeeded' and 'way to go' and 'get after 'em.'" I just thought that was one of the classiest things; he's a good guy.

For years I have refereed in the ACC and Big Ten, and a little bit in Conference USA and Big 12. I don't know of any other athletic director who officiates. For a long time, we thought we should – you know how they do these model calendars? – well, we ought to do a referee calendar and put all these faces that all these basketball fans in the SEC and ACC and Big Ten communities know; have a little fun with it, put a little bull's-eye on them or something like that. I've always thought it would be heck of a marketing idea but no one's ever liked it but me.

> To be a Division I school in football, your stadium must have 30,000 seats and you must average 17,000 in attendance.

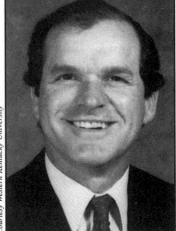

Courtesy Western Kentucky University

WARNER WAS A HARD DOG TO KEEP UNDER THE PORCH... BUT HE DIDN'T HURT US IN '94
JACK HARBAUGH

In the mid-1970s, a father stood at the side-lines of a Catholic grade school in eastern Iowa and watched his son loft a long pass toward the corner of the end zone. Little did that father know that 20 years later that son would launch a similar pass – a pass that if caught would send his Cinderella team to the Super Bowl and cap off a Cinderella season for his son, the quarterback. Gene Warner at All Saints School playground in Cedar Rapids, Iowa? No! It was Jack Harbaugh watching his son Jim throw the pass at St. Patrick's grade school in Iowa City, Iowa. Jack Harbaugh is currently head football coach at Western Kentucky. Before that, he was head football coach at Western Michigan. Prior to that, he was an assistant to Bo Schembechler for many years at Michigan, and during the early '70s, he an was assistant to Frank Lauterbur at the University of Iowa. In 1995, his son Jim, while playing for the Indianapolis Colts, threw that pass that, if it would have been caught, would have propelled the Colts into the Super Bowl. Jack Harbaugh is just a great guy and one of the few coaches with knowledge of sports trivia. Harbaugh coached his Western Kentucky Hilltoppers against Kurt Warner during Warner's senior season at Northern Iowa in 1993.

I think it was '93 when UNI played here at Western Kentucky. He threw four touchdown passes and they just wiped us out. The quarterback position is such a unique position. If somebody is not willing to have a little patience with you, I think a lot of guys can get lost in the shuffle. When you come out of college, people put raps on you: "He can star in the NFL." "He can start in the NFL." "He can be a third-stringer in the NFL." "He's not gonna make it." Once you get pigeonholed, it almost takes an act of congress or a situation like Kurt had at St. Louis

Coach Jack is applauding NFL quarterback Jim at an appreciation night at Western Kentucky.

with the Rams to get that opportunity. I think he's one of those guys. The Lord blessed him and presented him with an opportunity and he demonstrated that he had the skills to do it at that level. The Bears gave up on him.

> **The Lord blessed him and presented him with an opportunity and he demonstrated that he had the skills to do it at that level.**

Jim was in about fourth or fifth grade when I went to coach at the University of Iowa under Head Coach Frank Lauterbur. Great place. The thing I loved about it there were no pro teams in Iowa so they took their college football very seriously.

When I first saw Kurt, I thought this guy is so blessed, he's got great receivers and he's got Marshall Faulk coming out of the backfield. Then I watched him more closely in playoff games. Boy, he can throw. He's got the receivers. He's putting that ball places; he's got talent. Just picturing where they were a couple of years go. I can just see his wife in the stands. And here they are on the threshold of the greatest sporting event in history and everybody's rooting for them. Everybody. Can you imagine?

WHERE WERE YOU, MY WATERLOO?
RICK COLEMAN

Rick Coleman is with KWWL Television in Waterloo, Iowa. He has covered Kurt Warner since Kurt's freshman year at the University of Northern Iowa.

I did a coach's show for the Northern Iowa football team during the '90s. When Kurt was a sophomore, we started doing the show. At that time he was sitting on the bench behind Jay Johnson. He had a lot of ability, but according to some of the coaches, they didn't think he had the football savvy to be a starter, but it was a situation where Kurt was a year behind Jay Johnson in the pecking order. I would listen to some of the players talk, and I think you can learn a lot just listening to them talk. Some of them thought Kurt was a much better passer than Jay so I observed. When you hear it enough you sort of try to investigate for yourself to check it out. At practices, I would see Kurt, and in the drills he would definitely, in my mind, outperform Jay, and I would say, "Why isn't Terry starting this guy?" And obviously it would be a risk to bench an upper classman who had been winning like Jay to take a risk on a guy who hadn't started a game. Even though the guy was outperforming Jay Johnson in practice. The team was winning and Jay was a decent quarterback.

Kurt's not starting and I thought he was a real nice guy. I said, "You've got a pretty good game and from what I understand a lot of the players believe you ought to be starting." He never said, "I agree with you." He just said thank you. He was always a team player. I remember a spring game before Kurt's junior year where the teams were divided up and Jay had one team and Kurt had the other team, and Kurt's team won the game 17 to 7. I remember interviewing Kurt after the game – I think I still have the interview on tape – and he was saying, "Yeah we just made some plays and were able to win this game." I said, "Do you think this opens up an opportunity for you to start next year?" He said, "Well it depends on the coaches and what they think and feel."

> **At practices, I would see Kurt, and in the drills he would definitely, in my mind, outperform Jay...**

Courtesy University of Northern Iowa

Some may have felt Kurt was a better quarterback than UNI starter Jay Johnson (above), but Johnson had seniority and, more importantly, the team was winning.

He's too good to be true – a little skeptically. But I've know Kurt for seven, eight, or nine years, and I would see him out on occasion. I know about the situation with him and Brenda. There is no flaw in his character; he's human, of course. He gets tired of the media pressure; he gets tired of the invasion of his privacy by the fans. But he's still a good guy.

After winning the spring game, 17 to 7, I interviewed Terry Allen. He said, "Jay's still my quarterback until we have to see how the fall workouts go." Jay Johnson ended up being the quarterback three years his sophomore through senior years. That season, Jay Johnson took the team all the way to the semifinal round of the Division 1-AA playoff, and this was as far as the team had ever gone. You have to remember this team had an all-star cast of players for Division 1-AA football. They had a team talented enough to win it all. I don't know what Jay's statistics were in that semifinal game against Youngstown that day, but they weren't very good, and a lot of it was that Jay short-armed balls. Jay was a smart bright kid. I don't want to take anything away from his abilities as a football leader, but he didn't have the talent Kurt did. I think everyone saw that. The thing about Kurt, even though he was a better player than Jay, he was the perfect soldier. He didn't go to the media. I've seen other players who would go and plant seeds in the media about their frustration with what was going on, but he never did that. He just said maybe, hopefully, I'll get my opportunity. He waited patiently in line like a good foot soldier. That senior year they didn't have quite the talent. The junior year they had a championship defense and some definite weapons.

Around Kurt they didn't quite have the weapons but he still led them to the first round of the Division 1-AA playoffs. Bryce Paup was there only one year when Kurt was scout team quarterback – Kurt's redshirt freshman year. As a redshirt freshman, Bryce Paup was a senior. Kurt did a lot of scout team play. I would joke around with him a lot about his relationship with Brenda. I knew eventually they were going to get married. I think he was just looking for a situation financially where he would be able to take care of her and the whole family. I would always tease him about that. I would say, "Well, when are you gonna make that woman an honest woman?" "In due time," and it finally came around.

> **I've seen other players who would go and plant seeds in the media about their frustration with what was going on, but he never did that.**

The second day of the draft, in 1994, I was at Kurt's home. We covered Trev Alberts press conference held at Holiday Inn in Cedar Falls. Trev was a local kid, a terrific All-American at Nebraska and the fifth player picked in the entire draft. For a small community like this there was at least 150-200 people there. Mel Kiper Jr. was on television lambasting Indianapolis' selection about Trev with that high a draft pick. We were interviewing Trev, who was gonna sign for a multimillion-dollar deal. The very next day, I find out that Kurt Warner had signed a free agent deal with the Green Bay Packers. I told my colleague, Brian Lesley, sports director here, "Maybe we should go out and get an interview with Kurt." It's just a free agent deal; he didn't get drafted but I thought he always had a great deal of potential. He said, "Sure, let's do it." We

Kurt (middle) with Matt and Mom after graduation ceremony at UNI.

went over to his girlfriend, Brenda's house, a modest apartment on Waterloo Road in Cedar Falls. Kurt was there playing with the children and Brenda was cooking a modest meal, hot dogs, and macaroni and cheese. Kurt came outside and did the interview – real nice, genuinely excited about the situation, looking to go up there and show the Packers what he could do. And if he didn't make it there, he felt like maybe some other teams would get wind of what he had done there. They were the worst team in the world to try to break in with.

After being cut in Green Bay, I saw him at a few different places. He would say, "No I'm not gonna give up on my dream." We didn't cover the Barnstormer games as frequently as our sister station in Des Moines,

Academic All-American teams have been picked every year since 1952. Nebraska leads all colleges by a wide margin in number of players selected. Maybe the *N* on Nebraska's helmets stands for *Knowledge*.

Courtesy University of Northern Iowa

Kurt (13) gives instructions in the huddle at an arena game.

who would send us tapes. So unless Kurt would come up here to visit, I didn't see much of him, but when I was down there in St. Louis, just recently, we have kinda renewed acquaintances. This year we went down to about three or four games in St. Louis. As soon as we knew he'd been given the opportunity to play, our station decided to go down and cover it. He was glad to see we were there covering the games. We were all glad he was getting the opportunity because we felt he had the ability and was trying hard and hadn't had the opportunities, so our conversations were about that. I may have even tried to bait him early on about college when he may not have had the opportunity to show what he could do, but he always kept it positive. I can't tell you, it renews my faith in the fact that if you work hard and don't give up…

After the Super Bowl, he was walking through the tunnel and I was going down to interview him. He told me, "Thanks for your support; I love you." It made me feel good to have him talk to me. I knew he would never forget me because I had been one who tried to encourage him early on when he was down.

Words can't really pinpoint what it's meant to have him come from here and do so well. It puts our little area on the map. This area, this community has created a good person, as well as a talented athlete. I think in the long run, people will see that he really is that – just a down-to-earth, good man.

Joe Montana did not start until the fourth game of his junior year at Notre Dame.

Chapter 4

Steve Mariucci

Dave Jensen

Ron Pearson

Green Bay,
Greenhorn,
and Green Beans

*Bonnie Bell and other Hy-Vee employees had a blast when
Kurt Warner visited Hy-Vee's corporate headquarters in Des Moines.*

HE COMPARED HIM TO BRETT FAVRE. COMPARED TO FAVRE, HE SUCKED.
STEVE MARIUCCI

Steve Mariucci is the head football coach for the San Francisco 49ers. He came to the 49ers after a head coaching stint at the University of California. Before coming to California, Mariucci was quarterbacks coach for the Green Bay Packers. In 1994, he had the unenviable task of releasing Kurt Warner because the other three quarterbacks in camp were Brett Favre, Heisman Trophy Winner Ty Detmer, and Mark Brunell.

In 1993, we signed Kenny O'Brien from the Jets cause he had 12 years in the league. We had Brett who had one year, and Ty Detmer who had one year, and then we drafted Mark Brunell in the fifth round and then we had Kenny O'Brien. We thought we might keep four. Well you don't keep four. Somebody had to go. We felt the best guys were the young guys and we said, "Gee, do we want to do this? It's gonna be the youngest group of quarterbacks ever assembled in the league with nobody with more than a year experience." We ended up doing it.

So, when Kurt came the next year, we still had a young bunch. Yet, luckily Brett played every game; he didn't get hurt. Not that Ty or Mark couldn't have done it, it's just that when you're training young guys and they don't get all the practice work – Good Luck! It doesn't happen like it's supposed to when they're not getting all of the work so luckily Brett stayed healthy. We had to alternate Brunell and Ty Detmer active and inactive every other week, just to keep them happy. I don't know if that was the best thing or the worst thing to do but then, eventually, you can't hang onto all those guys. If they're all good enough to play, you simply can't hang on to them all. They're gonna go elsewhere because they all want to start. They all deserve to start so you can't hold them back.

In '94, with Kurt Warner at the Packers, proves timing is everything. You have four quarterbacks on your team: Brett Favre, Ty Detmer, Mark Brunell, and Kurt Warner, and it was not Kurt Warner's time. He was a youngster who didn't get a lot of reps at all because the others were very young and deserving to show us what they could do. They were all second-year players or so. So Kurt was there as a youngster, just getting his feet wet, just learning what pro football entails. You'd love to be able to keep all those guys and know the future and be able to predict. Needless to say, the Packers have only one of them remaining and it's Brett Favre, and he hasn't missed a game. So the others move on and they do their thing elsewhere. Ty has done it, so has Mark, and so has Kurt now. It's a matter of being patient and waiting for the right time and the right place and being opportunistic when you get that chance. Whether it's because you've been traded to the right team, or there's an injury or two in front of you, or whatever the reason might be when you get your chance. All four of those people have done well when given their shot. It just took Kurt just a little bit longer to show what he's got.

We were handed him. He was signed by Ron Wolf, the Packers general manager. Back then, Kurt was not ready yet. He was just beginning, in the infant stages of learning what pro football was all about. We were in a situation where we didn't have the time to train him and evaluate him like you would hope to because of the other guys being so young and already on your depth chart and already having proven that they deserved to be there. So they're getting all the reps. Kurt was simply a young guy who'd sit and learn in meetings.

I know he enjoyed being there because Brett Favre and Ty and Mark gave him a lot of grief and had a blast with him.

I know he enjoyed being there because Brett Favre and Ty and Mark gave him a lot of grief and had a blast with him. Favre called him Chachi. He may have had a lot of nicknames. They were a fun group of guys. He did fit in, he really did.

I don't know who told Kurt he was being cut. Typically there is somebody from the front office who would do that as a general rule. After a guy is cut, you wouldn't know that you would ever see him again. I would be lying to you if I said, 'This guy I knew had potential. This guy is going to be an MVP some day. This guy is gonna do great things.' You'd sound like some sort of genius that could foresee this and see the potential in the young man. But I'd be lying to you if I said that.

The next time I saw Kurt after that was when he was on television playing overseas. He was playing well. I saw just a couple of games. It was nice to see that and to know that he was doing well. Even still, you would not predict an MVP of the league-type caliber.

As we prepared to play the Rams their fourth game of the '99 year, we were hoping that prior to playing us that Kurt was lucky or just playing out of his mind. Everything was falling into place and maybe it was going to be just a flash in the pan. We were hoping that it wasn't for real. Then I threw the film on and I started watching their offense. Typically I watch the defense 'cause I'm involved in the offensive game plan. But I always throw the other side of the ball on. I looked at it, and said, "You know what? This guy is playing real good quarterback." And I started to get a little nervous. "Hey, he's playing well. He's really playing well." Why? I don't know. And how? I don't know. He's just really playing well. And he did it every week. It didn't change. In some ways, I thought that was very refreshing to see. You didn't prepare quite so much for Kurt. You prepared to stop their weapons, to double their receivers at times. You do that knowing full well he was gonna take shots down the field. You had to try to put a fence around some of those receivers and offensive weapons that they had. He was so good about distributing the ball and he was just not missing his throws. He was so accurate and he was poised and he was making good decisions. He was playing like a veteran, a guy who has been there for eight years. That was the thing that impressed me the most. Even Dick was shocked; he hadn't let him play last year when their quarterback was struggling. I didn't know who Kurt was competing against and it didn't surprise me that he latched onto a team. Not at all. I didn't know that he would be a starter.

Kurt and I talked before the game how his family was doing. I was telling him he was doing a great job and all that kind of thing. I told him I was proud of him. He was the first guy over after the game to shake my hand. He's a gentleman, as you know, a class act. It's nice to see good things happen to the type of person that Kurt is. He's had to work for everything he's earned. He's had to be very patient. Nothing has been given to him. He's earned it. Then when he had an opportunity, God, did he respond! He is a good, solid human being. He is out here this weekend doing a card show in the Bay area. I heard him on the radio here for about a 20-minute interview a few days ago. From a year ago, when he could just about go anywhere and do anything he wanted. He was virtually a nobody. This year he can't even leave the house without autograph seekers and everybody else hounding him every minute.

From one extreme to the other. That's what happens when you live in this fishbowl that we call sports.

I have a picture of Dick Vermeil right here on my wall. When I first entered the league all the coaches, 30 coaches down at the league meeting, we take a little group shot. Of that group – and I know all of them – I would say that I speak to Dick more often than any of them. We got to know each other when he was doing college games and we hit it off and always stayed in touch and he was talking about coming back long before he did. And I was hoping I could hook up with them. We got to be pretty good friends. Then when he was back in the league, even though we're in the same division, we would still communicate during the season and talk about our week-by-week schedule, and Christmas, and training camp, and "what's your health like?" and just family and when are you coming out here to Calistoga?, and on and on. He and I probably were closer than anybody. I was delighted for him; it was tremendous for him.

On January 4, 2000, Kurt Warner was on the *David Letterman Show*. Letterman asked Warner what it felt like to be cut by Green Bay. Warner said, "Well, I was a little disappointed." Letterman responded, "It made you feel cheap! It made you feel cheap and dirty and like a loser, didn't it?" Both Warner and the audience roared.

Speaking as a competitor, I certainly hope Kurt Warner can't keep this up.

> Lombardi never said, "Winning isn't everything, it's the only thing." That line was said by John Wayne in the 1953 movie, "Trouble Along the Way."

> The first coaches' TV show was in 1952, hosted by Bud Wilkinson at the University of Oklahoma.

YO, KURT. THERE'S A SPILL IN AISLE THREE.
DAVID JENSEN

Dave Jensen is the now-famous manager of the Hy-Vee food store in Cedar Falls, Iowa, who hired Kurt Warner at minimum wage - $5.50 an hour back in the fall of 1994.

K urt Warner was trying out for the Green Bay Packers. He got dropped and he came back to Cedar Falls, Iowa, and got hired on night stock. I was the night manager at Hy-Vee. He started working night stock for me for almost five to six months and then he was trying out for the Barnstormers, and he got the call from them and he put his two weeks' notice in and went to play for the Barnstormers. While he was with Hy-Vee, the jobs he did was stock the merchandise onto the shelves, a little bit of courtesy up front, sometimes he had to take groceries out to customer cars and load them up in the cars. Once we got done stocking the shelves, he had to face the store, clean up the aisles. He had a good, positive attitude toward what he was doing. He was very polite and he talked with customers. If I gave him something hard, he would do it; he never griped, something simple he'd do it. He was always willing to do his job.

Once we got all the facing done and all the work done, we'd have a football hidden in the back room, which was large and tall enough to kick field goals and had like a dock door. There was a railing where the door goes up and there was space in between where you had to kick the ball. We had a little round thing to put the football on and we'd kick field goals back there. Sometimes, when the store was slow, we'd take a paper towel or toilet paper that had got broken open, we'd have someone go across the aisles and we'd toss toilet paper rolls or paper towels over the aisles. Kurt's done that a couple of times.

Kurt told the media where he used to work back in Cedar Falls; he told them my name and to get in touch with me. So, I've gotten about 19 calls from media; some from New York, and ABC World News came in and I was on television for those guys, and I was also on television on Channel 7, KWWL out of Waterloo. CNN I was on TV for. Fox News I was on TV for. Then someone out of Tampa Bay called, Milwaukee, someone out of Atlanta, *ESPN the Magazine*, *Sports Illustrated*, someone out of Chicago, and then a radio station out of my hometown, Chero-kee, Iowa, then San Francisco, then Channel 2 in Cedar Rapids. Just finished an interview with them, and then a televised interview with WHO-TV 13 out of Des Moines, then I got a call from Kenny Kelly's show, a Des Moines radio show. It was kind of exciting to be inter-viewed by all these people. I hadn't expected anything like this.

We have his cereal, Warner's Crunch Time, in our store in a big display up front. It's made by his charity, PBL out of Pittsburgh. It doesn't say the name of any of the cereal companies who made it. Warner's Crunch Time is the official name on it. It's selling very well. We brought in two pallets full and it's down to half a pallet. I think we're the only one in the Cedar Falls-Waterloo area selling it.

The lowest-rated NBA finals game ever was June 17, 1994, the Knicks-Rockets, because most people were watching O.J. Simpson's Bronco being chased by police, the only white Bronco more famous than John Elway.

Rich Kotite, former head coach of the Eagles and the Jets, was once Muhammad Ali's sparring partner in Miami.

SACKS—NO HELPFUL SMILES IN THOSE PILES
RON PEARSON

Ron Pearson is the CEO, chairman, and president of Hy-Vee, a chain of 183 Midwestern supermarkets and 26 drug stores. Pearson started working at Hy-Vee in 1960 while in high school in Des Moines and joined full time upon graduation from Drake University. The employee-owned stores received an avalanche of positive publicity as a result of Warner's employ-ment at the Cedar Falls, Iowa, store when he was released by the Green Bay Packers in 1994.

A local writer in Des Moines wrote something about how we got more publicity at the Super Bowl than the people who had spent a million dollars for commercials. And another writer in Des Moines had some research that showed since this phenomenon started, we have had 148 mentions either on TV or in the newspaper. I don't know how they got those numbers but I suspect it's even more than that. There's been some from the *New York Times* to the front page of the Hawaiian paper so that's pretty much half the world.

I don't know that we can relate any direct relationship to hiring people. Any time that you get positive public relations for a public company that is really powerful. We work all the time to try to get out news stories and things we do positive because sometime, somewhere there'll be something bad come up. This has been all positive publicity. It's some-thing people talk about. They come in our store and talk about it with our employees. So it's a great source of pride for our employees and I think that's quotable. That's all over the Midwest.

I met him when he was with the Barnstormers; he was in our office signing autographs for a charity. I saw him play with them; I didn't have any idea he worked there. None of our people even said anything, but we're so big you don't do that. I suspect it was halfway through the season before somebody told me. About the same time I heard that Adam Timmerman, one of his key blockers on the offensive line, had worked at Hy-Vee in our Cherokee, Iowa, store.

When Kurt was at our office, when he was at the Barnstormers, he certainly wasn't the giant star right then, but I met him and talked with him and had photos taken with him. Almost all the employees came around to try to meet him and visit with him so that was really positive. He seemed like a nice gentleman. Little did I know that he was as nice as everybody has told me he is.

Several of the employees who worked with him have said, "If you think this religious thing is not real, you're mistaken. He is not a fanatic. He is just a very down-to-earth, proper, religious young man," and I think that speaks so well of having had someone in that position. His store manager, Steve Miller, has since retired, and he says the same thing. Kurt is an outstanding, great gentleman. He was just a nice person to have working for you. People didn't even feel any different about him.

How did Hy-Vee get its name? In 1930 two men by the name of Hyde and Vredenberg were casual friends and had little businesses and decided to form a partnership and start a little, bitty store along the Iowa-Missouri border, in Deaconsfield, Iowa. That stuck and they started a second one, then a third one. Then in 1938 they incorporated. They haven't been alive since 1950.

I just was at an industry meeting and there was not a soul there that did not bring the Kurt Warner thing up. Everywhere my wife and I went, everybody said to us, "My God, what are you paying for all this publicity?" I was at a charity fundraiser and the former governor of the state came in, Bob Ray, and said, "I thought Hy-Vee did everything, but I didn't know you grew quarterbacks." He carried on and on and on and wanted to know the whole story about it. Not just me, but my employees, whether they're clear down in Kansas or way up in South Dakota they're getting the same comments from customers so it's a phenomena that doesn't lighten up. His grandfather still works for us at the Fairbault, Minnesota, Hy-Vee. He's kind of a greeter. I do know that Kurt took him to the Pro Bowl. One of our officers was in the store and the grandfather started to tell him that Kurt was allowed to take six people to Hawaii and he was taking his grandfather, and he started crying while he was telling him about it.

I saw Doctor Bob Margeas a week or 10 days ago and, remember, I told you you'd better get the book out, there are other people writing about

Kurt. Bob told me he had a friend writing a Kurt Warner book. Little did I know that was you when I made that comment to you. All the legislators were out at our office recently and I made the comment that we're the company that employed Kurt Warner so, now not only employed him, we made him famous. The real fact is he's still working for us; we're just letting him do this for a while and if he doesn't make it, he's coming back. That gets a huge laugh from everybody. Everybody really is tickled about him. I've not heard one person, rich or poor, when you say his name, not say they hope he makes a mint. Anybody that nice – they hope he makes a lot of money.

I'm very proud of him and have written him a letter. I just told him we are very proud of him and were proud that he worked with us. I just thought I'd let him know from Hy-Vee, he's using our name. If anybody asks him, he comes right up to them and is very proud he worked for Hy-Vee.

Regular shoppers at the Cedar Falls Hy-Vee included Trev Alberts' parents and Robert Waller, author of *The Bridges of Madison County*.

Coach Jimmy Johnson and Janis Joplin were high school classmates at Thomas Jefferson High School in Port Arthur, Texas. Jimmy Johnson didn't know she sang. They hated each other. She called him "Scarhead" and he called her "Beat Weeds."

Chapter 5

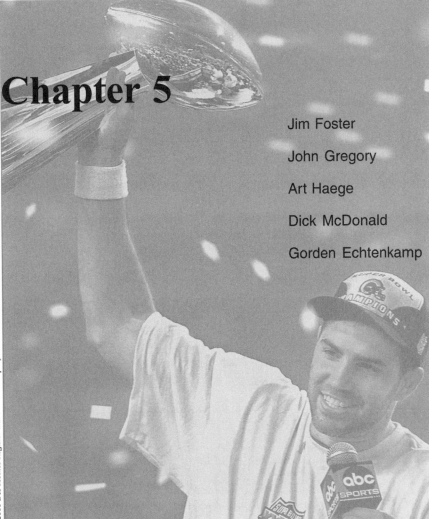

Jim Foster

John Gregory

Art Haege

Dick McDonald

Gorden Echtenkamp

The Human
Pinball League:
There are no Rest Areas
on the Highway to Success

John Gregory

Jim Foster

Dick "Mackie" McDonald with Kurt Warner in Kansas City

IT'S LIKE PLAYING HOOKY FROM LIFE
JIM FOSTER

Jim Foster is the founder of Arena Football and owner of the Iowa Barn-stormers, which starred Kurt Warner as their quarterback from 1995–1997. His story of epic perseverance and gutsy belief in himself parallels that of Warner and is deserving of a book of its own.

The Arena Football League unofficially started on February 11, 1981. I was at that time promotion manager of the National Football League in New York City, and I went to my first indoor soccer match, which happened to be the MISL All-Star Game, the old major indoor soccer league in Madison Square Garden. I took a colleague, Mark Fagan, who worked with me at the NFL, and we went down to see what indoor soccer was all about.

While we were watching it, I turned to him and said, "You know, if we can play soccer indoors, why not football?" He said, "How would you do that?" I said, "Well, you know I think there would be a way to do it."

I pulled a manila envelope out of my briefcase. It was from my Mom in Iowa City, where I grew up, which is 35 miles from where Kurt is from. I pulled this manila envelope out, which was full of press clippings on Lute Olson and the Iowa Hawkeyes. They had a great team in 1981 and went to the Final Four. My Mom was sending me press clippings because the New York press didn't cover the Big Ten very well. I started making notes on the back of it; drew the outline of a hockey rink and started making notes on how you play football indoors. Quite honestly, most of what is Arena Football today is on the back of that envelope. It's all mounted and framed now. On the back of that I schemed out that you'd probably have to play single platoon football to keep your costs down. Players would play both ways.

I grew up in Iowa City in the early '50s and '60s during the time when a great coach, Forest Evashevski, was at Iowa. I used to hang around the practice field. My Dad played football at Iowa before I was born and was a graduate assistant coach there and had recently retired as president of the I Club, so I've kinda grown up in football. I used to hang around the practice field as a kid. At that time, football was still single platoon; they hadn't gone to free substitution yet, so my memories of football as a kid were playing both ways.

What happened was, as I schemed things on the back of the envelope, I kinda went through a couple of different phases. The first thing was since you play indoors, how big would the field be and I guessed it would probably be about half the width and half the length, which is about exactly what it is – fifty yards instead of one hundred; two eight-yard end zones instead of ten – and just about half the width of an outdoor field so technically you could put four Arena Football fields on one outdoor field. Then I realized you would probably not be able to punt in an arena because the trajectory would be so high. So I thought maybe on fourth down you could just try a field goal so I wrote that down. Then I thought, well boy, all the kicks would be going up in the stands.

The NFL had just begun employing these loose nets to catch the balls. I thought we'd have to do that because so many balls would be going into the stands. I thought, "Wait a minute, first of all they're gonna make a lot of these kicks automatically." When I was a kid in Iowa City hanging around the Iowa practice field with Forest Evashevski's teams, he built a goal post which was real skinny with a high cross bar so his kickers had something to practice at and I always thought it was the darndest looking thing

> **To this day I always call it Evie's goal post and I sketched it in as being a smaller, skinnier goal post with a higher cross bar.**

when I was a kid so I sketched that in. To this day I always call it Evie's goal post and I sketched it in as being a smaller, skinnier goal post with a higher cross bar. What it ended up being was nine feet instead of eighteen, which is what the NFL post is. And it's fifteen feet high instead of ten. Of course that's made a big difference in our game, too, from a kicking standpoint.

And then the lightning bolt hit, and I thought instead of loose nets, when I was a kid in Iowa City, my parents bought me one of those Little League pitch-back nets which a lot of kids had. But I always used to

Ricky Nelson and John DeLorean married daughters of 1940 Heisman Trophy Winner Tom Harmon of Michigan.

throw my football into it and it would bounce off at strange angles and I make these diving catches and I make believe I was Jim Gibbons from the Iowa Hawkeyes or Harlan Hill from the Chicago Bears, who were my idols back then. I always wanted to be a Hawkeye and a Bear. So I'm here in Madison Square Garden thinking about all that and think maybe I could build the world's largest pitch-back net and hang it from the rafters in a typical arena so I sketched that in and that is actually the genesis for the patent.

Arena Football is a patented game. It is the only patented team sport in the history of the world that's actually played. Nobody's ever been able to do that before; it took me six years to get it. I applied for a patent in '84 initially and it was actually issued in March of 1990; a U.S. patent. There are also patents now in a number of overseas countries including Mexico, Japan, Canada, Korea, Great Britain either issued or pending.

Another interesting Iowa tie is Iowa's most famous football player of all time, Nile Kinnick, a Heisman Trophy winner, a scholar athlete, who went into World War II as a fighter pilot, crashed and died. A lot of people thought he would be president; he was such a gifted guy. The stadium is named after him. My son is named after him. In any case, Nile was a great drop kicker at Iowa. He played on the great Iron Man teams that was one of the top teams in the country in '39 during the depression. It was a huge rallying point for Iowa during the depression to have this great football team.

At any rate, as I'm scheming through this, I'm thinking now you can't ever quick kick in Arena Football because you're not gonna punt. You can only place kick. I thought what would happen if we made the quick kick legal by making drop kicking a part of this game? In Arena Football, if you try a field goal by drop kicking which we've had it done, it's four points instead of three. And if you try it on an extra point attempt conversion after a touchdown, it's two points instead of one. We've had a couple of guys who've been pretty good at it. They're soccer style drop kickers. They actually cradle it with their foot 'cause the newer ball from years ago is a lot skinnier. I got that idea that night because my Dad had played for Dr. Eddie Anderson who had coached Nile Kinnick several years earlier before he went off to the war and my Dad had learned to drop kick from the same coach. When I was a little kid, my Dad would drop kick to me in a field across the street from where I grew up, which incidentally is the high school that Tim Dwight, of the Atlanta Falcons, attended.

I'm thinking, "Why not make the drop kick a part of the game?" and wrote that in there, and you could actually quick kick. I got that idea from Hayden Fry, the Iowa coach who used to quick kick once in a while for field position. Very few coaches do that anymore, but it's an interesting concept. Then I got down to the economics of the game and the real question was: "Can you play professional football in a 14,000-seat arena and play once a week, which you've pretty much got to do in football?" You can't do like hockey or basketball or baseball and play two or three times a week and make any money. I thought, "Man, you've got a 47-man roster in the NFL. You've got all kinds of expenses."

I thought back to Iowa City one more time, as a kid, when I was real little, going down to the train station, and the Hawkeyes still took the train,. After that Iowa would charter a DC-3. They used two of them, which held 30-33 people each, and there would be 33 players on the travel roster in those days so I wrote that down.

So we have true iron man football which goes back to Nile Kinnick. I'm thinking about what would happen if we could get some really tough kids, limit the size of the roster and let them go both ways. So I wrote that down, and I knew we would probably play with seven, eight or nine players – couldn't play with 11 because the field was too small and we ended up testing all three and ended up with eight-man football. Most of that was on that paper which was written up that night – that envelope.

Well I get back to my office at the NFL next day and my buddy Mark Fagan told a few guys in the office, "Foster's got this wild idea for playing football indoors" and they asked me about it occasionally. Then another buddy of mine heard about it. He was in the advertising business with a large agency, Dentsu, in New York and he liked the idea. He said, "You ought to bounce this idea. You ought to tighten it up, get some rules written, have a marketing plan, things like that, and we ought to take it around to the television networks."

So I actually took some time. I was kind of intrigued 'cause I always have a lot of ideas, but when someone else actually tells you it's a good idea, that's when you listen – not when you think you've got a

> In 1935, Nile Kinnick was the catcher on his American Legion baseball team. The pitcher was Bob Feller.

good idea. Some of the guys said this is kinda interesting so I started working on it. Another mutual friend, a senior art director for Young & Rubicam, and the Cato-Johnson division, John Gagan is his name. He liked it, too, and he had a lot of connections in sports. He was doing work for me at the NFL marketing consulting for us. John did a water-color and acrylic drawing which hangs in my office of what an arena football field would look like in a stadium and it's amazingly accurate to this day.

So I get into NBC, CBS, ABC, ESPN, USA Network. I'm like "this is really cool going in to visit these people." I've got this great job with the NFL. I'm very happy. They don't know I'm doing this, incidentally. We spot meetings here and there. I go to NBC and meet with Ken Schanzer, who I think is still there; Art Watson, who was then president of NBC Sports; and a fellow named Sean McManus, now president of CBS Sports who also is Jim McKay's son.

They called back and said they would like to meet with me. They offer a contract to put a game together and see what would happen. They're going to put it on a Saturday afternoon Sports Anthology and gave me a couple of years to put it together. They offered me about $50,000 and fees to do it plus production costs. I thought, "Wow, I can't believe it." I've got this awesome job with the National Football League, and I've got this chance to go out and put my own football game together. I signed the contract and thought, "I'm not going to walk away from it, but how am I going to handle this?"

I got short-circuited about three months later because the USFL was announced. When they announced USFL, I said, well, good concept, off-season football which was always the plan for mine if I ever did anything with it and they had lots of money and seemed to be pretty organized and I can't compete with that. So I went back to NBC and told them, "Look USFL is gonna launch, I don't think I can compete with this. I don't know if my game mechanically works at this point." They said fine, let's chill it and put it on the shelf. ESPN had also been pretty interested in what I had but when I signed with NBC I hadn't pursued them any further. I then started getting phone calls about a month later from the USFL about the possibility of jumping ship from the National Football League. I loved my job but I really wanted to be a general manager long term.

I loved my job but I really wanted to be a general manager long term.

That was my goal in life at that point, and I never dreamed it would happen to me several years later, but I had several offers and opted to go with the Arizona Wranglers. I was assistant general manager going in. It was the last team put together in the USFL and it was kind of a disaster on the playing field, but we were pretty successful. We were third-largest in attendance and did pretty well in marketing. I went into the USFL the fall of '82, left New York, moved to Phoenix. I got great exposure to what doesn't work in professional football and how hard it is to compete with the National Football League. It was just a huge eye-opener for me and we did a good job out there. But every single day the fans and the media would say, all around the league, not just in Phoenix, "It's not the National Football League; it's not as good as the National Football League." You couldn't get over the second-class status and I kept thinking about Arena Football.

Ironically, the USFL was all first class. They had a couple of Achilles heels. The L.A. Express was a little weak in terms of the way it was operated. They had great players like Steve Young and entertainment – kind of a rebirth of the AFL. Dave Dixon, who put the league together, had a basic concept of not getting in the way of the NFL, play in the spring and the summer, don't steal their top players, and you're gonna survive and grow. But the problem was when Donald Trump got involved – and several other guys with big egos and a lot of money, they said, "Oh, to heck with that. We're gonna go right after the NFL." And that was the beginning of the end.

After a year with the Arizona Wranglers in Phoenix, I'm thinking, "I don't think this thing is gonna make it." The reason is not that it's not a good product but that it's never gonna get a chance to breed on its own; that it's a clone of the National Football League – the way most people look at it. It's an ugly stepsister. I thought the one thing about Arena Football if it works, and I'm not even sure it's gonna work yet, is the fact that it's gonna be a different game. When you walk in it's gonna be football and blocking and tackling, but it's gonna be a different enough game that you can't say this was an imitation of the NFL.

Then I got an opportunity to go back to Chicago, back to the Midwest, to take over running the Chicago Blitz, which George Allen had been with the first year and had a pretty good team. But George's owner was

> NFL footballs are made in Ada, Ohio.
> Each team uses one thousand per year.

a man named Ted Diethrich from Phoenix who really wanted to own the team in Phoenix. They arranged a deal for him to buy the Phoenix team and to come with George to Phoenix. I had an opportunity to stay in Phoenix with Ted whom I knew, but then I got the chance to return to Chicago and take over running most of the operations of that team.

I left Phoenix and the warm weather and a pretty good situation at that point to go to Chicago because I knew if the USFL didn't make it, I was not going to be able to put Arena Football together very easily from Phoenix. I needed to be in Chicago or New York. I had not sold my home in Connecticut yet because I was not sure what was going to happen to the USFL, and I thought I might have to go back to New York if it didn't work. I wanted to either go back to the NFL or maybe try Arena Football and probably end up back in New York to do it. I took a job, went to Chicago. It was a disaster. The team was bankrupted two weeks before the season by the owner because he didn't have the money he claimed he had. It was a mess. Marv Levy was our head coach. We had Vince Evans at quarterback. Doug Plank was playing for us. We had some other retreads from the Chicago Bears. It was just not a good situation. Actually, two weeks before the season, they bankrupted the team, fired most of the front office staff except a secretary and a couple of people so they could play the games. That's all they did – showed up at Soldier Field and played the game in front of about 4,000 people. It was a mess.

> **The team was bankrupted two weeks before the season by the owner because he didn't have the money he claimed he had.**

In the fall of '85 I was still in Chicago. I made another interesting decision – took an opportunity to do the marketing for the Chicago Sting indoor soccer team. It gave me a chance to work in the arena environment and understand how arenas work better. I had the football background but I hadn't worked with arenas. I did that for two seasons and then they suspended operations.

I said, "Now's the time to do it." I told my wife in the fall of '85, "This is it, Babe, I've gotta try this." My wife, Susan, just about the ultimate football widow of all time I think, and I went after it. I started testing the rules. I hired semipro players to go to a little arena in Rockford, Illinois. We videotaped on a soccer turf with tape down to create the yard lines, the gridiron. It looked great; we scrimmaged with seven, eight, nine players – eight-man worked well. I picked up a coach out of the USFL who had been a great running back as an Iowa Hawkeye, Ray Jauch. Ray had gone on to win two Grey Cups in the Canadian league and had come out of that league to coach the Washington Federals, which was one of the problem franchises in the USFL 'cause they weren't capitalized. The USFL was done.

Ray was still in Washington so he came down and we walked into the Rockford Arena. They had set the field up, the nets were hanging, the first time I'd ever seen it but they had used my drawings to actually put it together. Ray looked at it and said, "God, it looks like a postage stamp. I don't know how you can play football on this thing." He had been in the Canadian league for a long time and it scared the daylights out of me. My heart was pounding and racing and I thought, "Oh, my God. Every dime I had is invested up to that point to get to where I could do this." It worked well; the players loved it. They said this was so much fun. We knew we had a potential winner there from a mechanical standpoint, from a fun standpoint. So I made the decision to try and play a test game so we went back to Rockford. We invited the public and the media to come in. We held a little press conference – wouldn't tell them what it was. Said it would be football on a smaller field indoors. You have to come see it. We had a market research company come in as a favor and did market research and a fan audit to find out what the fans thought about it. The thing went off like gangbusters. I had so little money. I told the players – I gave them like $25 apiece to play on an indoor soccer turf which doesn't even have as much padding as an indoor football field. We jerry-rigged everything to make it work; I had to spend like $5,000 to get the first set of rebound nets built because they have to be out of a stronger steel so you can stretch these nets tight enough. If you don't use strong enough steel it just collapses the frames. I borrowed two sets of uniforms from two semipro teams I knew. I named one team the Chicago Politicians and the other team the Rockford Metros. They were playing in an arena named the Metro Center, which is still there.

The NFL since 1968 has given every player the Wonderlic test (a human resources test measuring the ability to acquire and use job knowledge). In a recent year, 118,549 non-NFL people took the test and only four had a perfect score of 50. In 30-plus years, the only NFL player with a perfect score was Pat McInally of Harvard in 1968. McInally starred with the Cincinnati Bengals as tight end and punter.

It's amazing what happened. We were only gonna play half a game as I was afraid someone would get hurt as they got tired. So I told the players you're gonna play two quarters and see how it works. We're going to video it and get fan reaction. I told every player if this thing works you will get a legitimate tryout if there's ever a league. I stuck to my word and about five kids from that game played in the league the first couple of years. So the game starts. Metro scores first and the place goes nuts – like they've been playing for 10 years. We couldn't believe it. I had ESPN there; Howard Balzer from the *Sporting News* was there. I've got a couple of potential sponsors there. Then, at halftime, with things going so well, the players don't want to quit. They said we want to play a second half. The team that was losing said, "We want to beat these guys." The winning team said, "There's no way they're going to beat us." So we played a whole game. The results are phenomenal. Howard wrote a full-page story, which I allowed him to release. Up to that point, everybody signed a disclosure, including the players: nobody could talk about what they were doing. I was trying to keep it under wraps. I did a pretty good job of it. I told Howard he could break it. ESPN was allowed to break it. It was national news a day later. They ran videotape on ABC Sports and ESPN *SportsCenter*. Howard had a full-page story that came out about Arena Football and the phone started ringing off the hook.

There were a lot of franchise wannabes and a lot of guys with a dime and a tire to kick and no money but wanted to be in the pro football business. We started flushing through it and I raised enough additional money to play a full-blown test game called the Showcase Game in the Rosemont Horizon in Chicago. Doug Buffone, the old Chicago Bear, got involved and helped promote it. We played that game in February of '87 – dead of winter, it was cold as heck. I was scared to death nobody was going to show up. Again, the same thing happened as at Rockford. We did market research again and it was kinda that old adage, "If it'll play in Peoria, it'll play on Broadway." Well, we went from Rockford to Chicago. People loved it; we had over 8,000 people there that night. We charged a nominal fee to get in and gave it to a local charity in Chicago that Buffone was involved with. Doug Buffone did the play-by-play to simulate television and I shot my wad to do that. It cost probably $10,000 to do that to make it look like a real TV game and it was a super success. People loved it, and we got some pretty good press from the Chicago area and some more national media.

Compared to those days, sports is so much more high profile and as a result of it you're seeing more and more of the wrong element getting involved as well. You're seeing that reflected in player attitudes on the field and you're seeing it in a lot of things around the edges of the business.

That's one of the refreshing things about Kurt Warner is that he's pretty much oblivious to that. I can tell you from negotiations with Kurt for salary which Coach Gregory basically took care of it, but Kurt wasn't a guy who said if you don't give me this, I'm not gonna play. He said I want to be paid fairly for what I do, let's get this worked out. Let's get back to the football field. Unfortunately, today there's too many players who have become affected with this attitude that "the whole world revolves around me. If you don't pay me what I want, I'm out of here." Kurt didn't have an agent here, and he went to the Rams without an agent.

Kurt was our highest-paid player and he made a little over $65,000 with bonuses. Our current quarterback, Aaron Garcia, who replaced Kurt, is making a little more than Kurt but that's just due to the fact that things have gone up. He's a very fine quarterback in his own right.

I was the first guy to ever use blimps indoors at sports events. We do a lot of things first. We don't get credit for it 'cause we don't have the platform to publicize it, but it will all come out in time. In 1987, when I started the league, I picked up Hardee's as a presenting sponsor. I was trying to come up with ways to give them more visibility. We were doing signs on the sidelines which at that time hockey was not doing; we were kinda ahead of our time on that. So I had our signs on the sidelines and I also spray painted Hardee's logo on the nets on either side of the goalposts but that didn't show up as much as I wanted it to. I happened to be reading a magazine. I am a pilot and have an interest in aviation, and saw these miniature blimps that a company in California was making and they were really kind of in their infancy doing it. I called them and wanted to know what they cost and how they worked, and they were radio controlled. They were using them at that time for shopping malls and had never put them in a big arena. We joke about being out for the team coin toss and I tell the team captain if they win to take the wind and they laugh at me. But there are air currents from the air conditioning system in an arena, sometimes more than you realize. So I bought four of these blimps for Hardee's, and had

> **We were doing signs on the sidelines which at that time hockey was not doing; we were kinda ahead of our time on that.**

one in each of the cities. From the get-go, we had problems with them because they just didn't have enough power on them to turn the propellers. It was like maybe the second game we played in Denver. We had local radio-control airplane club members to fly them for us. The guy who was flying the one in Denver got it too high, too close to the rafters and it got sucked into an air exchanger – these huge ducts about four feet in diameter that move the air in and out of the big arenas. It actually sucked it up against the air exchanger; we couldn't get it down, even when they turned the air off, because it had sucked it so far in there. We had to get a pellet gun and shoot it down.

One of the things the fans and the media noticed about Arena Football was the intensity of the noise and the excitement. People were used to going to football games in outdoor stadiums. Even in a place like the Astrodome, it just wasn't the same. When you go to an Arena game, the players are in your face, the people are screaming and yelling, and it is just a very intense experience. So what happened in our very first championship game ever at the Pittsburgh Civic Center was they had told me they had a retractable roof. They originally built it for their sunset symphony series, and they would open the roof so the orchestra would play with the skyline lit up in the background. We thought why don't we start the game with the roof open, and just try it for a different effect.

I've always liked *America the Beautiful* better than the national anthem. The first four years of Arena Football we never did the national anthem. It wasn't out of disrespect; we just liked the other song better. That was supposed to be another tradition of Arena Football that would be different from the outdoor game. We did that for quite a while and now everybody's pretty much gone to the national anthem. We started doing the song. As they started singing, the roof in Pittsburgh starts to open, the sun is setting, beautiful sight. Everybody said "Oooh, wow." If I'd had the money, I'd have had fireworks going off outside and really jazzed it up. The roof opens, it's spectacular. We start playing football. I swear even down to the players, everybody at halftime was saying "What is wrong with the crowd tonight? They're just not into the game." It's Pittsburgh, and by the third game they had built this

> Joe Theismann holds the NFL record for the shortest
> punt that wasn't blocked – one yard.

reputation for being this raucous crowd who loved Arena Football, loved their Pittsburgh Gladiators, but it was not the same. A funny thing happened—just before halftime the building manager came to me and said, "I don't think we can continue to run the air conditioner and have any chance to keep people from sweating to death in here. I really think we gotta close the roof." We close the roof at halftime. We come back to play the second half and all of a sudden it was like a different crowd in there. We suddenly realized what the deal was – the roof held the noise in.

When I put the league together, I surmised I might someday want to own my own team instead of always being commissioner. I kept the rights to a team and when I started the league, I love Iowa and they have no professional athletics. I remember one day, as a kid seven, eight years old, we're out in the garage in our new home in Iowa City, listening to a Chicago Bears game, and I asked my Dad, "Why don't we have a Chicago Bears in Iowa?" He told me it was because Iowa wasn't big enough, and he didn't think they would ever have any pro sports. Then when I was in junior high, I read about Des Moines having a professional football team. It was in the old Continental Football league. The Des Moines Warriors became the farm team for the Minnesota Vikings, and I ended up playing for them for a year when I

As a kid, I wanted to go see this pro football team we had in Iowa but my Dad said that's not really pro football.

came out of the University of Iowa. As a kid, I wanted to go see this pro football team we had in Iowa but my Dad said that's not really pro football. It's ironic. I end up being the guy that brings legitimate pro football to the state.

When I was putting it all together and looking at different markets, I decided Iowa was a pretty good football state. I decided to try it at places that would probably never be big enough to have a professional football team but who have a decent-sized arena and who loved sports and football. I penciled in from the very beginning that I might want to do a team in Iowa someday, preferably Des Moines. I protected the colors black, gold and crimson (taken from the uniforms from the three state schools: Iowa, Iowa State and Northern Iowa where Kurt played) for my team. In the original paperwork for the league when we put it together I protected the entire state in case I actually did move a team there.

At the time I was putting it all together, and even before that when I worked for the NFL, when I had the original idea for Arena Football and was still doodling with it, I used to make a lot of flights over the top of Des Moines. You can see, on a good day, the roof of the Veterans Auditorium at 35,000 feet. It's a big solar roof, like a big square top of a barn, and I can't tell you how many times I looked out a plane window and saw that and to know my family is down there and thinking how lucky I am to be doing what I do for a living and thinking, "I wonder if I'll ever be able to put a team in my home state and make it work?" So there's a lot of emotion and a lot of passion on that whole subject. I actually bought a beautiful little home right on the Mississippi River over in the Quad Cities, which we discovered by happenstance last fall right down from the Interstate 80 bridge, the main road across America, and I can't tell you have many hundreds of trips I made from Chicago, back and forth from Iowa when I was trying to put this team together not knowing what would happen. Again, I remind you I wasn't doing it with a lot of money – just a lot of hard work and hope and hopefully smart marketing.

I would drive over that bridge, and every time I would come home to Iowa I'd come across the bridge I'd look at that shoreline and say, "Thank God I'm home and I hope I can make this work." It's ironic. I'd sit on a park bench at my house at night and look up at the traffic going across that bridge upriver and think about those days. God, how blessed I've been. I'm starting to sound like Kurt a little bit. Maybe that's why I appreciate him. That part of it has been an amazing story in its own right; the fact that I was able to come home and make this team work. I thought if I could make it work it would be so neat to come home and give my home state a professional football team, not something rinky dink, not semipro. It's something that's gonna continue to grow into something major that they can be very proud of. That's what's happening and it's pretty exciting.

I went through the '92 season doing work for the league and a lot of work for the owners. A couple of teams particularly needed help and I tried to get their product turned around – their marketing presentation

Before Super Bowl XI, there was no national anthem. Vicki Carr sang *America the Beautiful*.

and then after the '92 season, late '92 I really started to work on "could I make the franchise work or not?" I was also looking at Indianapolis, New Orleans, and several other cities as possibilities, but I knew in my heart I wanted to come back and do it here if I could make it work. I had to make a business decision. It was the spring of '93, and I tell you I made a lot of trips back and forth, and I couldn't afford to fly 'cause it was too expensive between Des Moines and Chicago. So I did a lot of driving back and forth, a lot of trips at two o'clock in the morning and driving through ice and snow.

I made a decision to do a test game. Nobody in the league had ever done this before but I thought it was a good concept. I thought before you go into a market, why not play a game and expose the product as a still relatively new concept. On April 23, 1993, we played the "Rumble Under the Roof." I kinda built it up like it was gonna be a big boxing match and we brought in the Arizona Rattlers with Danny White coaching and the Cleveland Thunderbolts. We played the game before a sold-out crowd in Vets Auditorium. The crowd went nuts. Media reaction was phenomenal. I had really worked hard to put it together and make sure it had a fair shot. I did market research that night and again that was very consistent with every other game we'd done market research on. People just loved it, and out of that, I made a decision to try and move forward to put an investor group together. I would be the majority owner but I was gonna have to bring additional money to the table.

Then an interesting thing happened. In the summer of '93 there was some serious flooding in the Midwest. Downtown Des Moines didn't have water for 30 days – the city water plant was under water. It was a real, real calamity. My Dad called me one day from Iowa City, where I grew up (he's been my biggest supporter all along). He said, "It would be neat if you could do some sort of a charity game – an all-star game or something like that – to help the people." I got hold of the powers that be in Des Moines and said, "What do you think?" And they said it was an interesting idea. In about six weeks time, we had put together the first and only Arena All-Star Football Game and it was a very successful run. We decided to tie a ticket to the all-star game with the right to reserve a seat if we have a team – put down like $25 on a season ticket deposit. This would be refundable. That went pretty well for us, and out of that I was able to build enough momentum to go ahead and put the team together. In early '94 I made a decision to go ahead with the team and spent most of the summer of '94 in Iowa. My family moved out. We took possession of a house the day my son had to start school, right after Labor Day weekend. We've been at it ever since, and it's been a real interesting experience. We've got a good coach and a good program. But as the league gets bigger and more competitive and there's more money involved, and we're in a small market, it's hard work.

Well, what happened with Kurt was, in 1993 I was in the process of putting the team together – working on the funding and the mechanics of it, etc. I knew it was gonna be important in this state, and I think it is in other parts of the league to try to have regional talent. So we had Iowa, Iowa State, and Northern Iowa, which was one of the top 1-ΛΛ programs in the country. I knew there would be players there that might fit in with what we were trying to do with the Barnstormers. Guys who in essence were gonna be "tweeners" with the NFL, weren't gonna get the real good look because they were 1-AA. Since I'd been living in Illinois for 11 years, I hadn't seen them play so I went out and watched them play a couple of games.

I got to see Kurt play twice that year. I made notes saying he looked like a good strong kid who could throw the football fairly quickly. I'm gonna tell you right now, I'm not an expert on personnel. I'm not a coach. I've never wanted to be a coach. I'm never gonna coach. I understand the game pretty well, having played it and been around it as long as I have, but I don't pass myself off as a football expert. I have enough marketing savvy and enough knowledge of football to wire it together and get it done but I'm not a specialist at football. I could tell that Kurt had some potential talent and I was also thinking if I could find a quarterback from one of the three schools, it would be helpful 'cause that's a guy that's gonna get a lot of visibility. I didn't even know if he would even play for us or what he would be able to do. I was told he had only been a starter his senior year. He'd had a pretty good year, but I thought maybe he won't get picked up by the NFL.

Art was truly a very good coach but he's a crusty old-school coach.

I got hold of Kurt and talked to him once. At that point I also hired Art Haege, who is still with me. He had been the head coach of the Milwaukee Mustangs. You could do a book on this guy, in fact a couple of guys want to do a book on him; he's an absolute legend in football. The guy's unreal – old, tough character. He coached with Jerry Glanville for a while. Art was truly a very good coach but he's a crusty old-school coach. When I talked with Kurt he told me he was waiting to see what was gonna happen with the NFL. He was hoping to get a shot and I don't think he had an agent at that point even then. Then he ended up signing as a free agent with the Packers. At that point, we just kinda said, "Well, nothing's gonna happen there." He went to camp in the fall of '94 with the Packers and didn't last very long. Then Johnny Gregory came on board as our head coach. John is a UNI alumnus and knew the head coach there pretty well.

At that point, he started talking to Kurt, telling him, "Hey, you got a chance to play football and nothing happened." This was while he was stocking shelves and sacking groceries at the Hy-Vee in Cedar Falls.

He finally made the decision to come down and take a look at us and that's really how we got him. So I'll take credit for having first seen him because Gregory had been up in Canada and didn't know much about him, and Art had been over in Wisconsin. But after I got first eyeball on him, I passed the information along, and Art Haege and John Gregory are the guys who got him to come play. Primarily John, in this case, because he knew the coach up there and knew a couple of other people, and I think he talked to them. They said, "Hey, Kurt, you probably ought to go take a look at this. It beats sitting around."

Kurt hasn't changed from the day I met him.

Kurt hasn't changed from the day I met him. Kurt is a guy, when you talk to him, in a certain sense you feel like he might be a little cocky 'cause he's quiet. But he's not so much cocky as he's self-confident. He doesn't stick it in your face. He never will. He's a self-confident young man. He has a lot of respect. He's very humble. He's not a real verbose guy – doesn't do a lot of talking.

Although he's funny, 'cause every once in a while he gets this grin on his face and gives you a little zinger. He's got a little bit of a wit with him that kinda comes out of nowhere. He can be a guy that I would say that on a day-to-day basis, you don't think of as being a real talkative, yak-it-up kind of guy or free spirit. Yet, every once in a while, he'll kinda give you one of these looks and stick you with something. He's got a little bit of a cynical sense of humor at times, too, actually.

His first game was a nightmare for us. We went up to training camp. I've got a coach, John Gregory, who's spent 13 years in the Canadian

No NFL players wear protective cups.

League. He's not coached Arena Football. That in itself was kind of a real challenge for me because ideally I felt, and still feel this way, I wanted to bring a coach in who had coached Arena Football already because there are some real differences in this game. But I also felt it was real important to get someone who had Iowa ties so they would understand the nature of this state 'cause it is different than going into some big city in a franchise situation. We really sell Arena Football. The Barnstormers are sold statewide. It's a real bonding process so we work with a real grass-roots process. John is from Webster City, north of Des Moines, and has a lot of friends back here and was well thought of. The thing I felt comfortable about was he had a reputation for working well with quarterbacks and knowing how to throw the football. If you follow Canadian League football, you gotta throw the ball – just throw the heck out of it. I felt he could make the adaptation and a couple of people who knew him felt he could so I went with him.

We got these kids, quarterbacks, in camp that first year and he felt that Kurt had the most potential, physically the biggest, strongest kid we had. He seemed like a pretty smart kid—pretty levelheaded. I think that's the thing I have to say about Kurt that I remember. He always struck me as being a levelheaded kid. He wasn't a guy you thought was gonna be up and down. Ironically, there was a period he went through with Brenda when her family died, that was really, really hard on him. I can understand that, although at the time some of the guys on the team didn't understand how close he had become with her. They just thought it was some gal he was dating who had a couple of little kids. You know how cavalier football players can be. They thought, "Oh, just blow her off and find somebody else – too bad her parents died but you know, so what." I know there was some of that mentality in the locker room. Some of the guys just didn't see it being that big a deal. They just didn't understand the relationship. I'm sure they felt sorry for her but to a lot of players, a girl's a girl. That's all they are. You're not supposed to get in a deep-seated relationship with them. At least not when you're playing football.

His first game for us, we went down to St. Louis, which I think is ironic, and he just played very, very poorly. His reads were bad, he made bad throws, he was intercepted three or four times. He just did not have a good game at all and was really struggling. John said to me after the game, "Boy I don't know if he's gonna be the guy." This really scared me because I had invented Arena Football, put the league together, been commissioner for six years, had this dream of potentially making this dream work in my home state. Here I am now, being that owner for the first time, sitting up in the press box area watching my team stink, thinking, "Oh my God, what have I gotten myself into?" It was scary.

We get back to Des Moines, and John says, "I'm gonna give Warner another shot." And he keeps working with him and you could start to see the improvements kick in. Once you had been through that first trial-by-fire battle of being on that little 50-yard field like being a human pinball machine member, he just started to come around. It just got better and better and he really started playing some pretty good football.

If he hadn't been from Iowa, we probably would have been more ready to let him go. We try to keep about half our roster from in state, which is kind of an exciting part of it because we've been able to win with kids from the Midwest. We tend to focus on our part of the woods where we know a lot of people. It didn't hurt that he was from Iowa, but I think in John's mind, he still was the quarterback in our camp who had the most potential tools. I know he was looking around to see who else was back there. We had a kid, for example, who had been a starter with Milwaukee that we picked up and had already brought in. Art wasn't sure he was the guy either, but he was a kid with Arena experience. I know there was some thought that maybe we needed to go with him since he had played the game before and understands the field and how you have to throw the ball. But John just decided to stick with Kurt. I also remember that John Gregory was a UNI alum. Kurt was from UNI. He had good ties to the school. I don't think John Gregory would ever consciously make a decision to play a kid because he was from his own school 'cause he's a guy who wants to win. So if he has to bring a quarterback from Mars he'd do it. We were really pushing that first year to try and market ourselves as an Iowa team.

We go back and decide to give him another chance, and the second game we play is against the Connecticut Crusaders in Hartford and we eke out a win. Kurt definitely plays a better game; he's starting to get a feel for the thing. Then we come back for our first-ever home game. This is 1995, our first season. He's now playing for us.

We opened up against the Miami Hooters, which were owned by one of the principals of the Hooters Restaurant chain. The Hooters Restaurant chain was started in Clearwater, Florida, by three guys who were originally from Waverly, Iowa, which is next door to Cedar Falls.

Ed Droste is a limited partner in the Iowa Barnstormers. He's from Waverly, Iowa, and he has two other partners, Dan Johnson and Dave

Lageschulte. They all came from Waverly down to Florida and they started Hooters in the league, and Dave was the one who owned the Miami Hooters. After he sold the Hooters, he and Ed bought a little kind of quiet interest in my team. We played Miami and we beat them pretty good. Kurt really kinda came around that night. You could just see that he was getting a feel for the game. Also, he was working with receivers who had never played the game. We had a lot of guys who hadn't spent that much time around Arena Football. The most veteran guy we had is a kid named Leonard Conley, who is still with us five years later. He was a tailback at the University of Miami, but they threw to him a lot. He helped Kurt a lot in the early stages. He was the only one who knew what was going on out there on that little field. Everybody else was learning as we went along.

The St. Louis Stampede was coached by Earle Bruce, the ex-Ohio State and UNI coach. It was a sad deal. They should still be there and be doing well, but what happened was the building bought the franchise. Kiel Auditorium – it's called Kiel Center now – is owned by a group of 30-something businesses in St. Louis. That group originally came together to try to keep the St. Louis Blues hockey team from leaving St. Louis. After they pooled their money to buy the hockey team they found out they really and truly needed to build a new arena 'cause the old St. Louis Arena was not adequate and was just falling apart. That's the same thing that's happening in Des Moines with our building right now. So they ended up building a new arena and then they realized they needed to get more events in the building than just a hockey team and a few concerts. They start looking around for other activities and they run across Arena Football and say, "Hey that's a pretty good idea. It looks like fun. We think it could work." They didn't have football in St. Louis because the Rams hadn't come there yet. So they make an offer to buy a franchise and they get it. The problem was the group that controlled the building didn't really run it day to day. They pretty much left that in the hands of the hockey operation. The guy that mans the hockey team was not interested in Arena Football. He could have cared less. He just wanted to strangle us to death and get rid of us and that's what they did. They did no marketing. Earle got so frustrated he finally quit after two and a half seasons. It was sad. They had a very, very good football team. We had some great battles – some of the best games we ever played –

I think St. Louis could return to the league and be very successful.

nail biters. We went into overtime, unbelievable games. I think St. Louis could return to the league and be very successful.

And I think with what's going on with Kurt Warner in St. Louis it would not surprise me to see somebody (and I've already heard there have been a couple of calls to the commissioner's office) say we need to put Arena Football back there. When the Stampeders were there, they didn't draw well because there was no marketing. They literally did not market them because the guy didn't want the team – he did not want the team in the building. Interestingly enough, six months after they give the franchise up and sell it, he gets fired. I'm told that was one of the reasons he got fired – this is the problem when you have a committee running something. They had Anheuser Busch, Monsanto, and May Department Stores – all these big companies that threw money into the pot. And the guys who run these businesses are not paying attention to what's going on with a football team at the arena. I used to talk to people I knew in St. Louis, and most of them didn't even know they had a team. That's how bad it was; they didn't know there was a team there. I remember calling friends to tell them we were coming down to play and they didn't even know there was a team. That's how bad it was – just a disaster. They drew 4 – 5,000 per game and that was probably freebies they gave away at the last minute. It was just a shame. It really bothers me when I see a good football team that's not getting the support of its ownership.

Kurt had a good game in Connecticut. We came home a week later, opened the regular season in Des Moines, and we beat the Miami in front of the home crowd – lots of excitement, near-sellout, people were really pumped up. Kurt was one of the first guys to come on the field.

I actually flew a plane down to southern Iowa and in the spring there was no corn standing. I wanted to replicate the "Field of Dreams." Our playing field in Vets auditorium is called "the landing field of the dreams," which is a takeoff on the Barnstormers and the flying. When I first started the team, a writer said, "So you think if you build it they'll come to Des Moines, huh?" I said, "Yeah." He said, "So you're building your own field of dreams." When we named the team the Barnstormers, I said, it's not gonna be a field of dreams, it's gonna be "a landing field of dreams." So I went down to a hunting preserve that still had standing corn that a guy knew about, in southern Iowa. We packed a four-seat plane full of cornstalks we had cut from the field, flew them back to Des Moines the day before the game. So the afternoon of the first game, I'm down in the basement of Vets Auditorium with green and yellow spray cans in each hand. I had to take the stalks and put them on a peg board so they would stand up and we had maybe five feet wide of corn and about three feet deep and I still have a stalk in my office. It looked like it was green living corn. I did a pretty good job of painting it. We put it out where the players come onto the field. We had fireworks going off and had strobe lights and spotlights; it was pretty neat. It was televised. I think Kurt was the second or third man out; they actually merged through the corn onto the landing field of dreams in Des Moines. It was very emotional for me, obviously, but was pretty spectacular for the fans that night. The guys came out one at a time, and we had the Iowa guys going first – the kids from Iowa. There was Roehlk, and Warner and then Chris Spencer and Carlos James – these were all really good guys from within the state that people knew. Kurt got to come out through the corn. Kurt was not All-League that first year. Years two and three, he was the All-League quarterback. He had a pretty good year the first year and people took note of him.

We created a program. My largest limited partner is a guy named Bruce Heerema who has done real well in business down in Pella, Iowa, a real, real strong Dutch community southeast of Des Moines. Bruce came to me one day. He's a really good guy, very kind-hearted man. He said, "I've got some money I've got to put into charity this year. I wonder if we could do something that would help the players, too – like some sort of program, where we could create a couple of jobs or something. I've always been an advocate of YMCA programs because it cuts across a lot of different social levels. They do a good job in a lot of communities and they are very good in Des Moines at what they do. I'd had some dialogue with them; they were a sponsor where they traded sponsor-ships with our players so they could lift weights and work out. So I went to the Y and said what do you think about doing a program with us? Is there a need for a program where we can provide some role models? And they loved the idea. What we did is we set up a program, which is still going to this day, called the Barnstormer YMCA Sports Alliance. Kurt Warner started a program for us and was the director that first year. He worked with Larry Blue, who was an All-Big 10 defensive end for the University of Iowa Hawkeyes. That program has had a tremen-dous impact on Des Moines.

> The revenue from one home football game at schools like Michigan and Tennessee pays for all the scholarships for all their athletes in all their sports for the entire school year.

I thought he had that opportunity to be an NFL starter some day. I'm not gonna sit here and tell you I thought he'd do what he's done. I just knew Kurt had a great attitude, was a competitor, very stable for the most part, other than that one little period he went through after his wife's parents died. That hurt him badly for a few games; he struggled badly. That was in his second year right after the season started.

Here in Des Moines, most of our players had nicknames as a marketing and publicity sort of thing, and I nicknamed him "Houdini." He was introduced that way and we had shirts out with this on them. He was Kurt "Houdini" Warner. The reason he got that nickname was twofold.

Kurt had an uncanny ability to escape the pass rush – he was awesome in our league and has done some of it with St. Louis. He's not that fast, not that quick afoot, but Kurt has eyes, I swear, in all four corners of his head sometimes and he has that ability just to put that hip shuffle on or to lean one way or lean the other. I mean, he's thrown passes off his back foot as he was going down. He used to drive guys in our league nuts. I could put a highlight film together you wouldn't believe. He wasn't running around very much. He reminds me of old guys who've been playing handball for so many years they just know how to walk to the right spot. They anticipate where the ball is going. That's how Kurt would be in the backfield. He's primarily a pocket quarterback but Kurt would always know where to position himself. He would see a guy coming, he'd give them a little hip fake, step to the side, throw the ball. Again, he's got that quick release so he could spot a guy, and that was the beauty of Kurt. Mainly, what he did for us is what he's doing in the NFL. John Gregory gets a lot of credit for helping him develop this. It was there, he just hadn't put it all together yet 'cause he couldn't do it when he came to us. But that was the ability to read three, four different receivers.

John Gregory brought in a different offense than most people in the league were used to seeing. It was pretty innovative. He brought it from Canada and it's what we call "a hot read." They do a lot of "hot reads." You don't call a play in the huddle and run a set play. You go to the line of scrimmage, as the quarterback and you've got receivers who are running routes. They run their routes depending on what the defensive backs are doing. There's nothing set. You'll come on a basic formation, but in essence you've got a couple of receivers, depending on which way the safety rolls or the cornerback zones up or goes into a man. The receivers work together and then they run routes – picks, deep underneath. The quarterback has got to be able to read that. You read the "hot" first to see if he's open. If he's not, you go to the secondary. That's what they're doing in St. Louis and John taught him that.

People are saying to me, "This has got to be the greatest thing that's ever happened to Arena Football and the Barnstormers. Personally I have mixed emotions about it. I don't think it hurts us. I'm not gonna say it's a negative but to me there's a little bit of Jim Foster who has spent an awful lot of time with Arena Football who feels like we had an awful lot going for us before Kurt Warner came along. There's just a part of me who knows that Arena Football is a lot more established than some people have given it credit for. To take my personal feelings and passion for the product and put my marketing hat back on, I have the reality to say, "Yeah, Kurt may be the guy that's doing it for the Arena Football League." That's funny because they say Red Grange is the one who made the National Football League when he came out of college at the University of Illinois and played for the Bears in the NFL. They were never on the radar scale till that. They also say that Johnny Unitas in that great game they played on television in 1958 – Colts and Giants – really brought the NFL to enter the television era. So there are certain players who can come along and be a watershed for a league. I think you can look at the NBA and say the same thing about Lew Alcindor and a couple of those guys and certainly Michael Jordan. There are certain players every once in a while who take the game to a new level – Babe Ruth with baseball. You can go on down the list. The exceptional athlete once in a while makes the league or brings it to a new level and you do have to say that about what Kurt's done. I guess the sensitivity I have, and I've told people, you know as this story develops it's gonna go from Kurt Warner plays in the Arena Football League for the Iowa Barnstormers to someday you're gonna pick up a story somewhere, someday that says, "This young man toiled in a barn in a cornfield, playing for five dollars a game, playing on a dirt/sawdust field." It's the romance of the story that journalists

> Barry Sanders was tackled for losses 14 percent of the time.
> On approximately 400 carries, he lost more than 1000 yards.

like to play with, and I understand that. I have to accept that. It's obviously good for the league and good for the Barnstormers. We're getting calls from players and agents right now, "We want to come and play for the Barnstormers. We want to be a part of this success story." I know the league is getting a lot of calls.

The other thing is that I'm aware the National Football League has now assigned a personnel guy to just pay more attention to the Arena Football League. At the Super Bowl a year ago I signed a very historical document, with my wife present, along with David Baker, our commissioner who also signed, creating a partnership between the National Football League and Arena Football. Actually they were the option papers for them to buy 49.9 percent of this League. The NFL had never done anything like that. They have a couple more years to exercise this option. From everything we're told it's gonna happen. This was not done just for the heck of it. We know enough about the NFL to know they don't jump on things overnight.

Kurt hasn't changed a bit. I don't bother Kurt 'cause I've got enough of my own things to deal with and I know he's busy and I try to respect that. A couple of guys on the staff call him every once in a while just to see how he's doing. Kurt's Kurt; he hasn't changed a bit. He's still business as usual – same attitude same philosophy on life.

Trent Green's fiancé worked for me when I was commissioner of the league in 1991 in the league office in Chicago. She was an assistant to me so I knew who Trent Green was. This was when he was playing at Indiana in college. I already knew about him.

I have always felt that Kurt was capable of playing. I was not sure that Kurt was ever gonna have – you have to look at it this way – does this guy have the tools to be a world beater? Can he be a big-time NFL quarterback? Those intangibles are very hard to measure. You don't know how he'll handle the pressure. The only thing that concerned me about Kurt, as stable as he was, was that one situation with Brenda with her parents dying and how hard that was on him. It was a different kind of deal, but it was always in the back of my mind. If he's in the National Football League, the pressure that's put on you in incredible. Would he be able to keep that stability that he has? He has obviously been able to do that and I think that's great for him and has been great for the St. Louis Rams organization. So I felt like if he got a chance to play his game, a chance to do the things he does well, he wasn't forced into the situation of trying to run an offense that didn't fit what he did well. That might be a problem.

Fortunately when they brought in Mike Martz as offensive coordinator, and with the help of Vermeil, they have been able to have an offense which very much mirrors what we have in Arena Football. A lot of what they do is the way we play our game, and from what Kurt's told me and other people, he's been able to work with Vermeil and the offensive coordinator to bring some things into the game plan that are very similar to the things with the Barnstormers in particular. I think there's a comfort factor there and it's helped them a lot. There's a three-step drop. You very rarely take a five, you got about two or two and a half seconds to throw it. If you don't throw it, your number 1 priority in Arena Football is to at least get back to the line of scrimmage. And Kurt was not a running quarterback and your whole concept is "don't get sacked." You've got to try to get rid of the ball quickly or at least not get negative yards. At that point just try to stick your head in there and get back up to the line of scrimmage. The average in Arena Football is to throw the ball 75 percent of the time. We averaged a little over 90 points a game last year in Arena Football between the two teams. The Iowa Barnstormers are the highest scoring offensive team in the history of the league.

Playing for the Barnstormers, Kurt was making in the mid- to high-60s as I remember with us in the second and third year. He was probably pushing $70,000 that third year. The way his contract worked, he got a base salary, which wasn't a heck of a lot more than most of the other guys on the team and he got a $200 win bonus like everyone else. Arena Football League is standardized and that goes back to when I established the single entity you still get a bonus as a player on the winning team. Kurt, then, would have individual incentives for throwing touchdowns, yardage, whatever, winning games by over a certain point. And that's where it kicked in for him and it was really set up for, "Kurt you do a good job, you're gonna make more money." I think he was pushing 70. I think the job with the Y was the better part of 30. He wasn't doing bad. He was happy. Kurt wanted to get a chance with the National Football League, but he wasn't saying, "God, I hate my life. I'm stuck in Arena Football. I don't like it." He loved playing Arena Football. And I say this with all sincerity although I invented the game. This was a guy who loved what he did. He bought a home in Johnston, a nice suburb. He got married. I was at the wedding, along with most of the guys on the team with the organization. He felt real good about his wife and he had a good income. You've got to put it in perspective. Yeah, it's great to make millions of dollars, but a hundred grand in Des Moines isn't too shabby.

I FOUND KURT WARNER DOWN AT THE CORNER OF WHAT AND IF
JOHN GREGORY

John Gregory grew up in Webster City, Iowa, played football at Northern Iowa, and became a football coach of note in the Canadian Football League. He is the only head coach the Iowa Barnstormers have ever had.

Terry Allen, the current head coach at Kansas, was head coach at the University of Northern Iowa (UNI), my alma mater. Kurt Warner was a quarterback who had started for him for just one year, but Terry thought he might be a suspect. He sent me a film of a game against Western Illinois, and he threw for a lot of yards and had played very well in the game. It was the only film I had on him. We brought him to Des Moines and worked him out. Like a lot of young guys, the number one thing he was trying to impress me with was his arm strength, and that was very good. He implanted balls in a lot of guys; we didn't necessarily have a lot of real good guys catching the football for him. I was impressed with him as a person. He came down and did a nice job in the workout and we progressed from there. This was our first year as a team. Both our other two quarterbacks had Arena experience on other teams, Lopez and Loots, and we only had about a week's or less than a week's practice then had a preseason game set up.

We went down to St. Louis to play the Barnstormers' very first game ever – an exhibition. Kurt was awful – at least four interceptions, fumbled the ball from center another four or five times. He just had an awful game. He wasn't the only one – we were all awful. I never considered cutting him, despite an article that appeared that said I was. I could see from practice he had a lot of good things in him. We lost that game real badly.

The next week we won – we kind of tricked them on that deal. It wasn't because we were very good, but we did show signs of being a good football team. Kurt did a lot better than the previous week. Then I had to make my decision on the starting quarterback and I'm kinda one of those guys who "If that's our guy, that's our guy. You've got to put all your nuts in his basket."

The next week we went up to Milwaukee and scored 72 points with Kurt as the quarterback. His attitude after coming back from St. Louis was being upset with himself. He doesn't make excuses; he's not one of those guys. Then in Milwaukee he played very well and we scored 72 points. That was the first inkling we might have had something special. As a new team in the league, we didn't have anybody, didn't have an expansion draft.

We just turned over rocks and found guys. We had a menagerie; we had the shortest football team receiver-wise that's ever been anywhere – just a bunch of midgets. Willis Jacox was a midget but he was a good player. He'd played for me in Saskatchewan.

After that first game, he came and said, "Get rid of Warner, he's not good enough to play." I said, "I think he'll come around." We did really well that first year. We had the most wins of any expansion team. We beat the world champions from the previous year, Arizona, in the first playoff game.

I thought if he got the opportunity, he certainly could play in the NFL. I don't think we were ever scouted by NFL scouts. At the Senior Bowl this year, Kurt Warner and the Arena Football League were the topics of discussion every place you went. Prior to that time, I don't think, although there are 23 Arena Football players playing in the NFL right now, that we were taken very seriously until this deal with Kurt happened. This has meant a lot in terms of credibility to Arena football. Ron Carpenter, Paul Justin, and Andy McCollom all are former Arena Football League players who were on the team this year for St. Louis.

Kurt could have played for a number of teams. In fact, I was talking to one of the scouts at the Senior Bowl who had gone over to Iowa State for their Spring Pro Timing in '97. They had a few guys that were playing actually on our team and others who worked out after that, and Kurt threw. This guy who is a good friend of mine, who is a scout, said, "Yeah, I watched him and I didn't see anything special."

> In 1951, Bill Veeck, owner of the St. Louis Browns
> (now the Baltimore Orioles) sent a midget to pinch hit.
> The midget, Eddie Gaedel, wore number 1/8. Gaedel
> borrowed the jersey of the Browns' batboy, Bill DeWitt Jr.,
> now an owner of the St. Louis Cardinals.

We suddenly got a phone call. I was at American Association meetings in Dallas, from McDonald, our PR guy, who said Kurt was signing with one of the World teams, Amsterdam. Al Luginbill, Amsterdam's coach, said he had a heck of a time finding an NFL team who would sign him and allot him because they have to be allotted to the World League to go there if they are a quarterback. He had a hard time and finally talked Charlie Armey of the Rams into signing him. The thing I was upset about was that they didn't go through me but that's the way it goes.

We saw a lot of the World League games on television. Kurt played very well. He was the top quarterback in the World League. After watching him, I was sure that we had lost him. We then had to replace him and the quarterbacks who came in didn't get the job done for us and we had kind of a sad year after he left. Kurt was a real neat kid, real smart, picks things up very quickly, really nice guy, fun guy to work with, has a sense of humor, really not a rah rah

I never would have cut him; if I had it would have been the end of his career I'm sure.

guy at all. He gets his job done and expects everybody else to get theirs done. But our whole team, we're not a rah-rah type of organization. He's very smart and did his job very well so I think everybody just kind of respected him. But he wouldn't be a guy who would be the spokesman for the team or anything like that. I never would have cut him; if I had it would have been the end of his career I'm sure. I'm real proud of what he's accomplished. I went down to St. Louis and stayed after the game and waited for him and talked with him about 15 minutes and have talked to him on the phone a couple of times. It's a real breath of fresh air to see a person like Kurt really become outstandingly successful. If there's a type of guy you'd like to see this happen to, it's Kurt Warner.

When the Dallas Cowboys Cheerleaders started in 1972, each earned $15 per game – the same amount they receive today.

Art Haege is a veteran of football battles— both indoors and out.

Courtesy Iowa Barnstormers

IF THE PHONE DOESN'T RING, IT'S THE NFL
ART HAEGE

Art Haege is defensive coordinator for the Iowa Barnstormers, a former head coach of the Milwaukee Mustangs, and well-respected veteran of pro football wars.

K urt Warner, the first time he ever saw an Arena game was when he came to Milwaukee in 1995. I had called him after I'd called Steve Mariucci in 1995, so when everybody says nobody knew about Kurt Warner and he was out there – groceries and all – that stuff is not true. I was interim head coach with the Milwaukee Mustangs in 1994. Lou Saban was fired in Milwaukee, and I was interim head coach. We were playing our last game against Cleveland. We knew Kurt Warner was a very, very good quarterback and Saban had mentioned about him that he'd gone to the Packers. Since we're right in Wisconsin, we thought it might be a good deal to get a guy right there. So we knew about him;

it wasn't that nobody knew about him. I called him and he came down and watched a game. He left in the fourth quarter when we were ahead and he said, "I thought you guys were gonna win one." And we got beat. About that time I did not come back as the regular head coach and ended up coming over here to Iowa. We kind of lost him at that particular time for a while. It went from there to Gregory finding out about him, this and that, and everything. We knew about Kurt Warner. It wasn't like a guy who just came out of the ground.

I didn't know whether or not he'd make the NFL. We went out to supper many times on the road, or breakfast, or out for a Coke. He was a kind of a teetotaler and I am too for the most part. I'm a hell raiser but the kind of guy who doesn't drink and a defensive coach, and I don't coach him so we hang around a little bit when we are on the road. I don't know how many times he told me, "Art, When are they gonna get me a tryout with an NFL team? Why don't you guys get me a tryout?" I said, "Take care of this job and the next job will take care of itself." I learned that a long time ago after I was too greedy to take another job when I was a young coach at the University of Wisconsin, as an assistant when I was thirty years old.

But did any of us really believe he was an NFL guy? I don't think so. To be honest with you, I thought he had great potential. But the one thing that he had was himself. Of any player I've ever been around, he *believes* in himself. He has such confidence it's unbelievable. I'm sixty-two and Danny and Frankie, my older boys, thirty-one and thirty-two. I've got a boy nine and a boy ten. I tell them confidence; that's the thing that'll carry on. Kurt just believed in himself. I went down and watched the Rams his first year and went out to supper with him. He said, "You know what Art, I belong here. I belong in the National Football League." He looked right at me and I'm telling you, I believed. He cured me. He's a believer. He said, "All I need is a chance." I'll bet he said that fifty times. "If I get a chance, I'll make it. I'll make it." Well that Green Bay thing there was no way in heck with all those quarterbacks up there. No chance. But I think he's one of these guys who got in the right spot at the right time; good height, quick release, good arm.

There is a difference between confidence and cockiness. I've seen a lot of these cocky players come along. "I can do this." "I can do that." And all that stuff. He just looks you in the eye and says, "Hey, I can get it done." No question. I've seen him fumble. He set a record here in fumbles – I think twenty-four or twenty-seven. He led the league in fumbles. So he never was MVP in our league.

His first game in St. Louis was a disaster. I was the only coach on the staff who had been around Arena at all and it was a screwed-up deal, it was unbelievable. It was a bad, bad game all the way around. Some of the owners went down and said, "Oh my God, we'll never win a game." The ball was on the ground, fumbling around and everything. I said, "Hey, these guys have talent on this team. Trust me. We'll win some games. Don't get all bent out of shape."

I give Gregory, our head coach, a lot of credit, for hanging in with Kurt Warner. And he's the guy who has to pull the plug or not as the head coach. I can remember he pulled him a couple of times in '95 and when Kurt threw interceptions, fumbles, things like that. All of a sudden, about the fourth game he just kinda clicked in – man just rolling. I saw him throw a pass against Arizona with five seconds to go from his own 30-yard line and take one right in for a touchdown, scramble around, come out of a sack and wham throw a ball and took a hit that almost knocked him into the next bleachers. And it was a touchdown pass. I've seen so much of that – that quick release, accuracy. And he'll hang in there. I've seen guys like Jeff George of the Vikings. I told Jerry Glanville the week before the Rams were gonna play the playoff game against the Vikings so Craig James at CBS said I'll tell you what the difference is going to be at the quarterback position. You know the Vikings have got an experienced

All of a sudden, about the fourth game he just kinda clicked in – man just rolling.

quarterback and the Rams have got a quarterback who's not an experienced quarterback – he's a rookie. I called Glanville and said, "Bet all your money and all those motorcycles and all those '49 Mercurys on the Rams. What has George ever done? He couldn't escape a sack, for crying out loud, against a Pop Warner team compared to a Kurt Warner, and I'm telling you something, "Kurt Warner has won big games. In college and in Arena, and in World. I'll guarantee you that George never has. He's lost all his big games. You better bet on Kurt Warner." There's no question on those two players. They're the same type of player, but Warner is a winner.

Former Colorado Rockies Manager Jim Leyland was once a second-string catcher for Perrysburg, Ohio, High School. The starting catcher was Jerry Glanville.

"Get rid of Warner." I remember some of our linemen used to say that. It's kinda funny because we had two meeting rooms. We have the line over there and the linebackers. In the other one, over there, we have the receivers and the quarterbacks. You know the guys watch the film and say, "Whoa, have that quarterback stay in the pocket for crying out loud! That cost us money on that sack. What the heck's the matter with Warner?" He's not the kind of a guy who comes in like Garcia, our quarterback does now, goes out for a drink with the linemen, smokes cigars, hollers at them. Kurt wasn't like that, just stands back, very calm kind of a guy. What a guy. They just don't come any better than that, let me tell you. I think he got in the right spot at the right time and he took advantage of his opportunities.

I saw Kurt after the 49ers game where he threw five touchdowns. I waited almost three hours to see him after the game. He came over and gave me a big hug. I said, "Man, I'm gonna tell you something, Kurt." I said, "I know you're all into this church business. I'm going to start going to church every Sunday." He said, "You better start going to church." I thought if this is a deal, I'm gonna start going to church, too.

It's an unbelievable situation. Every once in a while I looked down on the sidelines and he was just killing them. I saw Steve Mariucci shake his head down there. You remember I called him up and said, "What do you think about this Warner?" He said, "Oh he's gonna be a decent player." Things happen and he's just killing the 49ers now.

But it's a whole group of people working together there with the Rams now. He never won the Big One in Arena. He had two shots to win that championship. I'll tell you what, he did good things, no question about it. We dropped some passes, our secondary didn't do a good job. Had we had all those type of weapons that he has now, we would have won it two years in a row.

My two boys are the only ones wearing Rams shirts at Iowa Falls Elementary. Everybody else is wearing Vikings shirts. I took my boys down to watch the Tampa Bay game and we stayed overnight. Andy McCullom got me tickets. I had Andy at Milwaukee, and he plays for the Rams now. Played for us for three games and went to the National Football League. He gets me tickets when I ask him. I told the teachers, the boys are gonna miss school. They're really big into this thing about missing school now. She asked me why they would miss. I said we're staying for the football game. She said, "What football game?" I said, "Hey, it's the Kurt Warner game down there – the Rams." She kinda raised her eyes and I said, "He may stay two days."

All I'm saying is he's a guy who had so much confidence in himself – not cockiness, not brashness, just a truthfulness to himself and he believed in himself. He looks you right in the eye and says, "Hey, I can play." When I was down that first year with the Rams at camp and it's obvious. Sure, he's made some mistakes. I think quarterbacks get better with vintage. I don't think there's any question about that type of thing.

Kurt had asked me about an agent. I told him two guys I thought were pretty good guys and he called them but he wanted to get a guy with more experience. But, shoot, he could have gotten Roman Gabriel with that outfit, too. But then he went with another guy, which is fine. Kurt's a different kind of guy. You think he'll jump over a cliff for anything, but he won't. He's a smart guy; he wants to wait and see what's happening. He was chasing around trying to get a workout and ended up going with Amsterdam. Of course, the Amsterdam coach was a guy by the name of Al Luginbill, and he came and watched us play Anaheim in '97 out there. He went over to Hooters and he said, "That Warner can play." I said, "You better believe it he can play. " He wanted to go ahead and get him to go to Europe, which he did through the Rams.

What used to happen when the offensive team had the ball in our practices, and Kurt is very, very accurate throwing the ball against us. We're on defense so he'd be just shredding us down the field. He'd laugh and say, "We just killed your boys over there." So what I would do is send another linebacker in there every once in a while. You're not supposed to send both linebackers in there and then they'd hit him, actually tag him. We can't hit him hard, just kind of grab him before he threw the ball. He'd say, "Hey, you're cheating, you're sending another linebacker." I said, "No we didn't we actually just changed those linebackers." He's so competitive is what I'm trying to say. He'd throw a touchdown pass and we'd say that wouldn't have been a touchdown pass. We'd have sacked you anyway. He'd get so mad at me. You know, all you do is cheat. I guess what I'm trying to say is the competition of the guy, and his guts in practice. He wants to put every single pass in there. I tried to screw him up on defense over there and even though he was hitting most of them, I'd send an extra linebacker and say we were there anyway, we'd have sacked you. That pass doesn't count.

The day before games our special teams coach goes over the players, etc., and Kurt would be on one side and I'd be on the other side, not doing much just standing or talking. What he'd do is take the football and try to throw it to me as close as he possibly could by my head, and I'd just pretend he never threw the ball – bang, about a foot away all the way across the field. That would be about 28 yards side to side, sideways, and I'd pretend like he never really threw the ball. I say, "Who threw that ball?" I'd look over at some other guys. I'd see him smile and look away and try to hide. He did that about every time we played before the game when the special teams coach was lining up the players and going through a walk through. He'd always try to rifle that ball as close as he could to my head and I'd pretend he wasn't really throwing the ball. Just the little things that the guy is, the kind of a guy who was so much fun to be in practice because of his competition. Sometimes practice can be boring in professional aspect, not like college, with cheering and hollering and all that stuff. He always made it fun.

I think the difference between Kurt and a guy like Paul Justin would be his confidence, his inner competition in himself; he is so competitive. I saw that through him in practice. You know we're on defense against him all the time and we would get after him and stuff and he would get mad as heck saying we were cheating over on defense or sending the opposite linebacker or that linebacker would be out of the box. He would get out of the box sometime and get an interception; he'd run over there and say we're cheating and stuff like that. He'd get angry, upset, shaking his head. Art, all you do is cheat. This guy has that competition underneath his guts. He's not one of these guys hollering at the players and all that; he's not that kind of guy. He's got that inner competitiveness. He believes, you see, that's the big thing. He has so much confidence. I could see that from a defensive standpoint all the time. He wanted to complete every single pass – every single pass. He wanted to complete every play. We had to cheat when he was in there; we couldn't stop him.

Some of the guys would groan about Kurt rolling out too much or something – little things like that. Of course, they always blame the quarterback. I used to say, "Hey, I tell you one thing. We'd better have that guy or we might as well pack our bags and get the heck out of here." I've said that many, many times.

> The Arizona Cardinals are the only NFL team to play in a college stadium – Sun Devil Stadium, home of Arizona State.

CERTAIN TOLLS MUST BE PAID
ON THE HIGHWAY OF LIFE
DICK McDONALD

Dick "Mackie" McDonald is the Director of Public Relations for the Iowa Barnstormers.

Everyone who calls me inevitably asks if this guy is as good a guy as he seems like. It's true; he is. What you see if what you get. I've told people before. In this case, Leo Durocher was wrong. 'Cause this nice guy's gonna finish first. I've known him too darn long. You can't just come up with a story like this and have people believe it, but it's true. He's as close to one as there is. The thing is we still get along, we're still really close, but we're about as opposite as opposite can be. One of my favorite lines has always been the one Sparky Anderson said. When an athlete gets up and says I want to thank God for this home run, etc., Sparky's line was: "Where was God when you were 0-for-4?" In this case, this is Kurt. Everyone is a little skeptical about professional athletes – about "I want to thank God for this and so on." Yeah, right. It's true with Kurt. It really is. That's why, after each game, Kurt got up there and said praise the Lord and all that stuff. Anyone else getting up there, 'cause I don't know them I'd have a problem with, but I don't have a problem with Kurt because I know that's him.

He was awful his first game. We played in a preseason game our first year at the Kiel Center in St. Louis. We had about three players on our team who had never seen an Arena Football game before and now we're gonna play in our first one. Kurt was bad – oh man! A story going around, which is incorrect, says he was almost released after that game, but that is not true. But he wasn't very good. No one had played the game before, and it was ugly. But he got pretty good.

> Golfer Greg Norman's Turf Farm provided
> the sod for Super Bowl XXXIII.

Willis Jacox, one of our receivers, said Warner can't play. Jacox gets in arguments with Coach Gregory about Kurt. Gregory goes, "No, no, Willis, he's just learning, he's learning." At the end, Jacox said, "Maybe Gregory knew more about it than I did."

My son is the marketing manager and equipment manager during the season here. He and Kurt are real close 'cause they're about the same age, and they've got sons who are six days apart. We were gonna put together a bus in November and go down to St. Louis, figured out a price and sold it immediately. So we said we're gonna do another one and sold it out immediately. We could have done a caravan and have the first bus pull into St. Louis and the last one not have left Des Moines yet, but we limited it to two. Kurt and Brenda and the kids came over Saturday night to the hotel. We had a reception there and Kurt was Kurt and he signed everything, and there were a lot of people that he knew, and we just had a ball. It was a great time and was funny because we had long-sleeved white T-shirts made up for everybody. On the front was our big logo and on the back in blue was Warner #13. Two busloads and we get there and are walking to the TWA dome. All the St. Louis fans were yelling "You can't have him back! You can't have him back!" He's worn number 13 since college. I saw something the other day that he said he wanted to point out to everybody that 13 is not an unlucky number – I don't know.

I thought he had an opportunity to make it in the NFL but I don't think anybody foresaw this. I get probably three to four calls every day from national media – every day. They'll call up and say, "This is so and so with the *New York Times*." And I say, "Gee, who do you want to talk about?" Or they'll call up and say, "Hi this is so and so with the *Atlanta Constitution* – guess who I want to talk about?" Yeah! These started about halfway through – about the time they went to play Tennessee – they were five and 0 or something like that and all of a sudden it's, "Geesh, what's going on here?", and it's been ongoing ever since.

A guy by the name of Ron Jacobs, who lives in Hawaii, works and does some things for *Sports Illustrated* and he was doing a deal on Kurt's rookie card here which I put together and they're just ugly. But the darn things are going for $270.00. We didn't have any action shots, we just posed guys at midfield with a curtain backdrop and Taco Johns, a local restaurant chain, spent a little bit of money to pay for it. Jacobs is a Rams fan – always has been. So now at six in the morning, he goes to bars to watch the Rams games 'cause that's when they're on out there.

He's a freelance writer with *Sports Illustrated* and was doing a story on Kurt's memorabilia – it's just going crazy.

He says, "Your guys have jobs in the off-season don't they?" He asked if any guys here have really strange jobs – who maybe would have played with Kurt, etc. I said, "No, we had one, but he's no longer with us and he didn't play with Kurt; he's a kicker, but he drove a garbage truck in the off-season up at Minneapolis. Everybody in the Arena Football League has an off-season job. Kurt's job is being a quarterback with the St. Louis Rams."

Every game that he plays in on national television, sooner or later they get around to his Arena Football days and they show two or three clips of him playing in a Barnstormer uniform. Absolutely overwhelming!

I come in one Monday and go sit down with Gregory and go, "Okay, John, you've taught me enough about X's and O's to have an opinion and be dangerous." I said, "This stuff the Rams were using looked awfully familiar." He said, "No kidding!" I think some of our way of running our offense is starting to trickle in to the NFL. In the Detroit game, the Rams had scored and they were going for two. I'm sitting in one of my watering holes here in Des Moines watching the game. The owner was sitting next to me at Billy Joe's Pitcher Show, a local cinema/bar. I said, "I'll just draw this play up. Wherever Isaac Bruce is, he's gonna go down to the back of the goal line, cut across and Kurt's gonna hit him right at the goal post. Bill said, "Aw, come on." I said, "That's what's gonna happen." I drew it up and said, "Here you go. Here's the X's and here's the route." Bingo, that's exactly what they did. He said, "How did you know that?" I said, "I don't know what the Rams call that, but I call that 80 goal line. That's normally Chris Spencer catching that ball for us with Kurt throwing it." If anybody did a book on this thing, they would have to point out – this is not a novel. The Kurt Warner Story, and this is not a novel! Steve Sabol had a thing on the Internet which said this might be the greatest sports story ever.

> The Super Bowl was not called the Super Bowl
> for its first three years. It was called the
> World Championship of Professional Football.

THAT'S ALL WELL AND GOOD BUT WHAT DID KURT AND LARRY DO FOR THE VILLAGE PEOPLE?

GORDON ECHTENKAMP
President, YMCA, Des Moines

Kurt was employed by the YMCA for three- to six-month periods in the off-season. He worked in what we call the YMCA Barnstormers Youth Sports Alliance. It was a partnership between the YMCA and the Barnstormers to take advantage of a couple of pro athletes who had great values and who really were concerned and cared for kids, and we put them out in the elementary schools on a regular basis. They traveled to a schedule of about 15 schools each week for a variety of programs for the kids. They would go to a school and spend time on the playground providing structured activities for kids during recess. In fact, we were getting great positive role models out to where kids were playing and they got to know them and trust them. In some cases, Kurt and his partner would do individual tutoring with children who were assigned by the school – 20- or 30-minute sessions through a period of time. In some cases, they met in small groups of kids assigned by the school. It varied depending on what the school wanted to do. The result was they had good positive models in the presence of the kids. Kurt is a wonderful person. It was most impressive that he obviously connected with the mission of the YMCA.

In August, first week of September, and for a couple of years the team took a trip in September, went overseas, I think to France one year. They would start with us the first of October and conclude when camp started.

It was clear from the first day that Kurt was a special person. We were surprised at his abilities as an athlete but there was no question initially that Kurt was a fine person.

Kurt has drawn greatly from his faith, which has made him a strong person, but he also has a great value system. In the YMCA we talk a lot about values; that's what the Y does and we accomplish our mission through programs that build character and we build character by teaching and demonstrating positive values. That's what the Y is at its heart, and Kurt has been a great example of help and honesty and respect and responsibility and character; he believes those are important virtues.

I'm sure these values are instilled by your upbringing and by surrounding yourself with people who also have these values. But we also see people who have been brought up in horrible, horrible environments that come out with great values and conversely there are people who have been given every opportunity to do the right thing and for some reason they don't. Kurt is just a great example of having a great environment and doing the right thing.

Jim Foster, managing partner of the Barnstormers, recommended that we hire Kurt so I made the decision, but it was on Foster's recommendation. They kinda handpicked a couple of players. The other player was Larry Blue.

This is an original program and was not copied from anyone else. It was an original program unique to the Barnstormers and YMCA. It puts quality young men in front of kids. As professional athletes they have the unique opportunity to present themselves really bigger than life. You see them on television and read about them in the newspaper, but to get out and have them sit in the classroom in those little, bitty chairs with kids develops relationships with them. It's really a special opportunity. The Barnstormers, since coming to Des Moines, have been very concerned about creating a good sensitive connection to the community.

> **The Barnstormers, since coming to Des Moines, have been very concerned about creating a good sensitive connection to the community.**

nity. They're not doing this just to get their names in the paper. They're doing it, and helping with the funding for it also, 'cause they know they are making Des Moines a better place.

There are two impressions that I have on him. We know you've found somebody who can connect with kids when they walk into a room and you can count the number of third-graders who are hanging onto his legs. Kurt had the kind of personality that kids just clung to because he was such a great guy. But, conversely, he could walk through the lobby of the YMCA or walk through the gymnasium and adult members connected with him also, 'cause he's such a fine guy. I can imagine there were several thousand people in Des Moines watching the Super Bowl who were watching who they thought was their best friend. He has the ability to connect with people like that.

What is really unique about what Kurt and the other guys have been able to do, as opposed to the typical pro sports thing, often athletes are willing to come out and speak at fund-raising events, but they come in, talk and then they leave. Kurt came in every week. He didn't come in and just talk to the kids and leave. He was there every week to be with them for six months of the school year. Long-term behavioral changes in kids occur through that kind of interaction. He didn't just come and go; he was there for them. The city was alive with support for Kurt.

William (Refrigerator) Perry, "the Galloping Roast," had a grand total of three touchdowns in his career.

Pat Riley never played college football but was drafted by the Dallas Cowboys. His brother, Lee, played seven years in the NFL.

When Lou Holtz coached at Arkansas, his personal attorney was Bill Clinton.

Chapter 6

Al Luginbill

Charlie Armey

Europe – Nice Town. Experience is What You Get When You Don't Get What You Want.

Al and Sue Luginbill take a break from the rigors of
NFL Europe league training camp.

AMSTERDAM CUSTOMS: "DO YOU HAVE ANYTHING TO DECLARE?"
"YES, THE SCOTTISH CLAYMORES MAY BE SOME SORT OF HIGHLY EXPERIMENTAL SHEEP."
"ANYTHING ELSE?" "YES. THE CUBS SUCK!"
AL LUGINBILL

Al Luginbill is one of the real key parts of the Kurt Warner story. A former football coach at Arizona State and San Diego State, he has been with the World Football League since its inception.

Our league, the NFL Europe league is not set up for people to make a lot of money. I use the term "a league of opportunity." I got involved with NFL Europe with Bobby Bethard, who is now the general manager of the San Diego Chargers. In 1993, I had four years left on my contract at San Diego State and was terminated for whatever reason I'll never know, but that's past me. It took me about four months to settle with San Diego State University and during that time, Bobby approached me in relationship to what I'd be interested in. At that time they were bringing back a World League scenario. I really wasn't interested because I didn't want to be involved with something that was gonna be going down the drain. But when he approached me and talked to me about how it was being owned and operated, I knew I was interested. Because it's something you get in on the ground floor as a coach and a director of football operations, you run your own show, and you end up in professional football in a totally different environment. It was something that, as I learned about it and understood what they were trying to do, I became interested and was fortunate enough to be interviewed and be hired so I was hired in June of '94 and I've been with the league ever since and thoroughly enjoy it. I'm the only head coach the Amsterdam Admirals have ever had.

With Kurt's situation, this whole thing started in February 1997. The night before our draft, Amsterdam had a young man, Will Furrer, and he was coming back to us as a returning player, and he was someone we'd like to have back. But the St. Louis Rams signed him the night before our draft, which left us null and void at quarterback. So the next day there wasn't much to choose from in the draft. All the quarterbacks had been assigned. We went out and approached Kurt. At that time he had already made a commitment to the Iowa Barnstormers and we certainly respected that. He's a man of his word and he just felt he'd committed to Iowa at that time and I respected that. That was a one-time conversation and we moved on. I think nine out of 10 guys would have said, "I want to go to Europe." I had seen him play in the summer of 1996. We had a young man who had played for us in NFL Europe by the name of Gary Howell, a defensive lineman for us. After our season was over, he played for Iowa in the Arena League, so he was a teammate of Kurt's. They were playing out here in Anaheim and I was living in Del Mar at that time, and Gary had called and said they were gonna be in Anaheim. I had never seen an Arena League game in person or on television so I went to that game really to see Gary and watch him, and that's the first time I saw Kurt and was impressed with him. Then that brings us up to when I first met him. It hadn't worked out in '96, so in the summer of '97, when

I told him at that time, "Kurt, the worst thing that can happen in all this is you could end up in Iowa where you are right now."

the Arena season was over, I immediately called him and asked him if he would be interested in coming to NFL Europe. This time we gave plenty of advance warning to see if I could work out something with an NFL team where he could become allocated to our league. I told him at that time, "Kurt, the worst thing that can happen in all this is you could end up in Iowa where you are right now." At that time he wasn't married yet. He was just in the process of being married, and he only had the two children he was adopting. During that off-season he got married. Brenda became pregnant and he had a third one on the way. I never saw or met Kurt Warner until the day he showed up at training camp, but I had probably 50 conversations with him over the phone. Once the tryout was set up and we found a team that was interested and was willing to bring him in for a tryout, he had two tryouts that year. One was with St. Louis and one was with Chicago. Chicago never got back to him and St. Louis signed him. St. Louis signed him and at that time John Becker was vice president of player personnel and Charlie Armey had just come on the scene and so John's the one who worked him out and called me and said, "Hey, I really like this guy." That even got me more excited because I knew that I liked him.

He had an ability to throw the ball accurately. You can't teach that; quarterbacks either have it or they don't have it, and this young man had it. You could tell that he was a great competitor and it didn't seem that anything bothered him. As the game went on, he was able to roll with the punches and the ebbs and the flows of the normal football game and I was able to see all that in person. It wasn't hard to spot; it stood out. Everybody's got a different thing. I don't have a ranking of different leagues. To me, our game is not rocket technology. If you are productive with people coming at you, who's to say you can't be productive in the NFL doing the same thing. Everywhere he had been – bottom line – he had won. What makes you think all of a sudden he's not gonna win in the NFL? If he has these attributes, they're not gonna leave him; they're not just gonna disappear. He was very fortunate. The Rams by then had surrounded themselves with some excellent football players and he was able to go out and lead them.

After the workout with the Rams, he ended up signing with them. They allocated him to us. They taped the workout and sent the tape to me and I was able to see what Warner could do on a big field. Their excitement exuded to my excitement because I'm the one who brought him to their attention. John Becker and I have been very close friends for a number of years. I called him and a lot of other teams. I wanted a team to work him out, and if they liked him to allocate him. In my opinion, they were a quarterback-starved organization at that time and they needed somebody. Dick Vermeil had just taken over. The whole thing was in transition at the Rams so this was an organization where I felt Kurt would at least get a chance if he came into our league and did what we thought he would do. The training camp was in Orlando. It took him a few weeks to adapt to the big field again. As each day went on he got more comfortable, more comfortable. We had a nice group of receivers and a good group of people around him.

We leave for Europe and he comes out of training camp as our starting quarterback. Jake Delhomme was his backup. We go into the season opener and he opens up the first half of the game against the Rhein Fire down there. He's just lighting it up. I liked what I saw that day. The next week he had an excellent game against the Scotland Claymores and we won like 26 to 3. The following week Kurt lights it up down at Barcelona. We're down there and we're up by 28 points at halftime and he's hitting everything. We end up winning that game but he gets severely bruised ribs and he's hurting. This is a tough guy, but he's hurting. We've got seven games left. My feeling was if we sat him out a week, the medical people said we got a good chance of having him for six weeks.

So I sat him out; we lost. We didn't have much of a choice; he was hurting and it would have been very difficult for him to play. After four games, we're 2 and 2, but really we're much better than that and we all know it. But we go on a winning streak now and we end up going down to Frankfurt and our offensive team ended up having a horrible day and we end up losing down there. That was Kurt's worst game. I remember walking off the field with him that day in Frankfurt and saying, "Kurt there'll be another day on this." We left the field and he came back and played extremely well the next two games. We ended up tying for the league championship but we lost the tiebreaker because of our losses.

So Rhein goes on and wins it and this was disappointing because Kurt had a good year but never really got to play healthy. In St. Louis, I think there were certain people who were in his camp behind him and there were certain people who had doubts. Obviously none of those people who had doubts are gonna stand up now. And everybody, of course, knew he was gonna do what he did – right? My point was if I talked to him, or if I talked to their personnel people most of the time they said he would be very, very impressive in practice and do a heck of a job running their look team, etc. So I was really surprised when they put him in the expansion draft, and I was even more surprised that Cleveland didn't take him.

In Amsterdam, I felt as early as training camp that I had made the right decision. I just liked his personality; I liked the way he handled the football team. Those are things I don't think you can coach. As it went on and got more competitive each week, he made plays down the stretch at times that had to be made, that the ball had to be thrown to a certain spot at a certain time, and he made those plays. He made those plays under duress and hurting. He was not physically 100 percent. So if he could be successful in our league in a situation where he was not 100 percent, my feeling was wherever he went on as long as they had somebody who would believe in him and give him an opportunity, eventually he would do well.

> The Heisman trophy winner gets to vote
> in the next year's Heisman balloting.

Kurt's probably the only person that truly believed he could do what he did and that's why he did it. Any of us, his mom, myself, anybody who's been around him would understand why it happened. In my dealings with him, he's never been somebody who's full of himself. My feeling is that people still doubt him. I heard one of the heads of personnel of another NFL team said, "Well, let's see what he does five years down the line."

Each year's gonna be different, but if there's somebody who's gonna give you consistent effort, it's gonna be Kurt Warner. I don't even worry about his consistency. Will he throw 41 touchdown passes next year? I don't know, but I know one thing: there won't be anybody better prepared to do it than him.

The only Rams game I saw this year was the Giants game and I got to see him there. Marshall Faulk played for me at San Diego State. I recruited him out of high school in New Orleans and the main reason I got him to come to San Diego State is that I promised him that I would not move him to defensive back. Tommy Newton, the starting left guard for them, played for us on Kurt's team. Ron Carpenter played for us two years in Amsterdam and Jay Williams played for us. So we have five guys there I've got personal contact with through the years. When I saw Kurt at the Giants game, I said, "Man oh man, I can remember that day you and I walked off the field in Frankfurt. Did I tell you there'd be another day?" He just laughed and said, "Yeah, I remember that." He's one of those guys – you remember things like that. You remember the times when you're down and out and it makes those good times that much better. This has got to go down as one of the all-time great stories in sports history. If you were fortunate enough to be around him, it's not as shocking because you know him and that's why I'm not surprised at anything that would happen with him. There's no rhyme or reason for certain guys being like they are – Joe Montana, Tiger Woods – why is he able to just focus at times when the other people in his profession can't? I think that just is the innate ability to be great – a God-given talent that you are given and you work at it. Kurt goes right in the weight room and lifts with linemen. He doesn't divorce himself from the remnants or the parts of the team that are not important to him. I've had a lot of great things happen to me because of the sport of football. I love the game, but I don't know, to see him and

This has got to go down as one of the all-time great stories in sports history.

Marshall – two people I've been around on game day and have gone to war with – to see them playing in the number one game in our profession at the same time is certainly something not many people will ever be able to say, "I've had that opportunity." It's about opportunity, and I think Kurt's the first one to say that. He said to me before, "I'm so blessed that somehow the good Lord brought us together." And that's how he looks at it. He doesn't try to figure it out. His faith is the reason this happened. If you try to figure it out, it'll drive you crazy. There's no rhyme or reason to it. What have you got? 250 million plus people in this country and, out of all of those, two of us hook up like that.

Twenty years ago, two thirds of all NFL field goals were made. Now, better than 80 percent are successful.

Steve Spurrier was the only quarterback to go 0-14 in one NFL season, with the '76 Buccaneers.

THE ARMEY IS LOOKING FOR A FEW GOOD MEN – ABOUT 40 OF THEM.

CHARLEY ARMEY

General Manager, St. Louis Rams

Shortly after the Super Bowl, Charley Armey was named general manager of the Rams. For the three seasons prior to that he was the director of player personnel. Armey joined the Rams after the 1997 NFL draft and coordinated all the Rams' professional and college personnel departments. Prior to that he had been director of college scouting for the New England Patriots. Armey, a four-year veteran of the U. S. Navy, holds bachelor's and master's degrees from North Dakota State University. He and his wife Audrey have two daughters, Lisa and Kellie, and one grandson, Travis, and reside in Lake St. Louis, Missouri. It was Armey who pulled the trigger and okayed the signing of Kurt Warner for the Rams and designating him to the World Football League. Charlie has brothers and sisters from North Dakota to Atalissa, Iowa, to Washington, D. C., where his brother, Dick Armey, is the Majority Leader of the U.S. House of Representatives.

U sually the hardest thing to find in any organization is the personnel guy 'cause it's tough to find players. When you find players, it's really easy to forget the personnel guy 'cause once you establish your team, it'll cruise for a few years because you've got good players. Then the personnel guy's gone and you've got a hard time trying to find another one. An example of that is when Pittsburgh had Dick Haley and they would lose players to free agency he found a way to replace them and that team just kept right on rolling. All of a sudden Dick Haley goes to the Jets and they still have a good football team. But the next four or five or six years they start losing players and they don't replace them. All of a sudden their team starts going down and hasn't even bottomed out yet. It's all in the personnel guy.

Don't get me wrong, as a personnel guy, I don't expect to be in the limelight or get credit. In fact I'd prefer to be in the background because I work better with people who underestimate what I do. It's just a fact of what we do. Then we get very comfortable here and somebody comes along or if there happens to be a power struggle, there is none here. But if there did happen to be a power struggle in the organization and you weasel out the personnel guy, that's what happened with me at New England. I was running the thing, and there got to be a little bit of a power struggle, and I was the only one who would stand up to Bill Parcells and, what happens is, I wind up here. They start losing the players they shouldn't lose. It's really hard to talk about it, because it sounds like you're blowing your own horn, but it's just a fact of what happens in this business.

We grew up in the small town of Cando, North Dakota. I have a brother that lives over in Atalissa, Iowa. He was deputy sheriff there for a while. When you grow up in a small town, you rely on your neighbors a lot more than you do in a big city. You get closer to that and you see things differently and have a better background for reading people when they give you answers and in talking with them. But yeah, I'd thought growing up in North Dakota was a great little deal.

I had to fight to keep Kurt Warner on the team for a year and a half. Once Al Luginbill called me, I have a hard rule that anytime anybody with any credibility recommends a player to me, I follow it up. You never know where players come from, and I've had that rule for years. Al and I have known each other for years. He does have a certain amount of credibility with me. My first coaching job was in Graceville, Minnesota, and Mike Kolling, my first high school quarterback, was an assistant coach at Northern Iowa. Once I talked with Mike, he told me he would recommend that I take a good look at Kurt Warner. I had heard of him when I was at New England but we had Drew Bledsoe. But I knew about him when he was at Northern Iowa. Then Green Bay had signed him and didn't look at him,

The New England Patriots once played a regular-season home game in Birmingham, Alabama, in September 1968.

either. Then I saw his results and was tracking him when he was going on the Arena League and Al Luginbill asked me to work him out with the possible chance of putting him in NFL Europe.

Two things I look at in a quarterback are how accurate he is and how are the intangibles. A lot of quarterbacks have size and speed and arm strength. Billy Joe Tolliver's arm is stronger than any arm I ever saw a quarterback have. He could throw the ball harder than anybody I ever saw, but he didn't always throw to the right guy. That's one of Kurt's big assets. Immediately, when I worked him out, I knew that he had the ability to play from the physical standpoint because he never made the receivers adjust to catch the ball. He always gave them an opportunity to make the play. I think he threw 70 balls and none of them touched the ground. The other question you have to answer with a quarterback, is a question which most people can't answer, and it's very difficult, are the intangibles. In other words, how does he manage the team? That's why I flew over to NFL Europe. When I put him in NFL Europe and saw the results coming back on what he was doing over there, my suspicions were starting to be confirmed. I flew over there and actually watched him in a competitive situation and got to sit there and see the intangibles unfold, I knew this guy could play on our level, and the war was on. It was very difficult at first when we brought him back from NFL Europe that first year. Ten days later after he gets back here, we start training camp. These guys who were on our football team at that time had been through two minicamps and know the offense. He had never seen the offense so you could imagine the struggle I had keeping him on the team over Will Furrer. Our coordinator at the time was Jerry Rhome, who really wanted Will Furrer 'cause he fit his comfort zone; he knew his offense. Then the other thing I have to give Coach Vermeil credit for, he stayed with me on it. When we saw him in our training camp, it started to come to the surface that this guy was very accurate. The things we saw in the workout and we confirmed in NFL Europe were there. And Coach Vermeil became ignited by it as well, so he stayed with me. When it became time to make the cut we decided, hopefully, and I kept my fingers crossed, because when it comes down to the final cut you really have to defer to the coaches. But I stood my ground for keeping him over Will Furrer and Coach Vermeil stood with me.

> **When we saw him in our training camp, it started to come to the surface that this guy was very accurate.**

Football staff meetings can become very heated but they are maybe different than a big corporation staff meeting. Football coaches are very competitive, and you expect that. When I go into a meeting with my scouts I expect two or three times during the meeting to have a difference of opinion and some heated arguments and that's how you get it right. If you expect everybody to be a "yes man," that's kind of what Parcells likes, he just likes everybody to do what he likes, and if you do that you generate mistakes. I like to filter out mistakes. The other thing, if you're good at what you do, people recognize it quickly. Coach Vermeil pretty much stood with me on anything about personnel because I had a good track record before I came here and he recognized that early on that I knew what I was talking about regarding personnel. And that's what I do, that's what I'm supposed to do. Like I told Rams President John Shaw, "You're not paying me to be wrong." Naturally I'm going to be wrong sometimes because you can't always be right but if you don't have an opinion you don't have a chance. We made some very good moves. I try to stay as low key as I can, doing it so I don't call a lot of attention to which player I like. It's like a guy going into the casino 'cause he's a real hot gambler and everybody tries to figure out what he's going to bet on next.

The other thing is you've got to get them here and they've got to be coached, etc. But I pride myself on one other big factor, which I think is a huge edge. I know the personality of the coaches because I study that very carefully. I know the type of players that can play for whatever coach I'm working with. I knew the type that could play for Parcells. I knew the type that could play for Forrest Gregg. I knew the type that could play for Chuck Knox, Marv Levy – all those different people I've worked with who are successful coaches, I made sure I knew the type of player that could play for that particular head coach. And I tried to filter it down as much as possible for the assistant coaches. There are a lot of good players that won't fit in another system. I use the word "fit" an awful lot. They fit here; they may not fit someplace else. They may be an All-Pro someplace but can't do it here. And that 's why you have to be careful with free agency. You have to study free agency real careful. Because some guys in free agency could be an outstanding player in the system, and you spend a lot of money on them, and they come in here

The first televised NFL game was in 1939 between the Brooklyn Dodgers and Philadelphia Eagles.

and they can't quite do what they did there. So you have to be careful and know what you're doing in that area.

My vindication feeling on Warner is unbelievable. I believed in him, and I really believed hard in his ability, so when you believe in somebody and that person does what you think they can do, what I'm talking about now – I'm not talking about being the most valuable player and that kind of stuff. I believed he could play at this level, so when he proves that I'm right on the fact that he can play at this level, it's really self-rewarding. It means all the hard work you do in any particular player pays off.

I have the same feeling about a kid named London Fletcher. I think I'm probably the only guy in America who believed in London Fletcher's ability to play. So it's the same thing. When you see a guy you believe in, you see him come to the surface and do what you think they can do, they deserve the credit. I don't deserve the credit. I just was lucky enough to recognize and believe in them. Kurt Warner persevered through a lot of things to do what he's doing.

Kurt definitely knows I believe in him and he knows that I flew over to Amsterdam and watched him play and took him to dinner. What I wanted to find out, when we were at dinner, if what I was seeing on the football field – the personality and everything – was the same as I was seeing. I deal a lot with the psychological makeup of players and their personality. Kurt's was exactly what I anticipated he would be. He's really a clear-eyed intelligent guy with both feet firmly on the ground. What I liked at the dinner you could tell all he needed was an opportunity, and I just had my fingers crossed that we could give it to him. Of course, not at the expense of injuring Trent Green. When you hired Mike Martz to be your coordinator, he had a quarterback in Trent Green that was tailor-made for the offense he was teaching and rightfully so. He wants to bring him 'cause now he's got a huge starting point for his offense. What I liked about Martz was he had very little time with Kurt before he walked into the office and said, "You're right, we'll be fine with him. This guy can play." He saw it early on, too, the traits he was looking for and it was just a good fit.

It's so hard to get to the Super Bowl, which we did when I was with New England. But it's even more difficult to win it. When you win the Super Bowl, and there's only been 34 of them, it has to be the highlight. When you feel you won it, and you were involved in a big way in winning it, that really is rewarding. On Super Bowl day and all through the season, you're the forgotten party in the whole thing, technically, because they're on the field playing. You put a good driver in a race car and he wins the race – it's the car and the driver. You had to go out and select the car, and you have to go out and find the driver. But it's very rewarding and this is what you get out of it: to see that trophy and to be able to hold that trophy and to know that you were a part of it. That's very rewarding for everybody in the organization. And everybody in the organization contributes on different levels.

I learned a long, long time ago, most writers know when you are not telling the truth. I make it a point not to lie to them. If I can't answer the question, I just tell them I can't answer it. I won't lie to them because they've got a hard job. My job is extremely hard and extremely competitive and you have to find the players. You have to find the players that give your coach a chance to succeed. That's what's so much fun about it.

In 1969, the famous Joe Namath Super Bowl, Army assistant football coach Bill Parcells watched the game at the house of Army's head basketball coach, Bobby Knight.

Dean Cain, who played Superman on TV, holds the NCAA record for most interceptions in one season.

Race car spelled backwards is race car.

Chapter 7

Gus Ornstein

John Ramsdell

Cinderfella was Ramtastic

Warner in home arena action in 1997. Coach John Gregory is in white shirt.

IN THE FINAL QUARTER OF HIS CAREER AND PRAYIN' FOR OVERTIME
GUS ORNSTEIN

Think, if you were a backup quarterback going to the St. Louis Rams camp in Macomb, Illinois, in July 1999. You knew Trent Green was going to be the starter but you'd have to think that you had a good chance at the number 2 position. That was the feeling held by Gus Ornstein, a Jewish high school quarterback legend in New York City who played collegiately at Notre Dame, Michigan State, and Rowan College in New Jersey. Ornstein is a very enthusiastic and likeable young man who has had to endure somewhat similar paths that Kurt Warner had to overcome to make the NFL. In the spring of 2000 he signed with the Indianapolis Colts. An all-around athlete, Ornstein also played baseball in the Yankees organization.

The Rams came down to Rowan a bunch of times and saw me. I did not get drafted and then signed a deal with the Rams as soon as the draft was over. I checked the roster to see who was on the roster and had not heard of Kurt Warner before – just did not know who the guy was. I just tried to find out some things about him, but most people I talked to didn't know who he was. Most thought of Curt Warner as the running back for the Seahawks.

The first time I got to meet him was out at minicamp when the draft was over at the end of April '99 it would have been. Just right away, he's a real good guy, just real friendly – Trent Green, too. And Joe Germaine who they drafted in the fourth round, they all just seemed to get along right away. It was hard to meet him at that first minicamp; we were only there three days. The next time I went out, the whole month of June we were able to just come out and work out and had another minicamp.

That was the first time I got to know Kurt better as a guy whose locker was right next to mine. His story, where he had come from, was kind of what I've gone through. Him at the professional level compared to mine at the college career was kind of similar. I used to joke that he was a poster boy for what I'd been through: his resilience and ability to just keep battling no matter how many people told him he couldn't make it. We just got along real well because he was a super guy. During training camp, the coaches were all over his case because he was the backup, trying to put the pressure on him to see what he could handle. Kurt used to always come to me with his frustrations and stuff and just frustrated with the mistakes that Trent would make. Kurt would kinda do the same mistakes, but when Trent would make them they were okay, but when Kurt would make them they made a scene out of them to kinda show both of them what he was doing wrong. One night Trent took the four of us out to dinner. I hung out with them a bunch, just ate meals with them all the time.

Then when Trent went down in the San Diego game, it was all in Kurt's hands. It was a great break for the guy and I was talking to him at halftime and said, "Here's your shot." I was just hoping the guy would make the most of it. I could never imagine he would do what he's done with it.

I just spoke to him a couple of weeks ago, to congratulate him on the MVP and everything else and he's just exactly the same. I told him I was happy for him that he got the chance and was able to make the most of it when he got it. It's just been an awesome story. He's unbelievable. He's the most level-headed guy. I called him up and like I was "like Kurt, MVP you know," and I think I was more fired up about it than he was. He said, "We've still got a job to do here." You're the MVP, you know, going to the Pro Bowl! Come on – you know. He's got tremendous self-confidence in himself, which I think for all the stuff he's been through you need to have because nobody else is going to believe in you. If you don't have it in yourself you're never gonna get to where he's got. I was supposed to play the fourth quarter but when Trent went down they panicked and they realized Kurt was gonna be the guy and Joe Germaine was there, and I think I was kinda out of the picture at that point.

I thought the talent out there was unbelievable.

Honestly, when I first got to the minicamp, obviously I'd never been to NFL training camp and never really been around one except for what you see on ESPN's *SportsCenter*. I thought the talent out there was unbelievable. I was thinking this team had been four and 12 the last few years so maybe everybody in the NFL is this good or that much better. But I don't know, we've got a ton of weapons on offense. If this team can't win, the other teams must be phenomenal. I thought we were good, but I had nothing to judge it against. So I'm honestly not that surprised at where we were. The coaches always said this team has what it takes to get there, and I think the players believed. Just seeing what we had in training camp and what was going on they started to see that, hey, there was talent out here.

I had never heard of Macomb, Illinois, where the Rams train, and I can see why. Growing up in New York City, then having to spend six weeks in Macomb Illinois…There's not a heck of a lot going on in that town. It was hot; the air does not move out there. The drive from St. Louis to Macomb is like three and one-half hours of cornfields. Macomb is an interesting place.

We only had a couple of nights off. There was actually, believe it or not, a phenomenal Mexican restaurant in the middle of Macomb. I have no idea how that happened. We usually headed there. That was the first time I met Kurt's family. I used to hang out with Rich Coady, a rookie safety from Texas A&M, all the time, and Joe Germaine. We were just leaving that place one night and Kurt's family had come up to spend the night – got a chance to meet his wife and kids. That's usually what we'd do, or just rent a video or something. There was like one movie theater. After you'd seen the movie, you couldn't really do that again.

The coaches were all cool. That was the one thing at the pro level that was really different. They treated you like people. They had respect for you and kinda listened to your opinion, like I remember just looking at Mike Martz's relationship with Trent and it was just so cool, exactly what you'd want from an offensive coordinator and a quarterback I mean, he'd ask Trent's opinion on things. It was just such a different view from college. It wasn't like "in your face – always putting you down" kind of atmosphere.

I tell Kurt all the time. Everytime I talk to him, "Hey, man you know, you're like the poster child for resiliency and keeping after it." I've worked out since I got released. I went back to Michigan State and finished up school and graduated and I've actually worked out for eight NFL teams the past few months. I'm actually pretty close to signing with someone in the next couple of weeks. Kurt's stats are unreal. When the Rams played in Detroit, a couple of my buddies from Michigan State drove down to Detroit with me. I just kinda went to the hotel and said Hi to Kurt and went out to dinner with some of my buddies, Rich Coady and Grant Wistrom. I told him, "Man I'm so happy for you. It's not real."

One of my buddies was doing something like a rotisserie fantasy team or something, and he said, "Who can I get that nobody knows about?" I told him about Az-Zahir Hakim. Just from being in training camp, I knew this guy was gonna do something great this year. Then my buddy is like "Man you called it." Nobody really knew who he was, either. I should have told him Warner, too – I would have been a hero then.

Kurt and I talked a lot about a lot of stuff. He said at Green Bay he only got about eight reps like the entire camp. I just kinda voiced some opinions. I would have thought Trent had a pretty good shot at MVP. I thought he was really good and was real impressed with him.

The greatest Jewish quarterback ever was Sid Luckman, who starred in a critical Ivy League Game for Columbia the same hour his dad went to the electric chair at Sing Sing. The father of the 1943 NFL MVP of the Bears was a leader of Murder, Incorporated. The only other current Jewish quarterback is Jay Fiedler of the Miami Dolphins.

STRESSED SPELLED BACKWARD IS DESSERTS
JOHN RAMSDELL

John Ramsdell just completed his fifth season with the Rams, his first as the quarterbacks coach. John is a native of Lancaster, Pennsylvania, and played football at Springfield College in Massachusetts, where he was a two-year letterman at running back. John and his wife Brenda have a son, Christopher, and a daughter, Amy. They live in Ellisville, Missouri.

W e're real happy about the whole deal, and it's been great. The problem with all this is they don't give you much time to sit here and enjoy it all. We're on to the next year already. It's been quite a run and it's nice to be part of it all.

This is my sixth year here, but I became quarterbacks coach last year. I came in with Rich Brooks in 1995. The team was still in L.A., spent about four months there and then we moved to St. Louis, so I've been here a little while – saw the good and the bad.

Kurt Warner is a wonderful guy; he's something special. When you start getting involved with the guy, you see that he is great. In terms of seeing he's gonna be the MVP, I don't know if you ever can say that for sure. That's kind of how it all falls together. He was here a year ago and I was coaching what we call the "H" backs at that time so I wasn't coaching quarterbacks that first year here. But just being around him, you know he's a great guy. You know he's got ability. His role two years ago was he was our third quarterback and basically all he did was just service our defense. He came in to training camp from Europe and didn't get a whole lot of stuff 'cause we were getting Tony Banks ready. And the next guy was Steve Bono, who was new to our program, so those guys basically got all the reps and we just had to make a decision between Kurt and Will Furrer, who we were gonna keep. That was a tough thing there that we had to struggle through. Will had been in the NFL for a while, with a couple of different teams. He was on our team the year before ('97) so Kurt had beat out an established guy at least on our team. Our offensive coordinator at that time was Jerry Rhome, and Jerry had had Furrer at two other teams. Just to make the team was the toughest thing for Warner. Here was a guy, Kurt, who's never been in the league and just to break the ice to be in the league, that's big. Once you've been in the league a little bit, I guess you have a little more value, more worth. People believe in you just a little bit more, whether you've played or not, at least you've been in the NFL. You've been there and had those kinds of experiences. Not to have any of that, that's tough to make a team, especially when there's no drafted interest, no financial interest in you, either. You're sticking out when you give a guy a couple of hundred thousand dollars signing bonus or something like that. You're more likely to look at him more. To be honest with you, Kurt came to us late. He wasn't in any of our off-season stuff. From a coaching staff, we really didn't know who he was other than the fact that he was coming in from the World League. He was at our last minicamp

> **There's a picture of Kurt and his award was the "Defensive Service Award of the Year."**

in the middle of June. That was the only time we saw him; he had a lot of ground to make up. So that was bad but he did it. And he made it in spite of all that so that's pretty good. And then like I said his role was to basically service our defense the whole year. He ran off the cards, whoever we were playing that week, and Kurt pretended to be the opposing quarterback. The funny thing is we have a lot of awards here. Coach Vermeil gave out awards at the end of the year for different situations. All these guys' pictures are on the wall downstairs in this hallway. There's a picture of Kurt and his award was the "Defensive Service Award of the Year." He was the scout team guy so he got that award. He gave the defense the best look of our upcoming opponent. That's kind of a little joke around here. You go down that hallway and see his picture's still up showing Kurt getting that defensive award and now he's the MVP in the league. That's gotta be the all-time greatest improvement ever!

So now '98's over and I've moved from "H" back coach to quarterbacks coach. I really liked Kurt because of my relationship with him at that time, not coaching him but just knowing him. In pro football as opposed to college coaching, you're a little bit closer to guys because you're with them all the time and it's the same guys, and it's not as many guys. So I really liked the kid. What happened was we hired a new offensive coordinator, Mike Martz, and we're putting in a new system. Mike knew exactly what he wanted to do. Really, Kurt and I were on the outside. We're both learning it together. We kind of came up together and we brought in Trent to be the quarterback. Kurt was told that he was our backup, he was gonna be number 2 because we weren't gonna re-sign Steve Bono, and Tony Banks was traded. Really, Kurt was the only guy back from the quarterback position the previous year and he was excited about that. Everybody knows that you can change from being number 2 to being number 3 in a heartbeat because there are other guys out there and there was talk about bringing in a more established veteran. Again, Kurt's in the NFL now, but he's never really played, so many people in this league are much more comfortable having an established veteran kind of guy who's been in the league and maybe even started somewhere else as the backup as opposed to a guy who's never played. Actually Kurt, to be number 2, with his kind of background is unusual but we felt good about it because of what he's done. But then he still had to earn it through what he did in minicamps, what he did in training camp, what he did in preseason – all those kinds of things. If he didn't look good in any of that stuff, we could always have brought in another veteran, whether it be Jeff Hostetler or some other guy 'cause there's always guys out there who've played. So he still – even though he was told that he was second – knew he had to prove his worth.

We were tough on Kurt at Macomb to see if he could take it. He wasn't babied. He wasn't sugarcoated. You know a lot about a quarterback is how you deal with pressure, how do you react to stress? The things we knew about Kurt was we knew he was extremely accurate, we knew he was quick with the ball, we knew he was very intelligent, we knew he cared and that he had a great work ethic. Those are wonderful things to have. What more can you want. What you want is experience and being able to react positively under stress, duress, pressure. You never know about that till you do it. So all other things are kind of manufactured stuff and that's kind of the indication and it's practice for the real deal. And you just don't know till you see them in the real deal. So then his next big test would be how would he be in the preseason games. At least there are bodies flying after you and they don't have our colors on so that's a test. Then once you pass that, it's, "Well, that was only a preseason game, it wasn't a real game." So now you take it to the next level. But the real game thing came a little quicker than the plan was. So then it wasn't a test anymore. You are the guy. We hope you do good.

The University of Arizona football stadium doubles as a student dormitory.

In terms of technical, mechanical, and all that kind of stuff, our goal was to make Kurt be a real good second-team guy that we felt comfortable about if we had to go past Trent. That was the "A-Number One" thing. That was one of the number 1 things – not only for him and the position, but for the team. We spent all this money we brought in what we thought was and we still think is a great quarterback in Trent and we felt real good about that. We figured, "Hey we got a chance." We've got good people around him, Marshall, Isaac, so we felt good about that. In pro football if you don't have a real good second quarterback, you really can just fall off the face of the earth so we wanted to make sure that that insurance was taken care of so that was a huge team goal. That was a big thing. Just in terms of all the individual kind of stuff for him was just to learn the offense. Because if you don't learn the offense you have no chance no matter what your abilities are. Just getting him up to speed as quick as possible, learn the stuff and just be a good decision maker – get the ball into the hands of guys who can win for us. You don't have to force things. You can play conservatively, just don't get us beat. And he went way beyond that – way beyond that.

A lot of our problems of the Rams prior to this year – we beat ourselves particularly in offense, dumb turnovers, it was unbelievable. Many games in '98 we were down 17–0 in the first quarter because of just flat turning it over and doing dumb stuff and just putting ourselves out of the game. That's a big thing we stress with Kurt and all the other quarterbacks is that you can't do that. You've got to keep us in the game so we can at least play the game. And he was beautiful in that. I think he turned the ball over once or twice in the preseason or took an unnecessary sack – those kinds of things that everybody goes through. You can talk about it all you want in meetings but you have to experience it and get the feel for it, which he did.

Around Rams Park everybody just treats everybody else like people.

Around Rams Park everybody just treats everybody else like people. Coaches aren't way up on a higher pedestal than players. We treat each other like human beings. We're all in this together. It's not a coaches versus the players kind of deal. That's absolutely true. That's my feeling about our coaches and our players.

We were playing San Diego, second home game, third preseason game, and Trent had basically completed every ball. We scored every time we had had the ball. This may have been the third series of the game, I don't know, but we've got points on the board. As Trent gets whacked, he throws the ball down the field and completes that one, too, like a nice crossing route with a 20-plus-yard gain. You knew his injury was bad. All you could do was just pray that it wasn't what you thought it was. But it turned out to be. Then, of course, Kurt goes in there. I'm the one on the field who gives the quarterback the play through the walkie-talkie. Martz is upstairs so I actually talk to Kurt. It was toward the end of the half. He only has about one play to get us out of the half. Then we play him for maybe just a series in the third quarter, two at the most, and we get him out early. A lot of the thought was, "Why are you doing that? Here's an opportunity. If Kurt's gonna be the guy, you've got to get him work." Well, the thought was, "Hey, we can't lose him, too." We can't get him hurt, so we got him out of there and finished the game with Joe Germaine. So Kurt spent a lot of time on the sidelines that day contemplating what the deal was. I had told Kurt the reason we were not playing him and he said, "I want to play, but I understand." He's smart enough, he understands. He wanted to play – anybody would – but he understood the situation. That's one of the things Kurt and I discussed. Hey look at this. All these plays are happening. I don't know if we'll win or not but it doesn't matter, and we're moving the ball. Guys are making plays offensively, defensively. Jeff Wilkens kicks a 50-plus-yard field goal. "Look, Kurt, you've got a lot of good players around you. All you've got to do is just manage the game. You're gonna be fine. You don't have to win the game. You've got lots of guys around you, just operate. Be a game man." He's agreeing to all this – just talking about what he had to do to get ready, just be a good game manager and you've got playmakers around you. You just can't take us out of games like with Tony Banks last year we had a lot of turnovers – that kind of stuff. You just can't do that. That's kinda how it went. He knew he was gonna be the guy.

After that game where Trent Green got hurt, there was talk about our quarterback situation among the coaches. There were some who wanted to bring in somebody else to be a starter, absolutely. But we felt good about Kurt and he knew the system. Just being in training camp, he knew it better than anybody we could bring in with the exception of maybe Jeff Hostetler. And he knew all the situation so we just felt com-

Jim Thorpe was the
first president of the NFL.

fortable. I don't think we were in a panic mode, but we were devastated – everybody was devastated, even Kurt I think – just for his feelings for Trent. It was the worst situation I'd been around in my coaching career in terms of losing a guy. It was totally devastating. It was like a bomb went off in the whole city and it was in this building, too, and it was that way for several days afterward.

The fact that Trent was from St. Louis wasn't a factor in our feelings. The fact is we were looking so good even back from the very first minicamp back in April, all through training camp. The offense was so efficient and just clicking right along, rhythm, timing, it was just moving. Trent's whole preseason he was like 28 out of 32. His pass efficiency was over 140. His incompletions were drops; they weren't bad throws; they were drops. So he was unconscious. He threw one interception. It was because Torry Holt, our rookie, went the wrong way. What I'm saying is that Trent played basically perfect through the preseason and no one stopped us. Every time he was in there, we scored, so the hopes were growing by leaps and bounds. All it was was just all positive; we thought we had a real chance. Then my first thought when he got hurt was, "Oh, okay, we still are good. The fact that Trent's hurt doesn't mean that Marshall isn't a good player or Isaac's not a good player. We've still got good players. We've still got a chance to be a playoff team as long as we don't beat ourselves." That was my theme with Kurt. But I didn't know that we would win the Super Bowl. I had really thought we had a chance with Trent. After that I thought we still had a chance to be a playoff team and still be a good team and maybe we'll grow and Kurt will get better through the process. Hey, who knows what'll happen?

The whole situation was bad. It may have put a little more pressure on us, but I just felt sorry for Trent, just the whole situation. There's no secret we had to win from a coach's standpoint, too, 'cause we were on the block, too. That pressure's there, but you just gotta deal with it. Let's put it that way.

Kurt played just the first half of the last preseason game at Detroit still because we didn't want him to get hurt. We wanted to get him "game ready," so to speak, get him a little confidence in moving the team a little bit, get a little chemistry going, and once we felt good about that we were taking him out because we didn't want to risk getting him hurt like the Trent deal. He played basically like Trent did; just went out and the first series of the game he throws a strike to Az-Zahir Hakim and its a touchdown but Az drops it and so maybe we get a field goal out of it or something. Kurt comes back out again and just about like we scored every time we had the ball the first half with him operating. So he played marvelous. We got him out there and, "Well, gee, this isn't a whole lot different than the other preseason games." In the second half, we just wanted to get out of there healthy so nothing much happened the second half. I don't even know if we won or not. We were very encouraged after that game about our chances. It was just a preseason game and now we've got to do it in a "real" game. You're going against the other team's best players all the time. Baltimore has a real good defense and they're not gonna put in guys that they're gonna cut now. They're already cut; they're not looking at anybody now. They're not just trying to get through the game to stay healthy; they want to win.

We felt comfortable with Kurt all along, and it just grew game by game. It took a big step that night in Detroit and then as well as he played in that first game against Baltimore. That was huge, really huge. Then to back it up again the next week against Atlanta, the defending NFC champions, that's huge. Then to do it against the 49ers was huge. Like every week, it was like, "Man, that's unbelievable. Just do it all the time." And then it became, "That's the way it's supposed to be, you know." So we're spoiled quick, real quick.

This is an incredible story. I'm just so grateful about the whole thing. I'm the first one to tell you, "It's Kurt, not me." He's the one who did it all. I'm just happy to be part of it. With Kurt, what you see is what you get. What I'm telling you is, he's the greatest guy to talk to. He's genuine, very sincere, matter of fact, tells you what he feels, and he has no selfishness to him at all. All he wants to do is help the team win and do the best he can do.

When people started recognizing him from a national standpoint, and the media was coming around, he preferred not to have any of the glory. Here's another part of it, Kurt is so focused, he understands the commitment, the undivided attention and effort that is necessary and required of what he does. All that other stuff is a distraction, taking away from the real game, and so he understands that. He understands how fragile the whole deal is, that he cannot be sidetracked at all. He really likes Trent and respects Trent and wants the best for Trent. There's no doubt about it. Believe it or not, Trent's the same guy as Kurt. You won't believe it, but they're the same guy.

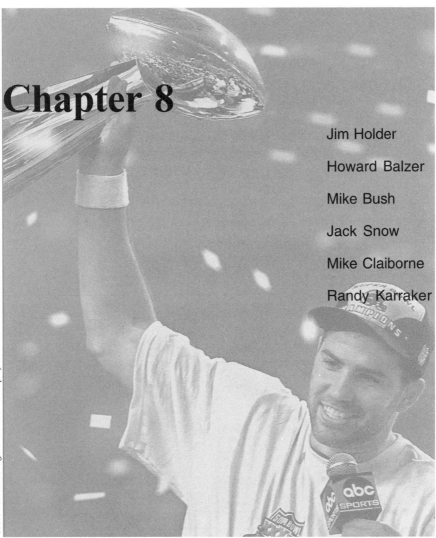

Chapter 8

Jim Holder

Howard Balzer

Mike Bush

Jack Snow

Mike Claiborne

Randy Karraker

Turn Your Radio On

Jack Snow with son J.T. at Busch Stadium, St. Louis.

Courtesy KTRS Radio

THE CYCLONE FROM AMES
JIM HOLDER

Jim Holder was raised in Madison, Wisconsin, and graduated from Iowa State. Jim has 24 years in the radio business. He is the sports director at KTRS, the Big 550, in St. Louis, and the public address announcer at Rams games.

E very Wednesday is the big media day for all NFL teams including the Rams in early '99. It was my suggestion to my boss that we get Trent Green and do a "Trent Green Show." Let's try to do something with Trent Green because he's a St. Louis product, Vianney High School, Indiana University. He was a clean-cut guy that people were all excited about. Let's get Trent on the Big 550. His agent's Jim Steiner, from St. Louis, who's got a lot of big people. Jim Steiner and I go back a long way. I suggested to Brian Jordan's mother that when they start talking agents, be sure to talk to Jim Steiner and Jim Turner. Steiner does all the NFL guys and Turner does the baseball guys. They still owe me a big steak dinner on that one. He made a lot of money on that one.

The Rams got Trent Green in February of '99, and Steiner was happy. I know the day Trent was introduced that Steiner was at the news conference. I said something like, hey, you know I had suggested to my boss, Tim Dorsey, to talk to you about having Trent Green so they were able to get together. He was on Monday mornings, and pretty soon, Boom, Harrison breaks Green's knee. Now all of a sudden, it's Warner's turn to quarterback the Rams. We said, "Well, let's get involved with a Kurt Warner Show." It was kind of a mutual thing, but I think it was Tim saying, "Hey, let's go after Warner." I contacted the agent in Chicago, Bartelstein, and said I know they want to do something and basically I just put them in touch with Tim and they work it out and said we're gonna have Warner twice a week on Tuesdays and Fridays. And it went well. Right from the get go you could tell, like at 7:40 in the morning on Tuesdays and Fridays, there were three people in the studio, Dan Dierdorf, Wendy Wiese, and Kevin Slayten. The three of them did it. I wasn't involved in that aspect of it because they're the co-hosts for our morning show. So we just did it 'cause it wasn't gonna be all meat-and-potatoes football stuff.

As a matter of fact, I think I still have a tape of the first show with Trent Green. We just kept Trent's show on the air; there was no reason to get out. Trent Green was under contract with us so we had to keep paying him. As it got later into the season, he was actually going to the games. He still was doing a lot of things with the club. He was the best the Rams had; people couldn't get enough. He was the one who was to have been the starter, and I'm sure people sat and were interested in whatever he had to say. When they were 6 and 0, you couldn't get enough here. It worked well.

> **I'm sure there aren't too many quarterbacks who can't talk a little bit.**

Kurt was just outstanding right from the git go. It was obvious, I remember telling him after doing the first one. "Hey, I thought you sounded great." I'm sure there aren't too many quarterbacks who can't talk a little bit. He was very good, fluent, not a lot of hemming and hawing around, very direct, and he would show a sense of humor. A lot of that, of course, is determined by how he is asked the questions. Again, this was done over the phone, a lot of times he would be on his way to the stadium, or he would be at home helping Brenda and getting the kids ready and doing that sort of thing.

Warner's number 13 jerseys made people go nuts. Somebody just told me last night that Kurt and Brenda walked into a restaurant and immediately they got a standing ovation and I know that happens. I'm sure when Ditka would walk into a place or Walter Payton or certainly Michael Jordan in Chicago that ovations occur. At our station, Dan Dierdorf is friends with Bobby Knight. He played for Bo Schembechler at Michigan, and Dan recalled the story about going into a restaurant just outside of Bloomington – I think Bobby owned it – and Dan said he walked in with the General and Bo Schembechler himself. There might have been 125 people there and everybody just shut up. Nobody said anything. They walked to their table and Dan said the silence was so eerie that he would never forget it.

But somebody was just telling me out in West County here that Kurt and Brenda went out and when they walked in the restaurant, he's now afforded that standing "O." I know probably five, six weeks into the season you could begin to track his popularity by the number of things he couldn't do. Or at least to the degree that the Warner family used to be able to just come and go in St. Louis and do whatever. But the little trips to the grocery story, family quick stop at some fast food stop, or whatever the place, it got to be too much of an effort. I know Kurt talked about maybe coming close to stopping and just grab a couple of items for the family, it became obvious he was not going to be able to go out. From having those kinds of reactions around Halloween time, fast forward to Christmas time, and it was probably tripled. It literally got to the point where – they love him here – he can't go anywhere.

In regards to his faith, it's kind of how you perceive things. There are, I think, some people who might be turned off by his religion but that might be the person who never discussed religion in any conversation. Whether it's in the 19th hole after having a great round of golf on a Saturday afternoon, or sitting in a bridge club with his wife and some other friends, that might be an individual who just might never get involved. Other people, I suppose in their own families, maybe used it to discuss religion or taking a little different view of Christ and what religion means to different people. I think people kinda did it personally. I think a lot of people probably took what he and Brenda talked about and did and then would discuss it kind of privately in their own families.

I was the emcee at a Quarterback Club function about midway in the season and it was the first time I had met Brenda. She came in with a little baby and we had a chance to talk briefly. Then she got up and made a presentation about Camp Barnabas. That was the first time I had heard anything about it. They were selling some kind of a product, a frozen bread or whatever that you buy and put in your freezer. When you had guests over, or that special dinner, bring out this bread and stick it in the oven. I just remember being very impressed with her; it was obvious that I remember thinking, "She's very good." She made quite a presentation about the camp and was well versed and you could tell the interest. And I thought she made an interesting selling point. She made some people laugh and she made a few people even kind of "well up" a little bit in talking about what this camp means to different families and the things they didn't have and what they were hoping to be able to do, so I was impressed.

> Tex Schramm's first name is "Texas" even
> though he was born in California.

We were always looking for a different angle and talked with the Barnstormers people and got their coach John Gregory. He was a pretty good storyteller. We had him on with the Warners. Now you're getting into the sixth or seventh game and Warner just continues to throw half a dozen touchdowns per week and hardly any picks. I called Coach Gregory up and set him up to do our show. He used to stay in contact with Kurt and Brenda, but he was having a difficult time getting through and I remember he gave me his cell phone number because I think maybe Kurt was turning his off because of the volume of calls. I just remember the coach saying, "Hey, Jim can you do me a favor?" There was something that came up and he needed to talk to Kurt within a reasonable time. It may have been something to do with a bus trip. As far as Kurt with the coaches, I'm sure if you talked with him, he'd say Kurt was a heck of a basketball player, and he thought he could probably have played for Northern Iowa. Something that stood out, I thought, was the fact he talked about what a precision passer that he was.

When this thing is going, you're always looking for these little bullets and different angles and looking for people to say different things. When Kurt was running the scout team, you don't normally question one of the starting tackles: "How the heck is the third team quarterback doing?" Once he took over and started having all this success, people did say, "You know what, the guy was pretty good in practice."

I know there were certainly a lot of media people who were hoping Warner would get an opportunity to show his wares.

I wasn't alone in the media, at the end of the '98 season, that wanted Warner to play. You've got Warner and you've got Bono. You know you're not gonna take the next step with Bono, so why not play Kurt Warner? You know it was kinda like when Jamie Martin was here, he looked like he could do some things and basically wasn't given a chance. And Warner didn't get a start. I think he threw 11 or 14 passes in the second half of the last game against San Francisco of the '98 season. He didn't even start that game, so from the Rams' perspective, what they said, I know there were certainly a lot of media people who were hoping Warner would get an opportunity to show his wares. I don't think anybody was overly excited about Steve Bono, in all fairness to Steve.

From somebody who's been around here as long as I have, in the last three years, we've had two of the most amazing seasons ever with McGwire and now Kurt Warner. The days pass and the home runs would go or the touchdown passes and the wins for the Rams and homers for McGwire. It kept going and it was basically like a dream. You say, "I hope this thing never ends. This is a long-running film, let's just continue to let it run." It was obviously fun, not only witnessing it, but, of course, reporting on all the achievements with Big Mac and with Kurt. You talk about historic events – and since we just finished a century of sports – probably there haven't been two better stories than that coming out of the same city by two fabulous guys. These guys weren't jerks.

The PA announcer for the Houston Astros (Colt 45's) during their first season in 1962 was Dan Rather. The PA announcer for the Brooklyn Dodgers in 1937 was John Forsythe, the actor.

Yvonne Davis is married to 1946 Heisman winner Glenn Davis. Before that she was married to 1954 Heisman winner from Wisconsin, the late Alan Ameche.

THE SAGE OF ST. LOUIS
HOWARD BALZER

Howard Balzer is a writer for Pro Football Weekly, *for* Rams Update, *and hosts his own sports talk show in St. Louis. He's also the author of* Kurt Warner, Quarterback, *published in the spring of 2000 by GHB Books.*

T he book I'm writing is called *Kurt Warner*. I'm not sure you could even call it a book. It's more geared to a younger audience, basically telling the story of Kurt Warner. It's not that long and includes a lot of pictures and is more like a "magazine" book. This local company here in St. Louis has done it on hockey before on the St. Louis Blues and they decided to try it on football.

The irony on this is before the training camp I had talked to the same publishing company about doing one on Trent Green. We were set to do it and then it got to being late summer and Trent didn't have the time to sit down to interview, etc. He just said, "Let's put it off until maybe next year." Of course, the irony of it is what happened.

When I was doing this thing all year where – and had a lot of people doing it – we were burning sage for the Rams. It was kind of a bizarre story how it all started. It was right after Trent Green got hurt and a lot of people believed that the Rams were cursed – no matter what they do, something bad happens.

My wife and I go to a festival every year in Texas and they have booths, and a lady psychic has come to this for years and I've gotten to know her 'cause she camps near us. So I happened to call this psychic last August and I started telling her things that have happened – bad decisions and all that. I say, "Read in your cards and tell me if there's some kind of curse over this football team." So the weird thing is she starts to tell me, "Yeah I'm getting this feeling that there's this really negative energy around this football team." Then she said, "I don't know what it means, but it seems they brought it from somewhere else." I hadn't told her the Rams had moved here from Los Angeles so it was kinda freaky. She said, "There is this negative energy but there is something you can do about it." I said, "What?" She said to burn sage. I said, "Sage?" She said, "Yes, it's a native American thing that's tradition. (I've since found out that native Americans are not the only ones who do this, a lot of people do it.) You burn the sage, you come up with a chant, and you ask God to cleanse the negative energy that's around whatever it might be. A lot of people do it when they move into new homes. They go into the different corners of the house to cleanse whatever negative energy might have been there from before. She says it cleanses and purifies and you just ask God to cleanse the negative energy. Come up with a chant. So I came up with a chant: "You gotta believe."

One night before the final exhibition game – it was two days after I had called the psychic – I had announced on the radio the day of the final preseason game saying I was gonna have an announcement the next morning of how we were gonna remove the curse of the Rams. So that Thursday I'm talking with some other guys at the station after I was on the air, and they started talking about Marshall Faulk and the Greg Hill trade where the Rams had traded him and people were criticizing it. They said, "Well no one will even talk about this at the end of the year if the Rams do well and Marshall Faulk has a great year, unless Marshall Faulk gets hurt." I said, as a joke, "Well we won't have to worry about that once we start burning sage."

Then it was really weird. As I was driving home from the station, I started getting this weird feeling. Now this was five days after Trent Green got hurt. I said to myself, "What if Marshall Faulk gets hurt tonight?" I got this weird feeling so I actually went to the supermarket and bought some sage leaves in the spice section. Honest, I'm not putting anyone on. Peter King talks about it on CNN. Skip Bayless wrote about it in *the Chicago Tribune* during Super Bowl week. That night, half an hour before the game, I go out in my backyard. I'm the only one

"You gotta believe" just came into my head. So I just said "You gotta believe, you gotta believe."

doing it at this time. No one else knows. I start burning these leaves, and I said, "Rid the negative energy around this team," and I start talking about Kurt Warner and Marshall Faulk and all this stuff and saying the names of the players on the team and I said, "Oh, I've got to call it a chant." So that's when "You gotta believe" just came into my head. So I just said "You gotta believe, you gotta believe." That night in that first game, Warner takes them down the field and gets three scores in the first three drives and they're winning 17– 0 at halftime. So I called my wife who was out of the town at the time – she was the one who had given me the number for the psychic. We were talking and I said, "Yeah, the Rams won, and I burned sage." She said, "Well it just shows you gotta believe." And I swear I had not told her what the chant was.

So anyway, I get on the radio the next week and began talking about this thing: "We're gonna burn sage." You can get it in different forms. I did a pregame show at Planet Hollywood right across from the Trans World Dome and I was telling people to come to the show, bring sage, the whole bit. I said even if you're not coming to the show, burn it at your tailgate parties. And people did it; people bought into it. People brought sage to where I was. I found out later that people had it at different tailgating parties all around the Dome. Of course, the Rams won that game. And weird things happened in that game where the Baltimore kicker hit the upright on a field-goal attempt. Then Chris McAlister, the Ravens rookie cornerback, intercepts a Warner pass at like the 20-yard line and is running in toward the end zone for a touch-down. There's no one there, and he just falls down at the 5-yard line. It was just totally bizarre. The Rams were winning at the time, but who knows what would have happened if the Ravens had made those two scores.

I kept doing it all year and all around town. People were burning sage and some people were taking it on the road with them to games. People in the organization, I mean that Stan Kroenke, a minority owner of the team, would come up to me in the locker room after games and say, "Howard, keep burning that sage." John Bunting's wife was burning sage all year; Jim Hanifan was. Different people in the organization kept coming up to me and saying, "Hey, keep burning that sage." I'm saying, "Hey, it's all positive thinking; just think positive. You gotta be-lieve!" So anyway, this goes on all year.

The night after the first game, the Rams have a dinner to honor this new "Ring of Honor" they've started for Rams Hall of Famers and Cardinal Hall of Famers – guys who've played pro football in St. Louis. So I'm talking to Kurt and I mention to him how I had burned sage the day before. He said, "Do me a favor, don't burn it at the next game." I said, "Why not?" He said, "Well, because I have faith and I get strength from above, from God." So I was a little troubled by it but I explained to him, "Well, Kurt when you burn sage, you don't just burn it and expect things to happen – people have to believe. You don't just burn it. We're praying to God as well. It might not be the same God you're praying to but it's God. We're praying to God to remove this negative energy, etc." So he said, "Okay."

I went ahead and burned it before every game, including the Super Bowl. Most players on the Rams never said anything to me about it all year. However, the equipment manager, Todd Hewitt, burned some in the locker room before the Super Bowl. In fact, he said NFL security came and were sniffing around, wondering what the strange smells were and what was going on in their locker room. A lot of people made the comment, "You're sure you're burning that and not smoking it." The only player I knew that knew something about it was Todd Collins and that's another crazy story.

The night before the first game of the season, when I'm getting ready to burn sage, I go running out that day to find some. I didn't want to use the leaves because they burn out real quick. I found some in stores that were like incense sticks, others look little cigars, and the weird thing was a lot of them were packaged in Sedona, Arizona, which is where Georgia Frontiere, the Rams' owner, has a home. Sedona is famous among psychics because it's supposedly one of the few places in the world known as a "psychic vortex." I thought that was kinda freaky when I found that out. But anyway, the night before the first game, I'm reading this NFL packet the league sends out right before the season. It's about 60 pages of stats and different things. I'd had it for about two or three weeks and hadn't even looked at it. For some reason that night I decide to look at it to see if I could find a couple more notes for ideas for the first show tomorrow. I'm looking through it and get almost to the very end. There's a list of players' superstitions. I start looking at it. There's Todd Collins, the linebacker for the Rams, the first player listed. It says he has an Indian fetish made of stones and charms, which he keeps in a pouch. He rubs it on his body before games, especially in places where he's had a previous injury. When I read that, I was mad at myself that I hadn't read this thing earlier and I could have talked to him earlier in the week about what I was going to do.

The next morning, I get downtown and park my car in the parking garage and start to walk about eight blocks to Planet Hollywood. I'm coming up to this street which is about two blocks from the Dome. I found out later there's a parking garage there where some of the Rams people

> The Rams, who began as the Cleveland Rams, were named for the Fordham University team.

– coaches, players and different people come and park their cars. Usually they get out and someone parks their car for them. This car pulls into the street and three players get out – Grant Wistrom, Jeff Robinson, and Todd Collins. I swear I start getting chills because if I hadn't read the thing the night before, it would have meant nothing to me. And obviously two or three minutes either way for either of us arriving and I don't even see the guy – our paths don't cross.

So I go up to him. I said, "Hey Todd, I was reading about your Indian fetish last night." So he kinda gives me a look and says, "Yeah, you don't think I'm like crazy or anything do you?" I said, "No, wait till you hear what I'm gonna do." I showed him the sage and he said, "Yeah, I've heard of that – that's great, that's great! Go for it. Go for it."

Here's the thing. I mentioned that missed field goal where the guy hit the upright. On the possession right before that, I think the Rams were winning 17 – 10, early in the fourth quarter. Warner fumbled on his own 30-yard line and everybody said, "Here we go. Same old Rams!" The Ravens get the ball and on first down they try a screen pass to the left to Priest Holmes. From where we were, it looked like he just had a clear cut down the sidelines. Out of nowhere comes Todd Collins and tackles him for a six-yard loss. That leads to the 54-yard field goal. So he makes a good play in the game. Then I go into the locker room and I say, "Hey, burn that sage – great play." Five weeks in a row we met in that same spot. Course, I knew he was gonna get there around that same time so it was almost like…then it was funny. I got to the point where I felt we HAD to meet for good luck. Then the last couple of games, we didn't but at that point it didn't seem to matter. But he was the only player who I was aware of that knew about it. I figure guys knew but it was never talked about.

So anyway, after the Super Bowl, and after all the interviews, I was hanging around the locker room. That's where I found out that Todd Hewitt had done it. I had given him some, and he had told me he had burned some in the locker room on Friday after practice. But then he told me he did it before the game, and so it's in the locker room and Kurt Warner's in there getting dressed after all the interviews. There's hardly anybody around. I just went up to him to congratulate him. I didn't want to talk to him. I had listened to some of the other interviews. "Hey Kurt, congratulations, amazing year!" He says, "Hey thanks." And then as I'm walking away, he says, "Oh by the way, Howard." I said, "Yes." He said, "I just want you to know your sage had nothing to do with it."

Sedona is supposed to be a very spiritual kind of place. But who knows? Everyone always talked about this season and this year being a team of destiny and so many things happened that are just incredible that to dismiss something is like – who knows? I'm sure there's a lot of people who believed in it. I know that there were people sitting in the stands at games and when things would start to go bad, instead of getting down and saying, "Same old Rams, here we go." They would say, "No, no, no, you can't think negative. You've got to think positive. Think positive – you've gotta believe. You've got to have that belief." There's no question a lot of people were doing that now. That collective spirituality, does it help? Who knows? That's the thing. No one can prove that it doesn't.

In '98 you always saw Kurt around but no one talked to him much because he wasn't playing. He was the number 3 quarterback but I had talked to him because I knew what he had done in Arena Football. In watching him practice at training camp, you could see the guy had ability and there were a lot of people during the season who felt he should have been playing some at the end of the year in '98 when Banks got hurt. But no one talked to him that much. The one thing is he didn't say, "I threw those three touchdown passes because of God." He never did that. Isaac Bruce said that, which was kinda weird.

I think Kurt is the real deal. It's hard for me to imagine that he's not. As long as the team has so much good talent around them, and can be kept together for a decent stretch. We would sit there at times, especially early in the year, in the press box, and would just start laughing at what was going on. We couldn't believe it. Like with another touchdown, or, "Well, now Warner's completed 10 in a row!" So be it, you know. We were sitting there laughing. It seemed so easy. It was incredible.

I've not seen anything like it in any sport. A story like this with a guy – I was analogizing it to someone – it would be like somebody in basket-

> Bronco Terrell Davis demands that the name tag above his locker always must read "Joe Abdullah," and Bronco center Tom Maler won't wash his practice gear during the year because he feels that he's giving the equipment "natural seasoning" to shield "evil spirits."

ball who played a couple of years in Europe, and then the CBA, had one tryout in the NBA and got cut. Then all of a sudden gets signed by an NBA team, doesn't play a whole year. One guy gets hurt the next year. He steps into the lineup and then averages 50 points a game. It's almost as crazy as that.

There was a six-week stretch, from six games prior to the final game where his passer rating never deviated after the game by more than like .2. For six weeks in a row, it was 111.2, 111.4, 111.0, 111.5 – always 111.something for six weeks in a row! That's how consistent he was. That would be like someone in baseball, after 100 games, they're hitting .400. Then they go two-for-five every day for 30 games – never go 0-for-5. It's a little different because they're playing every day. Football's only one game a week. But that's the consistency he showed. It's just unbelievable, unbelievable.

I was saying on the radio show, probably after the San Francisco game, that Kurt Warner and the Rams were for real and we had a shot. No one knew at the time that loss to the Rams was gonna start a string of six straight losses for the Niners. They came in at three and one. They had beaten Tennessee the week before with Garcia at quarterback. The Rams just totally took apart the 49ers. It was like, "Whoa!" Then the Rams won the next week in Atlanta, and everybody was saying, "Okay, this is a test now. They beat Atlanta at home, now they've got to go on the road again." When we beat them, that was when we started saying, "I don't know how good this team is, but who's better? Look at the NFC. Tell me who's better and no one could say who. So you could see right then. Minnesota was off to a slow start at the time. You couldn't look at any team at that time and say they were better than the Rams.

What a year!

Courtesy KSDK-TV

THE VOICE
MIKE BUSH

Mike Bush is the sports director for KSDK-TV in St. Louis. Bush anchors three sportscasts each weeknight and anchors and produces the top-rated Mike Bush's Sports Plus *program on Sunday nights. In addition to his anchoring duties, Bush has been the TV voice of the Saint Louis University Billikins basketball games for the past eight years. He has also been the play-by-play announcer for NFL games on NBC, college basketball games on ESPN and Raycom, the Missouri state high school basketball and football championships and the Pro Bowlers tour on ESPN.*

I n all my time of broadcasting and covering athletes, I don't think I can remember a story like this, where an athlete basically comes out of nowhere – at least in the public's perception – and goes on to have the kind of year he's had: NFL MVP, Super Bowl MVP. And he's handled the pressure and the media spotlight with such grace and poise. He's as good off the field as he is on; maybe even better off the field, and that's really saying something.

This is how well I read characters. I saw Kurt coming out of the Trans World Dome the night Trent Green got hurt. After talking to him briefly, saying, "I guess it's up to you now," I said to one of my broadcast partners, "I'm not sure he's ready for this; he looks scared." And boy did I read that one wrong. He wasn't scared at all. I talked to Kurt, did an interview with him at the end of the year, right before the Minnesota game for the playoffs, and I related that story to him and said how did you feel that night. The first thing he said was that he felt really bad for Trent. The second thing he said was that he was looking forward to the opportunity and he knew he would be successful – he knew it!

I said, "Come on, are you serious?" He said, "No, I knew I would be successful. I've been successful on the field every time I've gotten the opportunity. I knew if I ever got the opportunity I would be successful." I said, "You had no doubts?" He said, "No doubts." That's his direct quote. I said, "You had no doubts." He said, "No doubts." That's amazing. And it's not a cocky attitude; it's just an inner confidence.

There are a lot of guys who – and I don't think you can be a successful professional athlete unless you have some kind of ego – unless you believe in yourself, unless you have the ability to believe you're better than the next guy, I don't think you can compete at the level that these players do, whether it be football, hockey, baseball, basketball, and not have confidence in your abilities. But I don't think I've ever seen somebody who had such poise when there had been no media spotlight. Not only had he had no media spotlight, nobody even knew who he was except for those of us who had been around the team and knew he was the backup quarterback. I don't think I've seen anybody who was just thrown into the spotlight and really had no jitters whatsoever and handled it with such grace and such poise. Never, ever, I don't remember a story like this. I know it's been said, and I know it's a cliché already. If they had a script for this in Hollywood, nobody would believe it; it's too schmaltzy.

I talked to Charley Armey about Warner never having failed in any level. He said he thought players get into a situation where they are labeled in the National Football League. If you're labeled a backup quarterback, you may be good enough to start but if you're labeled a backup quarterback, you're a backup quarterback. And I think the same thing happened to Trent Green for most of his career in the National Football League. He was a backup quarterback. Well under some circumstances that occurred for him in Washington, he got an opportunity to start and all of a sudden he's a starting quarterback and he gets a big contract coming to St. Louis.

I think the same thing happened to Kurt. He's a backup quarterback. He had a tryout with the Green Bay Packers. He didn't make it. He plays

> Almost every good football team at any level in America is one play away (injury) from being average.

some Arena ball, some European ball, and he comes here and he's a backup quarterback. But our biggest question last year when we went to training camp was, "Are you gonna sign up somebody to back up Trent Green? You've gotta sign somebody. It's not gonna be Kurt Warner, is it?" Somebody saw something because they didn't sign Paul Justin until Green got hurt.

The first preseason game we did, in Detroit, after the Green injury, I was duly impressed. I thought this guy would come out and have all kinds of jitters. He had looked good already in the preseason, but I expected now all the pressure is on him and that's a pretty good Detroit team they're playing. He looked poised and he looked good, and I immediately thought maybe this won't be so bad after all. But as the season grew, every single time, you thought, "Okay, this is the week. This is the week." There were no weeks! It was an astounding display. I sat up in that play-by-play booth; we'd go to commercials, and I would just shake my head and say, "I can't believe this. I can't believe what I'm seeing."

> **Every time you thought it was going to be a fluke, it wasn't.**

It is an amazing story and is a story certainly worth telling. Every time you thought it was going to be a fluke, it wasn't. He did it game after game after game and if he would have, like in the Tennessee game, they're playing the Tennessee Titans. They're getting to him; they're knocking them down. They're knocking the ball loose. I've seen so many quarterbacks fold under those situations. That's it for them for the rest of the day. That's the kind of game they have and in the second half the coach says we better let somebody else play because you're rattled. But Warner came back and had an unbelievable second half and put the Rams in a position to tie the game at the end. That to me showed the kind of confidence he had, what kind of ability he had. To me the word that sums him up is poise, both on and off the field. He's got so much poise.

I have not been around any athlete who has been nicer, more accommodating. I did a long-form interview with him right before the Minnesota game. We sat down and talked about the fact that he had no doubts. We talked and I asked him, "What was the best moment of this season?" I'm thinking he's gonna go to a particular play – a particular game. Kurt said, "The best moment of this season was getting to speak at the Billy Graham concert." That just shows you what kind of person he is. The

Billy Graham Crusade was in St. Louis; they wanted Kurt to speak, and Kurt said that was the highlight of this year because that's what he's all about. Seriously, I've never met anybody who's more genuine. I've done several long-form interviews with him this year. He couldn't be nicer. One Sunday night after a game we had him on our studio show, and apparently some guy had followed him and his family (Kurt spends a lot of time signing autographs, but at some point you have to get in your car and go) and he was so upset. This guy had followed him and his family to the car and was harassing him and his family a little bit. He apologized on the air about having to get in the car and leave. He said, "But at some point, you know you've got to get on with it." I meet so many athletes who aren't like him. They don't understand who pays the bills – the fans. Kurt, I think has a great understanding for that, an understanding that goes way beyond his experience.

> Until the year 2005, each NFL team will get
> $75 million dollars a year in television money.

JACK SNOW WAS NEVER
AS YOUNG AS HE LOOKS.
JACK SNOW

Jack Snow enjoyed an 11-year career with the Rams at wide receiver. He ranks third in team history in receiving yards and fourth in career receptions. Snow also had a stint with the Rams in the coaching ranks, coaching receivers in 1982. He was a first-round draft choice in 1965 out of Notre Dame by the Minnesota Vikings before being traded to the Rams. His son, J.T. Snow, is a gold-glove first baseman with the San Francisco Giants, and his daughter, Stephanie, works in the Rams' front office.

As a Ram in Los Angeles and with them in St. Louis there's a big difference, to be quite honest with you. I grew up in Long Beach, in the Los Angeles area. We could play a big game and have probably 70,000 people in the Coliseum. But no matter how many people were there, you always had a certain percentage, 10, 15, or 20 percent who would be for the opponent because of the fact that maybe they grew up in that particular part of the country. So if we played the Giants or we played Philadelphia or we played Chicago or whomever, there would always be a good contingent of road people there so we never had basically what I would call 98, 99 percent backing. Here in St. Louis, it's just the opposite. They sell out 66,000 seats plus every game and you may have a thousand people or a few hundred people who are for the team coming in. But other than that, it's all Rams all the way.

I first saw Kurt Warner at training camp in '98. I liked him. I was watching him during practice, obviously. Then the first time our backups went down and he worked against our number 1 defense in the red zone, I watched him throw the football and thought this man's got something on the ball. He fired the ball and hit an open receiver and I really liked what I saw. Then toward the end of the '98 season we were so terrible, I was doing the broadcasting up in the booth. I was thinking, "Come on Dick, let's get him in there. Let's see, in fact, if he can play at this level." From what I'd seen in training camp and all through the regular practices, the regular season, he looked pretty good.

It's really amazing that most people thought he would fail when, in fact, he had never failed on any team he had quarterbacked. When he was in college, he wasn't allowed to play until he was a fifth-year senior and was Player of the Year in his conference. He went to the Arena Football League and was Player of the Year a couple of times there. Then he went over to NFL Europe and was MVP there. So, from that standpoint, granted the level of competition is not what it is in the NFL but in terms of his production, he's been right on so I'm not that surprised.

I have no answer to the question: Why did people just assume he couldn't do it? If I had the answer to that…you know he was in the Green Bay training camp and they cut him. So from that standpoint, I guess you could say everybody was wrong. It's an atypical situation where a guy falls through the cracks, then gets a shot, and, BANG, away he goes.

He got in the final game of the 1998 season and he looked okay. I don't have the stats in front of me, but I think he was somewhere in the area of four of 11. It didn't set the house on fire but it was in a situation where he didn't have a lot of time to be groomed and get in there with a solid game plan. We just put him in there to see what he could do. I liked what I saw in that game, just as I had liked what he had done in practices. I wanted to see what he could do on a consistent basis during the regular season, but he never got the opportunity.

He was backing up Trent Green in the summer of '99. Trent was our guy coming in, and, as everybody knows, Trent went down against the San Diego Chargers in the exhibition season. From that point on, I think everybody rallied around Kurt. Mike Martz gave him a rough test, so to speak, and was just filling his head with all kinds of stuff. And away he went. He responded very well. I think you've got to give the credit to Mike Martz and John Ramsdell, the quarterbacks coach. They both worked with him on a daily basis. It was unbelievable. They got him ready to do what he could do. The first couple of games, it was minimal in terms of exactly what he had to do on the field. But what he did do is he responded very positively and, my God, the rest is history.

> Even when *Monday Night Football* ratings hit
> an all-time low, it still ranks in the
> top five during prime time for the entire year.

The way he started out, he threw three touchdown passes in each game. I think he set a record – may have been four, I'm not sure. I would sit there in the booth and think, "This is absolutely remarkable." You keep wanting to wait before you pass judgment, and you say, "Is this kid for real? Will he blow up his next game?" Well, he never did. I think, probably, it was the midpoint in the season when it became obvious. I think a key point was the Tennessee game. We played them on the road. We were down 21-zip and he brought us all the way back and had a chance to tie the game on a last-second field goal attempt by Jeff Wilkins. Had we made that we'd have been in overtime. We were 21 to nothing down on the road against the Tennessee Titans and we came back and almost won that ballgame. Now I definitely went, "This kid is something. I like what I see; I think he's gonna be fine."

Kurt is a very quiet guy, stays to himself, very religious individual. From that standpoint, you walk by, you say hi, you give him a high five or a low five or something like that. But as far as going out and sitting down and talking to him at length, no. I'd drop by and say "Hang in there. Stay within yourself and you'll be fine. This is the opportunity you wanted." One key, too, is that he's an older guy. He's not 22, 23 years old; he's 28, 29 years old. He continued to play after college, and he's matured and I think he was definitely ready to get in and give it one heck of a shot, which he did.

At the end of the Super Bowl, I sat in the broadcast booth after the game was over and all the awards had been given out and started to turn the lights out. A huge cloud of melancholy settled over me. I couldn't figure out what was wrong. This was on Sunday night, and it took me till Tuesday to figure out I was sorry the season was over because it means the following Sunday there will be no football game.

We may never have this again in the history of the game or in the history of this franchise.

The season was such a fantastic roller-coaster ride. It was unreal and all of a sudden, BANG! It's over, it's done. We may never have this again in the history of the game or in the history of this franchise. Yeah, it was really fun. I was really down for a couple of days.

Luck had something to do with it. If you look at our season, we didn't have any serious injuries for a very significant amount of time. Nobody saw us. I think our first nationally televised game was against the Minnesota Vikings in the second round of the playoffs. Everybody took a look at us and said, "Who the heck are these guys?" You read about them in the paper but you don't see them 'cause we're not on national TV every week. After that game we realized we had run up 49 points on those suckers and had them 49-14, and they've got a pretty darn good football team.

Kurt Warner has a great sense of timing. He had two things: He put the ball in the zone. And when I say zone I'm talking about an eight- or nine-foot rectangle; nine foot high by three foot wide, which means every ball is catchable. You don't have to be diving for balls and pulling balls off your butt; the ball is right there. Another thing I liked about him was he had a good touch, and also the timing of coming out of the break. When the receiver would come out of the break, that ball would be right there. Or, if he was breaking on a post route, once he gave a little head fake to the outside and took one step in that ball was on its way and maybe three or four feet from him. So Bang! The receiver's got it right now and he can do something with it after he made the catch.

You can't do the things he's done in his first year, basically, in the National Football League and not be a little nervous.

As the season wore on, he became a little more nervous. He won't admit to it, but you have to. You can't do the things he's done in his first year, basically, in the National Football League and not be a little nervous. That's where I think he really reached down and tried to stay within himself and like I said, he's very much of a Christian kid and that's when he really went to God to settle him down and if that's what it took, hey, man, that's fine with me.

I've been in this kind of great situation twice in my life – once as a player and once as a broadcaster. The '64 year at Notre Dame was my senior season; '63 we were two and seven. We would have been two and eight but that was the year President Kennedy was shot, so our game at Iowa was canceled. When we came back for Ara Parsegian's first season in 1964, my senior season, our first big test for us was against Wisconsin; we played them up in Camp Randall. I think we beat them like 32-7 or 32-13. This was basically a bunch of no-name guys. We had John Huarte at quarterback and I was a wide receiver. Nick Eddy was an untested sophomore at halfback. The front four were led by Alan Page, and they were all sophomores. So that was a storybook season. It reminds me a lot of what we went through this

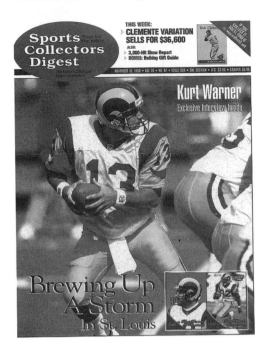

The most popular personality in St. Louis

year with the Rams in 1999 – very similar. A quarterback who had never been tested and some guys who hadn't played a whole lot, and away we went and played very well. It was awesome.

My youngest daughter, Stephanie, works for the Rams. She is the assistant and administrator of player contracts for the president.

I work with the receivers on the field and I'm there three days a week during the regular season so it keeps me around young people. You listen to the way they talk and they think and I love that.

The first Super Bowl, in 1967 at the Los Angeles Coliseum, had 32,000 empty seats even though the most expensive ticket was $12.

FIRST-TIME CALLER, LONGTIME LISTENER
MIKE CLAIBORNE

Mike Claiborne is an on-air talent and program director for KFNS Sports Radio in St. Louis

When Trent went down, there was a fear factor because we didn't know anything about Kurt's ability, and things were going so well. Dick Vermeil was pretty confident in Kurt right off the bat and made it clear that he was the guy. Once the confidence level was established for him by his coach, from that point on, it was smooth sailing. Some callers felt we should bring in a quarterback, but there weren't that many of them around so we were kinda relegated to him. The Paul Justin acquisition was one that was a safeguard because he was familiar to Mike Martz being at Arizona State when Mike was there. Other than that, there wasn't anybody out there as far as who the Rams were gonna pick up, so we were either gonna sink or swim with Kurt Warner. But even if Trent Green was healthy we were expecting to go 8-8 or 9-7. That would have been all we'd have hoped for. And had they done that, they'd probably have let school out for the kids when the season was over!

When the Rams caught fire, it meant so much, not only to the station, but to the whole community. Everybody shows up at work on Monday morning feeling good about themselves and their team. It's a positive influence. Kurt Warner, as an individual, did a lot of things that were positive for his team and for his community and he was a very likeable person. He always said the right thing. I just can't say enough about that. He had great faith in his God. Twenty years ago, it was unheard of for an athlete to talk that openly about his faith. I think that in our society, for people who are in search of some sort of fulfillment, he came at the right time. Now, he made some people who were religiously insecure a little bit uneasy. He was able to deal with that. People supported him and respected him for that. They didn't have to necessarily agree with him all the time, but you know Kurt never brought it up unless somebody asked him. He wasn't trying to get people to sign up. He was just an honest guy about what was going on. You couldn't find a better storybook ending as far as what he was able to do, for a lot of reasons.

Warner was successful for a lot of reasons:

One, he was in the right environment as far as the offense.

Two, he had a coaching staff that believed in him

Three, he had the right weapons in Bruce and two good young receivers in Az-Zahir Hakim and Torry Holt, and, of course, Marshall Faulk, and an offensive line that bought him plenty of time. He had a team that was behind him, he had great faith in his God, and all those things rolled into a great season for him as an individual. He had great family support.

In the 19 years I've been in the business I've never seen anything unfold in the manner that it did. It was discussed on some of our shows in St. Louis. "Who's the most popular guy in St. Louis, Kurt Warner or Mark McGwire?" and it's gotta be Kurt Warner because he's a nice guy off the field. At least when he's been in that environment, McGwire hasn't been as friendly as he used to be. Kurt Warner might turn that way down the road but now I think people are just enjoying the ride for what it's worth. I think for a couple of reasons, Warner thinks before he talks. He doesn't put people in compromising positions. He gives you an answer he believes in and he never says "me" or "I." It's a team concept. He's a guy you want to ask good questions, compared to some of the dumb questions that McGwire received. There have been times when he has been probably a little testy about a couple of different issues that have taken place. He was interviewed one night on a TV show about an interception he had thrown. He threw for over 400 yards that day but they wanted to pick out this one interception which showed him slightly upset about it, which he rightly should have been. Other than that he's been a straight shooter. He's been a genuine person that looks people in the eye when he talks to them. These days, the way interviews are conducted, you don't see a great deal of that. He's a good player and the guy's time is pretty heavily consumed. To try and get him on the air from here is a little bit of a challenge so we try to respect the guy's privacy to a certain extent. We've had him on different shows where's he's been interviewed. He's been very accommodating; we haven't had any problems with him.

> He's a guy you want to ask good questions, compared to some of the dumb questions that McGwire received.

The baseball Cardinals have tradition on their side whereas the Rams have gone out and done it in one year. The Cardinals have done it over the course of a century and I think that has a lot to do with why they'll continue to be the top dog. There are a lot of people pulling for each other in St. Louis. The Cardinals pull for the Rams and vice versa, so there's no animosity; there's no rivalry. It's just a situation where everybody feels good about what's going on in the community, and that's probably better for everyone.

The day the Rams got to the Super Bowl, that Sunday was when I first felt they had a chance to be at the Super Bowl! You look at the schedule; you thought they could go nine and seven, but once they started to steamroll teams in the manner that they did...Other teams were having tough seasons. You thought they could actually go three quarters of the way through the season because they were in uncharted territory, but from a playoff perspective, you just didn't know. I mean the teams they were playing – Minnesota and Tampa Bay had recently been in the playoffs, Minnesota having been in the championship game last year – all those things came into play. But to be honest with you, with the exception of the Tampa Bay game, the Rams didn't have a close one all year – at least the second half of the year. A year ago, it was ugly. It was brutal. They wanted to run Vermeil out of town and start over. It was a completely different situation. It was horrible – not a good town to be around.

What a difference a year – and a quarterback – make!

The halftime show at Super Bowl I was the New Christy Minstrels.

Courtesy KMOX Radio

THIS STATION HAS REAL KARRAKER
Randy Karraker

Randy Karraker is a personality on KMOX Radio in St. Louis.

First of all he's completely genuine. The Kurt Warner we knew during the '98 season when he was a third-string quarterback for the Rams is the exact same Kurt Warner we know as the Pro Bowler and the MVP and the Super Bowl champion. There are no airs about him. He's just a first-class, top-shelf person.

As far as his quarterbacking ability goes, his season obviously, statistically, is one of the greatest ever. And I think if you look at it objectively and watch the games, it was almost unbelievable how accurate he was. He very rarely misses the target that he's throwing to. He has unbelievable leadership ability. He took over that team. I think his teammates probably knew about as much about his personality as his fans did. From his very first start that last preseason game in Detroit, he took the leadership mantle of the team and there was no question who was in charge of the huddle. There was no question who was the leader of the offense. His teammates voted him an offensive captain so he has every element you want in an NFL quarterback. He's a terrific spokesman for the team. He's a classy individual. Obviously he's a winner and a real good player, too. I have asked everybody about this and the only story that I can think of that comes close is *The Natural*, the movie. The difference between Unitas and Warner is that Unitas played a year and struggled for a little while before he became a terrific NFL quarterback. This guy walked in and in his first NFL game threw three touchdown passes and led his team to victory. He set the record for the most touchdown passes in his first four games. Had his team at six and zero; literally had his team two plays away from going nineteen and zero if you take away one of his fumbles in the game at Tennessee, that they lost by three points, and you take away the fourth and twenty-six at Detroit that caused them to lose that game. They could have beaten Philadelphia if they wanted to and they could have gone nineteen and zero. They were literally two plays away from going nineteen and zero.

When Trent Green went down, it was one of the worst nights of my life. I'm a season-ticket holder, a big fan, and I was really thrilled with the addition of Trent Green. My number two team is the Redskins so I saw him play 14 games in '98. So I was thrilled when the Rams got him. As a matter of fact, I was so happy and so convinced that the Rams had done such a great job during the off-season that I predicted that they would go twelve and four. Once training camp started and I got to see some of the people who were participating, a big part of the reason I picked them was because of Trent. Then he comes in here and has his first press conference and he's as impressive a guy as you'd ever want to meet. He's from St. Louis. He was the All-American quarterback story, so I was crushed when he went down.

I also write for a publication called *Rams Update* that's distributed across the state. That's when I first heard the story about Kurt's son, Zachary, and the difficulties that he had endured in life. I had said "Hi" to him and we were acquaintances, but I was never aware of his deep faith so that's when I found out he's just a really good guy. I saw him occasionally during the off-season at Rams Park and we would talk. I found out how his family was doing and stuff like that. I knew what sort of a guy he was but I didn't appreciate the magnitude of everything until they beat the 49ers in the fourth game, until he threw those five touchdown passes against San Francisco. Every pass was on the mark – they're up twenty-one to nothing on the three touchdown passes to Isaac Bruce. It was just phenomenal. Then you see how Kurt is after the games. You see how he is during the week and his demeanor never changed. As the pressure mounted and they go into games where he's got a chance to win the division, he's the same guy. Before the Vikings game, he's the same guy. And even before the Super Bowl, it struck me, as I was in the upper deck in the auxiliary press area

> **I knew what sort of a guy he was but I didn't appreciate the magnitude of everything until they beat the 49ers in the fourth game, until he threw those five touchdown passes against San Francisco.**

and looking down on the field through my binoculars, and there he is, just playing catch. He's nonchalantly talking to Al Michaels while he's playing catch and warming up for the Super Bowl. His demeanor was identical right before the Super Bowl as it had been before the first preseason game he had played that he started against Detroit. He has the most low-key demeanor of anybody I've ever seen. I can't imagine him ever getting the "Yips" in any situation.

Dick Vermeil told us for several years that the reason he didn't take Jake Plummer was because the Rams had a second-round draft pick invested in Tony Banks. He wanted to make that draft pick work. My impression of NFL coaches and personnel people is generally, "Well, if we invest money or if we invested a draft pick in this guy, he's going to be our guy. And this other guy may or may not be a good quarterback, but we aren't even gonna give him an opportunity." I think that happens a lot in the NFL. I think there are a lot of good quarterbacks that should get the chance to play but for various reasons, they don't. I think Trent Green is a perfect example of that in Washington. They take Heath Shuler with the third pick in the draft so Trent's not their guy. So Gus Frerotte takes over for him and they give him a big contract so Trent's not their guy. Until it became a last-resort-type situation, they didn't give Trent an opportunity. I think that's happened a lot in the NFL. I have to believe Warner's success will change that a little bit. I have a feeling that some people who may have never gotten a look before will get an opportunity now.

Years ago I thought Chad May was going to be good. Rob Johnson never played and then he has that one good start for Jacksonville and all of a sudden he becomes a hot commodity.

I hadn't heard the John Daly comparison until Jim Nance actually brought it up during the playoffs; we had him on for an interview. But Daly wasn't able to sustain it. He had that one great tournament and he was okay for a while then he flamed out. I think there's such dramatically different personalities. I just can't fathom a situation in which Warner won't continue to succeed. He's got such a great attitude about it, and his physical attributes are such that now it's almost a shock when things don't go perfectly for him because he's such an accurate thrower. So I just have trouble finding a comparison. I guess the closest one you could make if he continues to flourish would be Unitas, but like I said, Unitas took a year to really get going. On our show Kurt became a big hero. Just to try to get people going the other night, I ran a little poll: "Who's the biggest sports star in St. Louis – Warner or McGwire?" Warner won in a landslide. I wasn't really surprised because Warner is such a likeable guy, such an accessible guy – always smiling and you never hear him snapping at anybody and he led his team to a championship. And as big as McGwire is, it didn't surprise me that it happened. That's the regard with which St. Louis people hold him. Right around Christmas time, my kid had dress-out day (he goes to a school where they wear uniforms) and there's maybe 150 kids in that school. So on the day when the kids go to choose their clothing, I'll bet there must have been two dozen Kurt Warner jerseys among all those kids – maybe twenty percent of the kids in the entire school were wearing Warner jerseys that day.

I think people were reasonably confident and thought that they could win with Warner but I don't think people thought they would win BECAUSE of Warner. He became a hero in town when they started winning BECAUSE of him. I think a number of people thought it was going to be a real rough year. In '95 they had started four and zero and five and one. I think with Green, people thought that was going to be the case, but I don't think with Warner people thought they would get off to that sort of start. I would say, at best, if you polled the Ram fans before that first game against

> **I think the big thing for St. Louis and the real sense of belief that this was a great team was when they beat San Francisco. They'd lost to the 49ers seventeen times in a row.**

Baltimore, I'll bet it was fifty-fifty as to whether or not they would win or lose. They didn't sell that game out. The local FOX KTVI, Channel 2, television station had to buy the last two thousand tickets to sell that game out. They had a "bye" the second week, then they just annihilated Atlanta in week three, in their second game. Then after that was when people started to get excited. They go on the road, they beat Cincinnati convincingly, and Warner was great again. I think the big thing for St. Louis and the real sense of belief that this was a great team was when they beat San Francisco. They'd lost to the 49ers seventeen times in a row. They beat them here 42-20, and the game was over by the end of the first quarter. That's when people really started to believe, not only in Warner, but in the entire team. Not only Kurt, but I remember the *Sporting News* specifically, speculating that Germaine would be the number one guy in St. Louis.

He was tugged every which way by the second half of the season. Everybody wanted to interview him. I walked in on Thursday, actually during their bye week, before they planed the Vikings. For the first time in weeks, he was there at his locker alone. I said, "What are you doing here all by yourself?" He said, "Well, the food wasn't ready in the kitchen so I thought I'd just come back here and hang out." I had to do an interview with him so he said, "No problem." So we did fifteen minutes and it's just like I was sitting down with the third-string quarterback. It was no different than when I talked with him in the middle of the '98 season. From a personality standpoint, he hasn't changed a bit. I interviewed his high school football coach down in Atlanta, and he said the same thing. He said – same guy, it's remarkable.

I think he can keep it up. You talk to the coaches, Vermeil and Martz, privately and they say he's not a fluke because I think if he was going to be a fluke, at some point during the season he would have had a bad game but he was great every single game. I think if he was gonna change, he probably would have changed this season. I have a feeling he's gonna stay the same. And the Rams do a pretty good job of protecting him and divvying up his time. But he's an extremely grounded guy and I would be surprised if he would change.

The undefeated 1972 Dolphins (17-0) beat only two teams with records over . 500. They were actually three-point underdogs to the Redskins in Super Bowl VII.

Chapter 9

Bernie Miklasz

J.R. Ogden

Doug Galloway

Kevin Robbins

Vahe Gregorian

Jim Thomas

The Fourth Estate
Doesn't Take the Fifth,
Your Honor

J.R. Ogden

NOT EVEN SAMSON
CAN TEAR DOWN HIS COLUMNS
BERNIE MIKLASZ

Bernie Miklasz, at the ripe old age of 41, has already spent half his life in the newspaper business. He started in his native Baltimore and has enjoyed widespread readership and a solid reputation as an outstanding columnist for the St. Louis Post-Dispatch. *Miklasz is a wonder raconteur.*

I told people, I think maybe Mark Hansen quoted me in the *Register*, that Kurt Warner came along at a time in my career where I was starting to question whether anything that I saw or anything I wrote about was really true in that we have these ideals of the way sports should be and it seems like in recent years, 98 percent of the time it lets you down. So there's a great disappointment, even when they achieve something, because you don't really respect the kind of people they are.

With Warner, he basically reaffirmed my faith that there can still be great people who accomplish great things in professional sports – that it's not all just a big act. That a guy can excel on the field and then, when he comes off the field, the way he talks and the way he treats people and the way he just acts in every phase of his life, it's genuine and it's sincere and there's nothing phony about it whatsoever. It was just very refreshing for me to watch this guy and the kind of quarterback he is and the kind of person he is. It kinda took me back to the reason why, like most sportswriters, I fell in love with sports many, many years ago as a boy. 'Cause a guy like Kurt Warner is just like the essence of what we hope sports can really be but in most cases fails to be.

So I kept thinking during the course of the season – I went through two years of Mark McGwire mania. Nothing gets bigger than that in terms of one individual and the attention he got. It was a two-year circus and I don't want to come across as critical of Mark, but I saw that Mark, as the circus intensified, really had a difficult time handling it in terms of his temperament. It made him very grouchy and very closed in where he just shut himself off from the rest of the world. He got to the point where it was hard for him to even have relationships with his teammates because everywhere he went he was just engulfed by people. His teammates, quite frankly, didn't want to be a part of it. It was freedom and peace of mind. They could go out to have a sandwich and a beer and not get hassled all the time, so Mark...I saw the affect the home-run record and everything else had on him. It made him a kind of an isolated figure and unhappy much of the time. Maybe only happy when he was actually in the batter's box. That was the only place he could get away from it.

So along comes Warner and he's just this incredible phenomenon in that he just came out of nowhere and so all of a sudden this guy's an overnight sensation, as we say. I hate that term, but he was just in the way that he broke onto the national scene. Nobody knew who he was. So I kept waiting to see how this was going to affect him. He got an incredible amount of attention in a very short period of time. It just exploded all around him. One day he's a nobody. A few weeks later he's got every morning network program, every magazine, every newspaper, you name it – the media culture just discovered him and there was a bull's-eye on the guy. Everybody wanted him. So I was waiting to see how this guy's gonna handle it. Surely it's gonna either make him surly or he's gonna get irritable or he's gonna withdraw or he's gonna lose concentration or he's gonna get a big head – some of these things or all of these things will happen to him. There's just no way you can take a guy who walks in from the Iowa cornfield and all of a sudden he's a national celebrity. There's just no way that that process can happen so quickly without doing something to change this guy and turn his head around and alter him in some way.

> **There's just no way you can take a guy who walks in from the Iowa cornfield and all of a sudden he's a national celebrity.**

But he absolutely did not change in any way, shape or form. He remained true to himself. He was polite to people. He was considerate to his teammates. He continued to go to the same church and worship with the people he had been worshipping with before he became a star. He was very accommodating and gracious to fans.

There was just nothing, other than the fact that the Rams, as they should have, began to limit access to him. There was no problem with that. The man was there to do a job, but other than limiting access to him and giving him time to do his job right, there were no changes at all. I know that it became a hassle to him because I did write one column where he had to turn down some people who wanted autographs. One guy started giving him grief. Warner didn't deserve that. I think he found it was really frustrating for him to have to learn how to say no. I've seen him out in public and even when he had to sort of get out of places or cut off autographs after a while, or he'd be standing there all night long. Even when he, in effect, rejected fans or withdrew from fans, he did it in the most polite way that you can possibly do those type of things. He was just a gentleman from start to finish and it just increased my respect for him all the more.

I have seen what celebrity and fame can do to people. Even though I'm a fairly young guy, 41, I'm kind of like a "young old-timer" in that I've been writing for a major paper for 21 years now. So I've seen a lot of remarkable stuff and he just astounded me in the way he remained levelheaded and in touch with himself and remembering who he was and also the way he continued to treat people which was very, very well.

First of all, there are three things – it's got to be his faith. Obviously it's a huge part of his life and it grounds him. There's no doubt in my mind. And the second thing is he's just a flat-out, nice guy. Sometimes we overanalyze things. With Kurt, he's just a flat-out nice human being. The third thing is he understands. Unlike, I think, probably 75 percent of "star" professional athletes, he completely understands how difficult it was to reach this pinnacle and how fragile it all is and how you can get lost in the system and just fade into oblivion and just disappear from the face of the sporting earth without a blink. Because of his struggle to get to this place and all the bad breaks that happened to him along the way, this is a guy who has tremendous perspective on the temporary volatile nature of sports stardom and how elusive it is and how difficult it is to get ahold of and how quickly it can change if you don't take care of your business.

He brought the perspective of failure to this place in his career and this place in his life. He wasn't a Peyton Manning and heralded, and almost trained from birth to be a star quarterback. He wasn't a Tim Couch who, again from the time he started playing high school football, was a VIP

> When Don Shula retired, he had more victories than over half the NFL teams.

and had developed a mind-set in how to handle these things and how to act and how to be a star and how to avoid the traps and things of that nature. Warner brought an experience of multiple failures to this place so he knew the other side. He'll never forget the other side, like having to work in a grocery store, having to go play Arena Football, and having been humiliated in the Green Bay Packers camp the year before, having to wait four years to start at Northern Iowa. He had a lot of rain fall on him so all of a sudden he's a star. But he didn't act like a star because he knew basically how precious it was to get to that point and, basically, how quickly it could all go away. He had been striving for that for many years and it just kept eluding him. He was not gonna lose control of himself or the situation because he knew how truly unique it is to arrive at a place like this 'cause he had taken a hard road here, there's no question about it.

I'm guilty, as most people are, of not paying much attention to backup players in my job. I had a couple of brief conversations with him in '98 when he was the third string quarterback, but I didn't really have much reason to talk to him. I remember late in that '98 season, I, and some other talk-show hosts, were kinda banging the drums to get Vermeil to give him a chance because in talking with the defensive backs and defensive players who used to just rave about him and the way he played on the practice field. "This guy's really got some game, I wish we'd take a look at him." Guys like DiMarco Farr, Todd Lyght and others, but those two stand out. He'd practice in '98 and he's a scout team quarterback basically, and the ball never hit the ground. After hearing these guys say how accurate he was – and it wasn't a major campaign to get him some playing time –

> **Vermeil kept promising that he was going to play him and give him a shot and he wouldn't do it.**

but I would drop notes. I do the Saturday Notes column saying, "Free Kurt Warner" or "What will it take for Vermeil to give this kid a chance?", stuff like that.

In fact, late in the '98 season Vermeil kept promising that he was going to play him and give him a shot and he wouldn't do it. We'd go into a game, and this was after Tony Banks got hurt and Bono was the starter, so in effect Kurt's the number 2 guy. So he'd say, "Yeah, I'm thinking about playing him in the second half or whatever." And he'd never play him. In fact, I was exasperated after one game late in the year. I do an additional column in Monday's paper. I do in effect, kind of a wise guy notebook – I don't know how else to put it. One of my lines was like, I finally figured this out – Kurt Warner doesn't really exist. In other words, we hear about this guy but yet, to the coach anyway, he doesn't exist. He's obviously a fictional character. I remember the defensive guys would always say very complimentary things about him – the way he ran that scout team, the accuracy that he showed, his ability to throw a variety of passes so that was the background.

The first extended conversation I had with Kurt was just very interesting. Trent Green goes down on a Saturday night. Sunday morning they learn that their worst fears were confirmed and he would be out for the year. There are a few hours of indecision on Sunday morning about, "What should we do, if anything?" They gave some thought to calling Jeff Hostetler to see if he would come in and maybe get him ready to run the team. But the coaches got together, Vermeil and Mike Martz, and decided our best bet is with Kurt, so we're gonna go with Kurt. They made it clear to everybody, had a big press conference. Jim Thomas and I were the only two media guys left after everyone else had gone away. We got Warner outside the locker room and there was nobody else there and we talked to him for about 20 minutes. And I just remember all the things he said were absolutely the right note. He talked about how he waited all these years for his chance, and he was confident he would be able to handle the job. There weren't any profound statements but he just really projected a lot of poise and a lot of confidence to the point where he changed my mind about what I was going to write. Saturday night I was like everybody else who was even remotely involved with the Rams. I'm not a member of the Rams organization but someone who's around them every day.

I was in the whole "Chicken Little" mode: the sky was falling. I was gonna write a column to that effect saying, "You know what, their season's already over." But Vermeil showed a lot of faith in him and I thought that was telling. And secondly, after talking to Kurt, he just sort of took us through his career step by step and what he had accomplished and what he had done, pointing out that whenever he got a chance – and he had to wait at virtually every stop and in some cases he never got a chance – but when he got a chance he always made plays and he always performed. So I was convinced that maybe it wasn't as bleak as it seemed. I remembered the remarks from late in '98, "Give the guy a chance, he really looks good out there."

So I wrote a column which I think may be the best column I've ever written as far as not doing the knee-jerk reaction which would be so typical and understandable in that situation. You would write a column saying, "The sky is falling." But my Monday column was actually very supportive and I made the points that, "Who was Trent Green a year go at this time?" Nobody knew who the heck he was. He had completed exactly one pass in his NFL career. Yet he got a chance and he made some plays and the next thing you know he's got a $17 million contract from the Rams. Then I said, "You know, let's take this a step further. Who were some of the great quarterbacks that ever played? Who was John Unitas? I actually brought up Unitas in that column. It was funny 'cause near the end, the last column I wrote on the thing really tied up Unitas – Warner. I explained how Unitas was making six bucks a game for the Bloomfield Rams (Pennsylvania) when he got a chance. People forget now, but Joe Montana was a third-round draft choice; people said he was too small, didn't have a big arm. So I made the point that you just never know with quarterbacks. The second point I made in the column is whenever he's gotten a chance to play, he's made plays and he's been a success. So I ended the column by saying, "Let's rally around the Barnstormer." That was how I ended it. Let's just wait and see, you don't know. Let's just not assume that this is a disaster, that there will be failure. There's something to this guy, maybe. I don't want to overstate I; I didn't write a column saying, "Don't worry, this guy's great." I just raised the possibility that we don't know what we have here. This guy could do a good job.

I wrote it from Busch Stadium in the baseball press box, and I remember sending it. I kinda made fun of myself. I turned to a couple of baseball writers and said, "You know what? I'm sure some people are gonna be laughing at me over this one. I'll probably look back on this one and grimace." Obviously I'm really glad now I wrote what I wrote. I looked pretty good. A lot of it had to do with the calmness and poise and quiet confidence Kurt projected that day. I didn't see a guy with his eyes all bugged out, who was stammering or a nervous wreck. I saw a guy who seemed totally in control of himself and the situation. There was almost a hunger there. You could see that he just couldn't wait to get going. He had to sound the right note 'cause he didn't want to look like he was celebrating Trent Green's injury so he had to be restrained. But you could tell there was something there, like, "You just watch me. You just watch me. I've been waiting and this is my time." It really did shape what I wrote. I was prepared to write him off and say the whole thing's a disaster but after talking to him and saw the way he was handling this, I really revised my thinking on it. He really had that effect on me. The first extensive conversation I ever had with him came when he was right at the crossroads there. He had inherited this job after a terrible thing for the Rams. Nobody knew who he was but he was ready to go. He couldn't wait.

Charley Armey, who is now the general manager, loved this guy from the beginning. He was the vice president of personnel. Even though last year the biggest competition in Rams Park wasn't whether the Rams would get to the Super Bowl, it was all these guys rushing forward to take credit for Kurt Warner. And Charley Armey deserves the credit for Kurt Warner. It was ridiculous. You had Mike White and Lynn Stiles and everybody's taking credit for Kurt Warner. Vermeil's a heck of a guy but he's got a bad habit of revising history. So he's pounding the table, this is after Warner had become a star, and saying like I knew it all along. I'm sitting there elbowing Jim Thomas and whispering in his ear, "Knew it all along? This is the same guy who wouldn't play him ahead of Steve Bono last year. The same guy that left him unprotected in the expansion draft where Cleveland could have gotten him? The same guy who was freaking out and gave serious thought to signing Jeff Hostetler when Green went down." Knew it all along? The evidence doesn't support that claim. Charley Armey is the one guy who, from the day he looked at Warner till the day he stepped in the huddle as the starting quarterback in his team, he's the one guy who believed in him 100 percent. Anyone else who tells you they knew all along is living a fantasy. They're trying to revise history.

In '98 in training camp, Charlie and I go out to lunch. He said, "Look, you're really gonna like this Warner. This kid can play." I'm like, "Yeah, sure, Charlie." And he said, "No, I'm telling you. This kid can play. We've got something here." Charlie had to save Warner's job in '98. It gets down to the third quarterback job and Jerry Rhome was the offensive coordinator then and he had a pet named Will Furrer who had been with him in three or four different cities. Jerry Rhome loved Will Furrer. So naturally when it came down to cutting time, Jerry Rhome campaigned hard to keep Will Furrer over Warner. Well, Charlie Armey went nuts in the meeting where they were deciding these things. He was banging the table and screaming at Rhome and telling him he was nuts and everything else. Vermeil, who was sitting on the fence, saw how passionate and how angry Charlie was, how much he believed in Warner, that it swayed Vermeil to Warner's side. Vermeil could very easily have cut Warner in the summer of '98, but Charlie intervened and did it with a lot of passion and anger. It was like he was a defense lawyer trying to save his client from the chair. He just gave it everything he had. He saved Warner's career here in St. Louis.

Charlie also, last year, was always saying I remember early on in the '98 season he was saying, "The guy we ought to be playing is Warner." He would always say that; always back in '98. If I knew then what I know now about Charlie – and the last year or so I've gotten to know

Charlie very well – I can't say I'll take 100 percent of everything he says as gospel, but I have learned when it comes to player evaluation, he's a very, very sharp and astute guy. He knows talent, and he just has a radar when it comes to detecting intangibles about players. A lot of scouts get caught up in a "40 times" – height, weight, how much he can bench press and all that stuff. Charlie's got an eye for intangibles – what kind of person he is, what kind of character does he have, does he just make plays? Some guys just make plays, some guys don't. No matter what they run in the 40, you either make plays or you don't. So many of these NFL games are decided in the last four or five minutes. Well, who makes plays with the game on the line? So Charlie's just played a crucial role in what happened with this team last year 'cause he found so many players for Vermeil and Vermeil really put his faith in Charlie. Charlie found a lot of Kurt Warners.

> **So Charlie's just played a crucial role in what happened with this team last year 'cause he found so many players for Vermeil and Vermeil really put his faith in Charlie.**

He found one in London Fletcher, too. Fletcher's like Kurt Warner on defense in terms of the story. Guy came out of nowhere, shunned by everybody, became like one of the best middle linebackers in football his first year as a starter. If I knew then what I know now, I would have taken what Charlie said in '98 more seriously. I didn't laugh at him, but I also thought, "Well all right, that's his guy, what else is he gonna say?" But obviously he meant every word of what he said. I know Charlie was very upset when Vermeil decided to leave Kurt exposed last February in the expansion draft. Charlie went along with it, though, because he thought there was no way Cleveland would draft a veteran quarterback because they were going to take Couch and they also had a deal to bring Ty Detmer in. Also as it turns out, they did draft a quarterback, Scott Milanovich, so Charlie didn't think there was any risk in leaving him exposed in the expansion draft, but he was very much against the decision. He's promoted and pushed Warner since the first day Warner got here.

The last two years, '98 and '99, I spent each year about 110 nights in a hotel room; a lot of seven-day weeks. When the Cardinals left, I actually left St. Louis and went to the *Dallas Morning News* to cover the Cowboys in 1988. Then the *Post Dispatch*, after 1½ years, offered me the column job. I loved this city and I wanted to be a columnist, so I came back. There was still a lot of interest in the football Cardinals here at that point. It's the second year after they moved. Coach Stallings was extremely popular in St. Louis when they were here. And even after they left, people loved Gene Stallings. They're having a heck of a year out in Arizona. They were like .500 or game above .500 the second year, later in the year, even though they had had an incredible amount of injuries and all these things go wrong. And I remember Bill Walsh, at that time was working for NBC, was doing Cardinals game. He said to forget their records, even though this was a .500 team or whatever their record was, Gene Stallings is doing the best job in the NFL this year. He's just kept this thing together so I thought, "You know what? Why haven't they given this guy a new contract?" This is unbelievable. So I called up Larry Wilson, the Cardinals general manager, and said, "Larry, what is going on with Stallings? This guy is keeping your boat from sinking and you're sorta making the guy squirm on a new contract. When are you gonna do something?" Larry – I'll never forget, it just blew me away – just started ripping Stallings.

It was the strangest thing. He knew he was on the record. It was just really bizarre. So I write this column and quote Larry extensively about basically how the Cardinals are not being fair to Stallings and it's about a personality conflict and all this other stuff, how people like Larry and Bill obviously just don't like Gene personally. And anyway it gets back to Stallings. He gets it the next day and he walks into Larry's office. He says, "You know, I know Bernie, and I know he doesn't make things up, but I want to make sure that there's not a mix-up. Did you say all these things, and is this accurate? Was this definitely on the record?" Larry said, "I said it." Stallings, who has a temper anyway, decides he's gonna quit. They're playing a game in Anaheim. This is like three or four days after the column is out so he goes in and tells the team the night before the game. "Gentlemen, I'm gonna resign at the end of the year. Let's just try to make the best of it." So he announces that he doesn't want a new contract, that he's gonna resign at the end of the year. So Bill Bidwill, the owner, did a "No, forget it" and they fire him and this happened within a week. Then he gets the Alabama job a few weeks later. I tell Stallings, "I'm still waiting for that national championship ring cause if I hadn't got your butt fired in Phoenix, you wouldn't have been available to take the Alabama job." I talk to him about two times a year and say, "Where's my ring? I'm still waiting."

THE WRITE STUFF
J.R. OGDEN

J.R. Ogden is sports editor of the Cedar Rapids Gazette, *a newspaper where his father was a legendary writer for many years.*

The first time I knew him was in eighth grade, when I coached him in basketball. He was a very good player, without a doubt the best player I had on a very average team. People have asked me, "Did you see anything?" I said, "No, I never did." 'Cause, geez, I don't look at a kid in eighth grade and say, "He's gonna be an NFL star some day." I knew he was a very good athlete. I knew he could do a lot of things. A very nice kid, obviously had some good upbringing because he was very easy to get along with. He was definitely the star player on our team that year but it wasn't a real good team – just an average team. He was head and shoulders above – as far as all-round athletics – anybody in that class as I recall. Just a good kid. Had a great high school career here later on.

I didn't hook up with him again until he was at UNI. I wasn't surprised at how well he did in high school. It was just one of those things. You don't really pay attention to a person while he's doing it and now that I look back, I think, "Geez, he averaged 20-something points a game his senior year in high school in basketball." He probably could have played some lower level, Division II or Division III basketball someplace if he wanted to. I think he did have some people talking to him about it. He was second-team All-State so he had some good stats. He was playing on a team that had a pretty tough schedule every year. It's tough for them because they're a small school playing in a city full of 4A schools, which were bigger. But they would always pull off an upset now and then. Dick Breitbach was pretty much of a high school legend around here as far as coaching goes.

When I went up to cover UNI football, it was his first year as a starter, his fifth year there. So I got to kind of hook up with him again a couple of times. We got to sit down and have some nice conversations and I remember saying at the time that this guy could make it in the NFL. He's got the arm, he's got the body, the size, and that kind of stuff. The only think that I would knock against him is his foot speed.

If someone was gonna sack him, he was gonna get sacked. He wasn't real elusive back then. I think Arena Football really helped him in getting that release off so he doesn't get sacked very much. I also think it helped him with his speed. But I always thought, especially his fifth year at UNI, that one year he played, he really could make it. Terry Allen used to talk about the arm he had that he could throw a ball straight up in the air and hit the top of the dome or something as a joke, but the guy just had a great arm. He had great size, the kind of size you see in an NFL quarterback, too. Those are the two things I really liked about him.

What I really liked about him, and I've said this to other people, is that he never once complained about his four years behind the starter. There are a lot of people up there who thought Kurt Warner should have been the starter ahead of Jay Johnson. I wouldn't have said Jay would be a great quarterback someday, but he was a winner. He was a leader. He led the team and they won with him so that's why they stuck with him. There are a lot of people who thought Kurt should have been there. The kids on the team would see Kurt at practice and say, "Geez, Warner should be starting ahead of Johnson." But Kurt never once complained. We talked about that several times. I asked if he ever thought about transferring and it never once crossed his mind. He stuck to what he wanted to do, and he knew he'd get a shot and he took it.

He stuck to what he wanted to do, and he knew he'd get a shot and he took it.

He wasn't really into the real religious stuff back then, either. He was just a nice kid; just stuck to it. I've done speeches since, telling kids, "Talent isn't always going to get you everything you want. Sometimes you've got to be very determined, stick to it, and be very patient." That's obviously what the Warner story is. He's been very patient in taking care of what needed to be done and waited his turn. Once he got it, every step along the way after he got his chance, he's excelled.

It's been a fabulous story – not only the fact that he made it BIG. I called him up a couple of years ago when he actually made the Rams team, and that was a big story. Even for him to make the team was a big story. Then all of a sudden he's the backup going into the season. Then all of a sudden Trent gets hurt. I did that story after Trent got hurt right before he started that first exhibition game. He gave me a call and we talked about it. That was a big story.

Then all of a sudden – BOOM, it's unbelievable! And it's not only our story, it's the world's story, too. And it's just been great for us. We had our sports columnist, Mike Hlas, cover him pretty much every step of the way. We were down for the majority of the home games and then we covered them all through the playoffs. People here just love it. We produced a full-page picture of him that appeared on the back of our section one day. I think that was the Sunday before the playoffs started. Then we did a Super Bowl wrap, obviously a lot of it on him. It was a four-page wrap and the majority was on him, showed a picture of him – a mug shot of him playing high school basketball – showing how much he'd changed. We were at the Super Bowl covering everything he did.

Most people realize this is a once-in-a-lifetime thing. A Cedar Rapids kid, not only starting as an NFL quarterback, but an MVP and Super Bowl MVP and winning the Super Bowl. It's just been unbelievable. It's not even just a local story anymore, it's a national story. Everyone's kinda taken off on that.

We were scrambling to find new angles, though, because we were tired of the same old thing about "How unbelievable is this?" "How great this is!" That kind of stuff. His mom has been real helpful and given us stuff. We've talked to his high school coaches and that type stuff has helped, too. He's just so humble and that's not an act; that's how he's always been. Even when he was at UNI, it was always what the other guys are doing for me. He'd say, "I've got great receivers."

It took a long time to realize how good he actually was.

He did have good receivers. Dedric Ward, who plays for the New York Jets, was a freshman at UNI the year Kurt started. Dedric's from Cedar Rapids, too. This is his third year with the Jets. Last year he had a real productive year.

It took a long time to realize how good he actually was. Like I said, it was a big story that he had even made the team two years ago, then this year when he got the starting job it was great. But did I expect it to last? No, I thought they'd bring in some veteran and he'd be a backup again. He'd been plugging away for so long, you just figured, "He's a great kid. God bless him for keeping plugging away, but he's never gonna make it." Then he has a big game and you think, "That's great." We were down there for that first game he started in the regular season and had a couple of good stories and then. You just kinda figure how much longer? When

Courtesy: University of Northern Iowa

Even when he got his chance to start at UNI, Kurt was quick to credit the other players on the team.

is the collapse gonna happen? I think everyone in the whole country thought that. "When is the collapse gonna happen?" Then you realize it's not, and you really jump on and start doing a lot of things.

Trent Green lived in Cedar Rapids for a short time when he was in grade school – like fifth or sixth grade. We haven't done much on him this year but we did when he was playing at Indiana and they played Iowa. University of Iowa sports is our big sports story so we did a story on Trent – being a Cedar Rapids native. If he had stayed on and had a big year, we would be following him, but probably not as much as Kurt. People just don't realize that Trent has the Cedar Rapids tie even though we have done it in stories here.

Two of the greatest quarterbacks of all time,
Johnny Unitas and Dan Marino, have the same
middle name, Constantine, and both are from Pittsburgh.

THE CHIEF WHO PUT THE EWE IN RAMS UPDATE
DOUG GALLOWAY

Doug Galloway, along with his wife, Cathy, own and publish St. Louis Rams Update *(800-578-2624). They also publish the* Kansas City Chiefs Report.

I t turned into a storybook situation, where Kurt Warner came through and did everything he was supposed to do. He just did a fantastic job. We had interviews with him and different stories about him. See, we don't feature just one player all the time, obviously. We rotate around to all the different Ram players. It's a team publication.

Our newsstand sales were helped dramatically, but the way our publication is designed, we do all our heavy promotion for new subscribers during the training camp and preseason and the first couple of weeks of the season 'cause they want to subscribe and get the entire season. Remember, at that time Warner was still unknown. The Rams had not sold out the first two games at home. The team and local television station had to purchase the remaining tickets in order to lift the blackout. So as far as direct impact on our circulation, it was not substantial.

Usually what happens is a team begins to progress and move up the chain of command as far as victories. The Rams had been down for so long. We felt the management structure was there to build a winning program. We started three years ago when they were four and twelve, five and eleven. At that stage, we went ahead and decided there are Rams fans out there regardless of their record and so we started publication at that time. I figured it would probably take four or five years, quite frankly, for them to get into the playoffs under Vermeil. And it took three years for them to get there. Usually though, when you get to the playoffs, anything can happen as far as making it to the Super Bowl. We thought that with a home-field advantage, the Rams would have an excellent chance of going quite a ways. Our Super Bowl issue that covered the game was mailed in early February to our subscribers. It was kind of a season review plus coverage of the Super Bowl itself. When you mail periodical mail you have to disclose what your publication's paid subscription is on that situation and right now we are probably

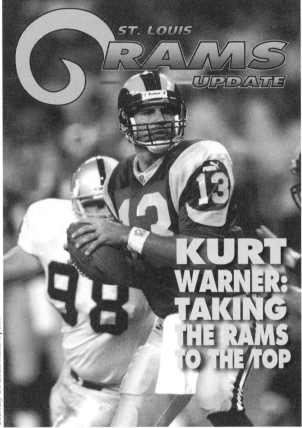

Courtesy St. Louis Rams Update

Kurt's success translated into success for other ventures.

about 3500 paid subscribers. We print every week the team plays so you print every preseason game and every regular-season and all the playoff games. We also print quarterly in the off-season. We do predraft, postdraft issues, and a season wrap-up-type issue as well.

Warner is down to earth, just a humble Christian individual. People look at that and say, "Is it an act?" No it isn't. He really is just...what you see is what he is. I've known people who worked with some of the organizations he was associated with before he became a starter and he and his wife were very active in those things. They devoted themselves to helping out other people. Many people at those organizations didn't know he was a quarterback. He doesn't brag about that stuff, doesn't hold himself up above anybody else. He's just a genuine human being, he really is.

We do a publication for the Kansas City Chiefs and are in our eighth year for that. It's called the *Chiefs Report*. We are located in Jefferson City, Missouri, and are about halfway between them.

YOU CAN'T GET INTO HEAVEN UNLESS YOU'RE A HAWKEYE
KEVIN ROBBINS

Kevin Robbins is a metro news and feature writer for the St. Louis Post-Dispatch *who trekked to Iowa to do an in-depth story on the Kurt Warner phenomenon prior to the Super Bowl.*

I learned more about the so-called work ethic in Iowa than I did in any part of my childhood. I was glad that one of my first jobs was there because I was in my formative years and was very impressionable, and when I was up there I really learned how to hit it. I think Iowa is just one of those treasures that, until people discover it for themselves will never know what it means to be there. I used to work in Iowa at a newspaper, *The Hawk Eye*, in Burlington. Kurt Warner was born in Burlington. So at any rate I knew Iowa, because I had worked there for three and a half years and sort of knew the way Iowans rally around their heroes – their hometown people who go on to do well. There's a certain pride in Iowa and I recognize that. It was really very easy. I just suggested to the editor in charge of all of the Rams coverage that we go up and do a story on how his hometown was responding to his success.

Actually it was not as encouraging as we had hoped. If you know something about Iowans, you know that they demonstrate their pride in real quiet, personal ways. They're not really very demonstrative or boisterous for the most part even about Iowa football. They get in the stadium in Iowa City and I guess they become a little more rambunctious. We went into these various bars and were hoping to find Rams memorabilia and Kurt Warner jerseys and helmets and posters and banners and people just really excited. That's not what we found, actually. In fact, there were very few outward symbols of Rams mania in these taverns. What we did find, though, was a lot of enthusiasm these people had for Kurt Warner as their hometown hero once we started talking with them. It's not like we walked into a tavern and it's just awash with blue and gold or anything like that.

I had done some perfunctory research finding out as much as I could about Kurt's growing up, but I found out nothing revealing when we got there. And that's not what we were really looking for. We had another reporter up there who was profiling him and was looking into that angle a little more than I was. My whole mission was to talk with people who didn't even know Kurt Warner. I did find a couple of people who did and they made it into my story, but for the most part I wanted to talk to people who had never met him but just felt akin to him because they were from the same town. I did end up talking with a teacher of his history class and a couple of his coaches from basketball and football. And they were just sort of bubbling with pride about this kid and how they always knew he would do something that would make them proud. They didn't necessarily think it would be in athletics but just that he would carry on the good name that Iowans have throughout this country as being good, hard-working, forward thinking, quality people. I really liked my time in Iowa as you can tell.

I had been to several places in Iowa but never had been to Cedar Rapids before and this was one of the reasons I wanted to go so badly. We were there for two days and two nights. My gosh, I was favorably impressed with the city, I suppose. It didn't really fit the whole storybook concept or myth built around Kurt Warner and this whole Iowa thing. A lot of people have their perception of Iowa as, maybe from the Kevin Costner movie or something out of some movie about farms that they saw. Cedar Rapids is a metropolitan area just like Des Moines and Iowa City. So it's not that Kurt Warner is from a small town, he's actually from a pretty good-sized city. I did want to explain that in my story, as well as explain to people that it doesn't matter where you live in Iowa you still have a connection to the land and a connection to those people who are farming out in northwest Iowa and that sort of thing. He isn't from a small town; he's from a very large city. We called his dad. He was extremely helpful. I called him in the evening before we headed out to these taverns. He insisted that I call him Gene. I told him, "We are up here and doing this story on people who've never met your son but who are proud of him. Can you lead us to a couple of places?" He said, "Well, you know, I think there's this tavern over in Irish district where people go to watch Rams games. You might start there, and there's this other place..." and by the time I had finished talking with him, he had given me maybe four ideas to go pursue. He was very helpful.

> **He isn't from a small town; he's from a very large city.**

Newspaper people are kinda fickle. They're kinda cynical. They're kind of hard-bitten. I haven't been here long enough to really know the personalities, but I think down deep inside, a lot of people were really,

Gene and Mimi Warner of Solon, Iowa, load up to head for Atlanta and the Super Bowl. Gene is Kurt's father.

really excited because never before has their home football team – the Cardinals, the Rams, whatever – never before had their football team made it to a home playoff game. By gosh, they did this year and they won it and they won the next one. I think there was a certain momentum in the newsroom here, a certain level of excitement about the Rams, but again newspapers are, like Iowans I guess, not ones to demonstrate their enthusiasm so that their colleagues may think they are excited about something as trivial as a football team.

I think this country is just so hungry for a good, pure, honest, genuine sports hero because even with Michael Jordan there was always something – his salary, or commercial ventures there was always something, I don't want to say dark or sinister, but a little bit impure, maybe. But with Kurt Warner, the whole thing about making the minimum salary, the whole thing about who he married and the family and the house he has in St. Louis, the car he drove, all that stuff. Everything was just like every man. A lot of my friends here in the newspaper business and I have talked about this in the past couple of weeks about whether any of this will in any way go to his head. I don't know enough about Kurt Warner to predict anything, but it seems now would be a very risky time for anybody in that situation. He's very susceptible maybe to – I don't know – turning into something he's not. Let's hope that doesn't happen.

THE POST-DISPATCH SAID, "GO TO IOWA." SO I'M THINKIN' ... MAFIA.
VAHE GREGORIAN

Vahe Gregorian is a sportswriter for the St. Louis Post-Dispatch. *He has also penned two sports biographies:* High Hopes *with Gary Barnett when he was head football coach at Northwestern and a book with George Perles shortly after he had been head coach at Michigan State University.*

Well, we just thought we hadn't done enough in amplifying him. We'd done something early in the season that ended up focusing a lot on his relationship with Brenda but we hadn't gone up there to Iowa. We sort of figured if you're gonna do the definitive story, not that we did that, but we did try to streamline it to his youth and his upbringing, we'd better go up there and do it that way. The Kevin Robbins thing was a little bit of "The Iowa Phenomenon" as opposed to sort of stuff on Kurt. My task was to go up there and just see as much of his childhood as I could and talk to people he either grew up with or knew. His mom was crucial in that story. She was pretty good.

I made a lot of calls before I went there to try and secure a couple of appointments – his high school coach, time with his mom, a best friend was going to come over to his mom's place. We had three or four things like that set up and Kevin had gone to his elementary school to do something else and gave me the names of some of his teachers that he hadn't talked to. In fact, I don't think they ended up being quoted in the story due to space limitations. So I talked to three elementary school teachers of his, and anyway it just sort of gathered momentum. I think some people do stories like that where they also mix the story Kevin and I did where they talk to the people around town about it. But we sort of did them as independent things.

I just thought that Kurt Warner...I don't think he's too good to be true, but he just seems like a very good guy and kinda bland. I guess you would take that over the outrageousness that you see everywhere today. Maybe you have to choose one over the other. Certainly not a particularly exciting childhood, but I'm a fan of those human interest stories even if they're about a guy playing "ding dong ditch it" and running if that's the most trouble he ever got in. You know, you never know if you really got the whole story. He may have gotten in some trouble we just never heard about it. The goal wasn't to find out if he'd been in trouble. I think we just thought this would be a good way to illustrate how clean he is. So I came away also thinking, as I always do when I go to Iowa, everybody there is just like "born nice." It's really amazing. Everybody I've ever met from Iowa, I've thought was just a nice person.

Everybody's just smitten with Kurt Warner – I don't know how else to put it.

You could see, about five weeks into it, that as preposterous as it might sound, this was gonna turn into a monstrous story. Obviously this kind of thing makes your engine run full steam. I think a lot of people were exhausted but also very excited. We put out a lot of stuff. Our beat writer, Jim Thomas, is just fabulous. Bernie Miklasz, our columnist is, too. Those guys…everything just sort of emanated from them, and they did such a great job for so long; kept the interest and kept fresh stories in the paper. It was a phenomenon really.

In the last 30 years, the record for the most touchdown passes thrown by a nonquarterback is held by Walter Payton, with eight.

JONAH WAS RIGHT. IT'S HARD TO KEEP A GOOD MAN DOWN.

JIM THOMAS

Jim Thomas is the Rams beat writer for the St. Louis Post-Dispatch. *Thomas was raised in St. Louis, attended George Washington University in Washington, D. C., and graduated from The University of Missouri-St. Louis.*

T he Kurt Warner story is unprecedented; he's the story of the year in all of sports. Again, you can explain a lot of stuff about the season – why this move is paying off, why this improved the team, why they did better in this aspect, Warner's emergence, just the kind of season he had, the numbers – you can't explain it. It just defies logic. I really do think it's a made-for-TV movie or a book. It's a great story.

The funny thing was in his first training camp in '98 in Macomb, not too far from the southeast corner of Iowa, it seemed like all of Iowa came to interview Kurt when he was struggling to make the team as the third and fourth quarterback. He was in a battle with Will Furrer for that third spot. Seems like every radio, TV, newspaper outlet in the state came. It was funny. He was one of the most-interviewed Rams players in the summer of '98. I thought this was kinda cute. I talked to Kurt a couple of times. As far as local media here, I was about the only guy who talked to him because, as a beat writer, you talk to everybody but the janitor. This year, he's the number 2 guy, a heartbeat away so to speak, and hardly anyone came down from Iowa. It was kind of funny – the talk of training camp. This is, until Trent Green got hurt. Actually the Rams had broken camp and were back in St. Louis by then even though it was still preseason. I guess they had all done their work by then. I guess a couple came down, but I even kidded Kurt and said, "Where is all of Iowa? They were all down here last year."

Obviously, when he became the starter that all changed. Heck, there was a writer, Tom Witosky, from *The Des Moines Register*, that practically lived here and covered almost half their games. I used to joke that if he spent anymore time in Missouri, he'd have to start paying taxes here. But he did spend a lot of time. I just thought Kurt was, in '98 even '99, a nice kid. But he's not a kid, he's 28 or whatever. I'm glad he's on the team and making a living.

We never really saw any of him in '98; he played in only one pre-season game, threw four passes, and completed all four. He completed the passes, but I remember he lost a fumble. He was back in the pocket; he kinda held the ball low. I remember Vermeil saying he has a tendency to do that sometimes in the pocket – put the ball down low, and then he lost a fumble, and it was real nip-and-tuck whether he was going to make the team. Will Furrer was kind of a favorite of Jerry Rhome, who was then offensive coordinator, and it came right down to the end his getting the job.

But there was nothing to base it on. Practice was practice. Maybe if you're a coach it's more of a measuring stick, but you couldn't really tell. He ran the scout team. He hardly ever got any reps with the regulars and so you just didn't see any...practice is practice. It's not like a guy necessarily dazzling and saying, "Wow." Even though I know some of the first team defense that was played against the scout team and get some feedback, "Hey this guy throws a pretty good ball. He's not bad." As the '98 season progressed and Banks struggled, I'd hear from some of the front office people. What sounded a little strange at the time was that they thought Warner potentially could do a better job than Tony Banks. As I say, it sounded strange. Even though Banks wasn't having a good year, this guy was in his third year as an NFL starter in '98, and had been a fairly high second-round draft pick. You go fast forward to the '99 preseason and I remember talking to Mike Martz, then just the offensive coordinator, now the head coach, saying that. I remember Mike Martz – this was about mid-August '99 – saying he was trying to get Kurt as much playing time in the preseason as possible. One, because he didn't know that much about him, and two, just in case something happened to Trent, he'd at least have some experience. He actually probably played a lot more in the first two preseason games than Trent, and then Boom, there is the third preseason game and Trent goes down and Kurt's the guy.

I don't remember a whole lot else about him. Even as a beat writer, you don't write about a third-string quarterback that much. I remember Tony Banks always used to kid him. Kurt was basically stereotyped as a kid from the cornfields of Iowa. Tony, very much the urban city kid from

San Diego, was kind of a hip-hop quarterback so Tony used to kid him quite a bit. Kurt used to kind of get run over by the weekly little informal press conferences that Tony would do in front of his locker. Kurt had the misfortune of having his locker right next to Tony's, so if Tony was trying to put his socks on or dress for practice, Kurt would have a hard time wedging into his own locker because there'd be 15 or 20 bodies there. Everybody always wants to know what the quarterback is saying and who would have thought that a year later those crowds would be around Kurt, and it would be Paul Justin and Joe Germaine who were getting wedged out of the way?

After Kurt became the starter, he was pretty much the same; I didn't notice that he changed at all, but I did have a lot more company standing around him. He seemed very patient. His story first came out right around that first San Francisco game, which would have been like October 10. San Francisco, at the time, was like three and one entering that game. Even though Steve Young was hurt, everybody thought, "Hey, San Francisco's still pretty darn good. The Rams have lost 17 in a row to San Francisco and the Niners had won before with their starting quarterback hurt. Anyway, that first wave, when his story was told and then each new wave, writers coming in from out of town or whatever and especially in the playoffs, seemed like he got just a little weary of that line of questioning, but he seemed pretty much the same. It didn't seem like he changed a whole lot, at least in his interplay with us.

There always seemed to be something, either a new challenge he had, then he started winning the awards, that was kinda neat, then he started showing up on the Letterman show, had the cereal named after him. There was always game-specific stuff and the playoffs were a whole new set of challenges.

Trent Green's brother, Troy, was a tight end/wide receiver at Northern Iowa. He was there the same time that Kurt was. They only overlapped about a year, but it's conceivable – I think Kurt might have been a freshman when Troy was a senior – that Kurt Warner threw passes to Trent Green's brother up there at UNI.

> Is Iowa the birthplace of NFL quarterbacks?
> Terry Bradshaw was born and raised, until
> seventh grade, in Camanche, Iowa.

As far as popularity in St. Louis, no football player is even close to Warner. Jim Hart had his day, Jackie Smith, Dan Dierdorf, and no one has come close here. Isaac Bruce had a big following and remains popular here but Kurt's right up there with McGwire. It will go down as one of the best seasons ever – second player ever to throw 40 touchdowns, his completion percentage, his quarterback rating, all of those are near the top that anyone has ever done in the whole history of this league. So you have the performance. You also have the fact that it was totally unexpected. Again it just defies logic. This just doesn't happen, where a guy comes out of nowhere and has this kind of impact in the National Football League. I mean, this is supposed to be the best of the best playing here.

Think of all the hundreds of thousands of dollars that NFL pereosnnel spend in scouting departments evaluating talent, looking at guys, having tryouts, looking at films, scouting games, etc. Nobody wanted this guy on draft day – nobody! Then he got cut. Then four years pass before he has another chance. This is kinda like *The Natural*. It just doesn't happen. Stories like this do not happen in the NFL. I even could kid him about this; you kept waiting for him to have a bad game. The only thing close to a bad game would be Philadelphia, and that was a meaningless game. The Rams basically played their junior varsity in that game – the regular-season finale. Okay, he threw a couple of interceptions against Tampa Bay, but he didn't have a bad game.

Partly it was the performance, and two, it was the fact that it was unexpected. You could never, in your wildest dreams, have expected this to happen. And the third part is the fact that he's such a character guy, a class guy, he's humble. And I hope he doesn't change – that success doesn't spoil him, so to speak. And so far it hasn't. Just what he represents, if he was a jerk and all this happened you'd say, "Wow, this is great, but he's a jerk." But he's not a jerk. He's just a fine person. People are relatively conservative. They love stories like this.

There are all different kinds of personalities, people from different backgrounds that cause people to react in certain situations how they can but he's certainly one of a kind – at least in this market. As a St. Louis native, I'm so happy for the town. It has just meant so much to them. They'd never even hosted a playoff game until this year, much less won a game. And now to top that off, to be Super Bowl Champions! That's amazing.

Chapter 10

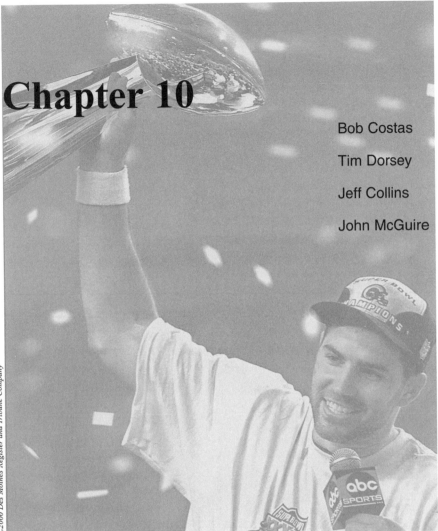

Bob Costas

Tim Dorsey

Jeff Collins

John McGuire

The Spirit
of St. Louis

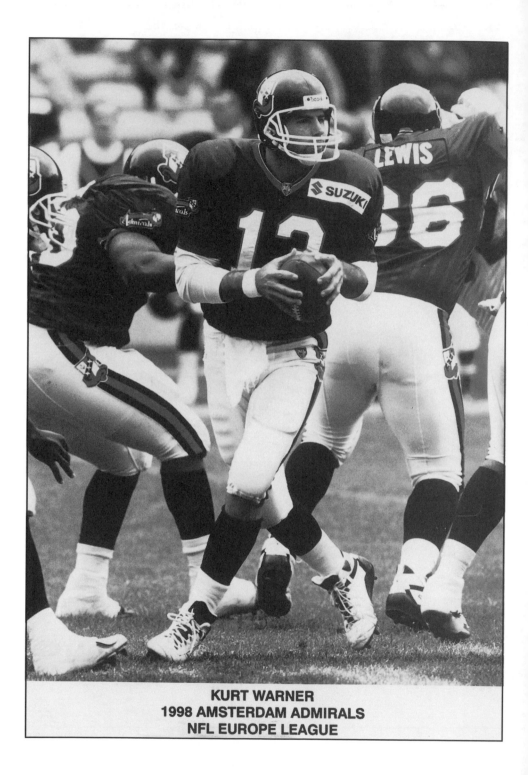

KURT WARNER
1998 AMSTERDAM ADMIRALS
NFL EUROPE LEAGUE

Courtesy Bob Costas

SO HE TOLD COSELL: "LEVEL WITH ME, HOWARD, OR I'LL PULL THE RUG RIGHT OUT FROM OVER YOU."
BOB COSTAS

Bob Costas is a native New Yorker who graduated from Syracuse University in 1974 and migrated immediately to St. Louis, where he was the voice of the ABA St. Louis Spirits. He is nationally recognized as one of the very top broadcasters in any sport today. He is also known for his love of the game of baseball and for his knowledge of sports trivia. Costas is always very cooperative in almost anything you ask of him, within reason.

I came to St. Louis right out of college. My first job was broadcasting the Spirits of St. Louis in the ABA. My wife's whole family is from here so those two things kinda led us to live here. We actually lived in New York for a stretch in the '80s, but when the first of our children was born we moved back here. Good place to raise kids.

The Kurt Warner story is a great story. Warner had one of the great years of NFL history. He was one of the guys who was not even a true rookie. He's been knocked around, done Arena Football, not protected in the expansion draft. A guy, kind of a "42nd Street," stepping out of a chorus line into a starring role sort of thing. Course, in the modern sports world, you can only do that once, because after that you become a mega-star. And he has become a mega-star. It hasn't changed him apparently in the way he relates to people and his perspective on things and that's part of his appeal, but he will never be obscure again.

The thing I want to emphasize, other than living in St. Louis, I'm no closer to this than anyone else who has a casual interest in football. I didn't cover it. I've never met Kurt Warner. I've never spoken with him. I have no particular insight into this. I don't want to position myself as something I'm not. I really have no particular insight into it.

Two things happened simultaneously. It was not only that he emerged, the team emerged. He had been obscure, to put it kindly, even at the end of the previous year, when he even sat behind Steve Bono, and he was not protected in the expansion draft. The team itself had not had a winning year in St. Louis and hadn't had a winning year since the early '90s really, hadn't been a playoff team, going back to Los Angeles. So it's a double emergence. This team comes out of nowhere to win the Super Bowl. There's no buildup to it. It's just – BOOM! And then he comes out of nowhere to throw more touchdowns than anyone except Dan Marino. So it was a wild and giddy ride.

When am I going to do a book? I have a book coming out in early April about the state of baseball. It's called *Fair Ball, A Fan's Case for Baseball*. It's kind of an extended essay; it's not a terribly long book – 160, 170 pages. It's an extended essay on the state of baseball with suggestions on what they should change, how they should go about it. It's kind of a critique of the positions of both the owners and the players and sets out a new paradigm maybe for the way the game would be best served in the future if all parties concerned could come to some kind of agreement on some of the approaches and principles in the book. As a first-time author, I have enjoyed writing it. I'm happy I got it down on paper. It's good for my peace of mind just to have gotten it said.

Some of the baseball people in power have grown up with the same sense of history of the game but not all of them do. Part of the problem in baseball is that since so many of the teams operate at a loss, the only way to recoup investments – sometimes you recoup that investment in spades – is to sell. And so you get a lot of turnover now in baseball and it inevitably brings in corporations or new baseball owners without a background in the game, with a different agenda than a lifelong baseball man would have. And sometimes even with a short-term agenda with no real allegiance to the basic future of the game, or to the best interests of the game. That's been part of baseball's problem. Ownership that comes from so many disparate agendas, and it's difficult to get all of them on the same page. I do think there are a number of owners and the, commissioner, Selig, who definitely have a love of the game and a knowledge of its history. That doesn't guarantee that you do the right thing either, though. Bud Selig definitely loves the history of baseball and yet he's been a proponent of radical realignment. For example, it makes no sense to discuss the Arizona Diamondbacks going to the American League. I like the National League better, without the designated hitter.

In the Chip Hilton series, it was an All-American story and kind of refreshing wholesome story like Kurt Warner but it wasn't a pro thing. But Hilton was the "star" of his high school team and teams – he was a four-sport star, so it wasn't like he came out of nowhere. Roy Hobbs, or Shoeless Joe from Hannibal, Missouri? I can only guess that Warner must not have been highly evaluated by the scouts. The fans thought that whatever high hopes – and I think at that time high hopes for the Rams was nine and seven, ten and six, that was high hopes – most fans thought that went out the window when Trent Green got hurt.

I'm trying to think of a comparison in baseball, but I don't know. Let's see: comes out of nowhere, all of a sudden becomes great, hadn't been, then does. Maybe like Brady Anderson, had never done anything and hit fifty home runs. He was a good player but didn't sustain that. John Beasley and Gene Bearden were kind of like one-year wonders. You know, it took Koufax a long time but he was highly touted. It wasn't like this.

I don't think stories like this have the same ability to affect us as it once did. But you know, some of that is just us – just age. Someone who is fifteen might not think that, might not realize it.

> Of all the great BYU quarterbacks, the only one to lead them to a New Year's Day bowl victory is Steve Sarkasian.

"DORSEY'S A REAL RING-TAILED TOOTER"
TIM DORSEY, KTRS

St. Louis native Tim Dorsey went from St. Louis Preparatory Seminary to Saint Louis University to KMOX Radio for 16 years to president of Charter Cable. On April 15, 1996, he and 40 illustrious partners started KTRS. The station has enjoyed outstanding success under Dorsey's leadership.

Kurt Warner is too good to be true. I've got a radio station in St. Louis, our morning guy is Dan Dierdorf from *Monday Night Football* fame. He's the number one analyst on CBS and is in the Football Hall of Fame, one of three guys from Canton, Ohio, to be in the Hall of Fame. The other two are Alan Page and Marion Motley.

Dan and I were talking and thought we should do something with the Rams so I went out and signed a deal with Trent Green who was the starting quarterback going into the preseason last year who came to the Rams from the Washington Redskins, a local guy, Vianney High School, All-American-type guy, almost a Kurt Warner clone. Another guy who's too good to be true.

Trent goes down – he's eleven-for-eleven his last game when he goes down. The whole town is deflated. We think the Rams finally have a chance to win a couple of football games and even at that time people were hoping nine and seven, best hope ten and six. And Trent goes down hurt, and we still have *The Trent Green Show*, and I'm thinking "Oh Lordy, Trent's out for the year, who's the backup?" I had no idea what the name was. I thought it was Curt C-u-r-t Warner, the guy who went to Penn State. I thought "Holy Cripes! He plays quarterback now? How old is he?" I called Kurt directly. I had no idea he had an agent or anything like that. I was told to call the Bartelstein people in Chicago.

I did a deal with a fine young guy named Rob Lefco, who handles marketing for Bartelstein and really handles Kurt's affairs. I told him what I was doing with Trent, and told him about the Dierdorf thing and asked if Kurt would like to do two days a week just talking a little bit about football and his family on our morning show with Dan Dierdorf and Kevin Slayten and Wendy Weise, and they said "yes." Week after week after week I became smarter and smarter and smarter. When Green had gone down, my initial thought was, "Oh Brother!" I wasn't gonna let Trent go just because he had the unfortunate accident so Trent was on the station on Mondays and Kurt did every Tuesday and Friday through the season. One day Kurt forgot about calling the station and doing the show – came on at 7:40 every morning. About 8:30 that day he called and said, "Tim, you should fire me. I am so sorry; I forgot. I was up with the kids and I was doing some things. If you want to fire me, I don't blame you." And he was as serious as can be. That's the kind of guy he is. He is very down to earth.

I will tell you that two days after the Super Bowl, they did the Super Bowl thing. He went to Disney World to do his shoot there. He called the station that Tuesday morning just a day and a half later at eight o'clock in the morning and said, "Guys, I've got a few minutes. Do you want me to do anything for you? Would you like to talk to me this morning?" Now here's a guy who's a Most Valuable Player, just wins the Super Bowl and is named the Most Valuable Player in the Super Bowl and he's calling to see if he can help us out and go on the air that morning. That's Kurt Warner, and that's the honest-to-God truth. He has sat in my office and signed footballs for an hour before and thought nothing of it – just a great guy. I've never seen anyone like him. No, I have not. There is nothing mercenary about this man. He's the real deal. And his family and religion both come before anything else and always will. I don't think anything will change that. I think this has actually sent some people to church and has made some people think about their religion. Certainly there are the naysayers who say, "Oh shut up. Enough of God already." I say that's their problem. I do not want to be hokey. I'm a practicing Irish Catholic but I even think this Kurt Warner is a type of missionary. I really do. And I think that's probably the main reason he's on earth. I do. I think he spreads the word of God.

> **I think this has actually sent some people to church and has made some people think about their religion.**

I don't think the same way Kurt does at all. My religion is very private, very Catholic, very parochial, but I truly do think that he is a missionary and I do think he is on a mission. You think of the Second Coming when you look at Kurt Warner. He has made me ask questions that I haven't asked since I was in the seminary. And I'm not that type. I've had thoughts that I haven't had in years.

I don't know Mark McGwire, but I will tell you just through Kurt's attitude only and publicly in the press, Kurt Warner certainly comes off as a much nicer guy – much nicer guy. Kurt is very accessible. I'm sure we'll have to up the ante to get the *Kurt Warner Show* in the fall of 2000, but because we were there first and because we asked, I think Kurt will remember that. I know his agent does. Because of that we'll have no problem working out something with him. These are very reasonable people.

We were probably more known as the football station than anyone else in town because of Kurt Warner and because of Trent Green. And when Kurt won MVP, we made about fifty thousand posters with Kurt's picture on them as MVP and passed them out to everybody going into one of the playoff games one day. In fact this poster was shown on the Super Bowl at the very end of the game, Kurt's picture on our poster. One of the *Tonight Show* producers saw that sign at the end of the Super Bowl, called up the radio station and asked if we would send them out for the people in the audience to hold up while they introduced Kurt when he appeared on the show. We said, "Of course, we'll do it." We sent them off.

Kurt Warner is a real ring-tailed tooter, that's what he is!

Tim Dorsey of KTRS, right, with Kurt Warner and nine-year-old Mike Dorsey, youngest of Tim's nine children

WHAT'S WITH ALL THOSE SUPER BOWL X CAPS?
JEFF COLLINS

Jeff Collins is a native of Davenport, Iowa, He has built a very successful chain of sporting goods and sports memorabilia stores about the United States and is the official Clubhouse for several major-league teams including the New York Yankees and the St. Louis Cardinals. Collins' stores stretch from New York City to St. Louis to New Orleans and points west.

We have three St. Louis stores – a Cardinals Clubhouse at the St. Louis Galleria, a Cardinals Clubhouse at Union Station, and we have a Sports Avenue store at Union Station. It's in our Cardinals contract that we are allowed to carry a certain percentage of Rams items during the baseball off-season.

At the beginning of the season, the whole Warner thing and the Rams thing went hand in hand. The sporting goods business here, like retail wise for the Rams, has been virtually nonexistent for the last two or three years

Even going into the season, we did not buy any Warner jerseys. Unfortunately, the way this stuff works, they import these jerseys and there has to be a certain demand. They have minimums in order to make jerseys for a certain player and to get somebody like Warner made at the beginning of the season, even though he was the starting quarterback, it just wasn't gonna be done. So at the beginning of the year, we had zero Kurt Warner jerseys – nothing. The other stores were the same way. He would have been one of the few starting quarterbacks in the NFL who would have had no personalized jerseys for sale in his hometown.

After the third week was when people started requesting his jerseys. Were we going to get them? When would they be in? So it took a good three-four weeks to get people to start asking for them. We did not have Warner jerseys, and neither did anybody else in town, until probably about the sixth or seventh week. That would have been almost halfway through the season before anybody had them. We were able to get them that quickly from Puma, the sideline apparel licensee for the Rams.

Our first order was small 'cause I think everybody was still – I hate to say it – but people were being more cautious. They didn't know how long this whole thing was gonna last and everybody was waiting for him to have a bad game. It took the first half of the season for it to really sink in with people that this could be for real. Our first order that we got in was very small, but after we had them in the stores for a couple of days, we were calling up to double and triple our original orders.

The problem was there's only three companies licensed to make replica jerseys with the player's name and number on them – Champion Products, Puma, and Nike. Actually there's a fourth – adidas – but they didn't make any Rams jerseys. So the three companies that could have made Rams jerseys – the only new player that the Rams picked up this year that got made at the beginning of the season was Marshall Faulk. Other than that, whatever everybody had was what was left over from last year. The manufacturers who make them did not have enough blanks (that would be Rams jerseys with no name on them) in stock to meet the demands on the Warner jerseys. What these guys do is take a few players and print up so many pieces of Marshall Faulk or Isaac Bruce, then they'll keep a certain amount in blanks. Then if a new player pops up, or somebody gets hot, like a Kurt Warner, then they will go in and print those blank jerseys with his name and number on them. What happened was all three of those companies did not have anywhere the amount of blank jerseys just to meet the demand of what everybody was wanting – Kurt Warner jerseys.

In St. Louis, we'd never seen anything like sudden demand. There's usually one player every year that this happens to. Last year I would say the closest it would be would be the demand for Randy Moss jerseys from the Vikings.

Now, at the end of this season, we have zero Kurt Warner jerseys – nothing left. We've been out of them since the week before Christmas. We got a really, really big shot of jerseys in the first or second week of December that really only lasted about two weeks. We went through and got the late shipment of 720 Warner jerseys in from Nike around December 10, and they were gone in three weeks. In St. Louis that's unheard of for a Rams jersey.

The Rams are changing their jerseys. This will be good for our business. They've changed the colors – it's a pretty dramatic change. It's a darker navy blue with an old gold trim. What happened with the Rams, when they came to St. Louis, most people thought they would make some kind of uniform or logo change just to kind of differentiate themselves from being the Los Angeles Rams, and it was something that was never done after they moved here. People always ask about it. It has always been a topic of conversation when the Rams got brought up. "How come the Rams don't change?" or do something to make them different than they were in Los Angeles? Anytime a team makes a change in logo or jerseys or anything like that it definitely means a boost in our kind of business. The possibilities are there to double what this would mean normally because there weren't enough jerseys in the marketplace last year to fill the demand for Rams jerseys. Nobody had any. We were going through the Super Bowl and that was the number one requested item was for Rams jerseys, Warner being number one, but all the other players being pretty close behind. People just wanted any Rams jersey with any player on it. Dan Marino has always worn jersey number thirteen and it has been a popular seller. It was mentioned during the Super Bowl broadcast that no quarterback wearing number thirteen had ever won the Super Bowl. We won't get anymore of the old Warner jerseys before the new ones come out because there's nothing left. The manufacturers knew that the Rams were gonna change this year; the league has to give the manufacturers a one-year notice on any jersey or logo or color changes. So they knew they were gonna change jerseys and did not want to have any excess inventory left over on the old. I don't think anyone had any idea at the beginning of last season that they would have to worry about having Rams jerseys for the Super Bowl.

It was mentioned during the Super Bowl broadcast that no quarterback wearing number thirteen had ever won the Super Bowl.

There also has been an increase in demand for Rams and Kurt Warner merchandise in our stores outside the St. Louis area. In the last two years I haven't bought any Rams jerseys for stores outside the St. Louis area, but last year was the first year that I did get some jerseys to those guys.

This is close to McGwire, but McGwire was more readily available. This is different, but it's one of those phenomenons that if we would have had 2000 of those jerseys we would have sold everyone of them and not had to mark a one down. We had a little bit of that hype down in New Orleans this year with Ricky Williams but not nearly like this.

It's just a nightmare to try to prepare for things like this. You buy, and inevitably you make mistakes. What happened to us in St. Louis was we bought a lot of T-shirts and all they wanted was sweatshirts. We were able to get them but now we've got a lot of T-shirts left. You never know exactly how it's going to go. You just try to wing it and get it done. The window's very short. You've got just a short period of time. It's getting it in, having a lot of it at the right time, then getting the heck out of it. If the team loses, we just move on to the next thing.

We're working on a deal to do a store with the Jets in New York and also trying to do one with the Minnesota Vikings. The key is to just getting associated with winners. These teams win and they put on formidable teams every year and you can do some business. But if it's a win you're on cloud nine, and if they lose, you're in the crapper.

We try to think different from the others. Like the Bears would want to do some signage for the store. They'd go out and hire an ad agency and would go out and spend twenty five hundred bucks doing a series of signs. I'll go to this guy down in Missouri I know that makes them and it'll cost me two hundred and fifty bucks. It'll look about as good as anything the Bears would do, so we've never had the luxury of being able to do things at the level they do so we have to scrimp to get a profit out of the business and somehow we get it out. They wouldn't do it that way. They'd hire a buyer and overpay him; then hire a manger and over-pay him. Before you know it, there's nothing left.

> The Saints' Ricky Williams is the cousin of baseball slugger Cecil Fielder.

BILL BIDWELL DROVE THE ST. LOUIS FOOTBALL CARDINALS SO FAR INTO THE GROUND THAT HE COULD QUALIFY AS A SENIOR PILOT FOR VALUJET.

JOHN MCGUIRE

John McGuire is a longtime features writer for the St. Louis Post-Dispatch. *A native of Kalamazoo, Michigan, McGuire is both a writer and an avid sports fan.*

There's so much fresh territory with him. He was overlooked for such a long period of time. The newly resurrected Cleveland Browns just kinda laughed, "We don't want this guy." Just turned him down. I was expecting the usual this season, and I'm not a rabid Rams fan so I guess I'm kinda unusual in St. Louis. I am so traditional that it bothers me when teams move. I just couldn't get caught up in the Rams thing for a while and when Warner came up I kinda giggled because I thought being a perverse soul, this is gonna be funnier than anything – this Arena Football guy, European Amsterdam Admirals – this is gonna be a hilarious season. They'll probably go one and sixteen or whatever it is. It's gonna be a disaster. The whole season I've been in a state of disbelief. I really have. I can't believe this guy's this good and I think with my little crowd of cynics, we are all kind of astonished because we thought this would be one of our glorious seasons where they're even gonna be worse than they have been in the previous four years they were here. So it's been wonderful to watch. Even though we were dead wrong about how it would turn out. I think that's why it's been so neat because it's just a total opposite of what we expected.

About five or six wins into the season, it became obvious this guy was not a stiff. He was really outstanding. I suppose in the beginning I didn't pay that much attention to him because we all felt when Trent Green went down, "Well this is it; this is the Rams; this is beautiful; this is what happens to them. It's gonna be another one of those years." I don't know how much any of us knew about the guy so it's been glorious for that reason. It's been almost like a movie – one of those Disney movies.

I think I felt like it was '95 all over again, when the Rams started off 4-0 in their first season here, until it became obvious they were certainly for real – very much for real. That took about two thirds of the way into the season. The whole season has had that Hollywood quality which is perfect for Georgia Frontiere because it really has been, as I said, a kind of Disney movie. Because who could believe it – that this guy, a total unknown, really has done what he's done. And I guess Charley Armey's the guy that everyone credits for putting this team together but it's been magical – it really has.

In St. Louis, a baseball town, football people can finally raise their heads!

In St. Louis, a baseball town, football people can finally raise their heads! They can smile and look you in the face. I wasn't a PSL (Personal Seat License) guy – didn't have tickets. My son was a PSL guy, and I used to tease him, but I said, "Well, it's a nice gesture. You're in business and I suppose you have to buy tickets to this thing."

But you know they were so bad last year that people were leaving tickets on their windshield wipers. The great story was a guy left two tickets under his windshield wiper and came back and there were seven there. They were beleaguered fans so I think they are celebrating in a way that far exceeds the normal euphoria over a winning team because they've been teased so much because they fell for a sucker deal and bought tickets to a really horrible team and now look – it's just unbelievable.

I haven't seen anything like it in all the 34 years I've been at *The Post-Dispatch*. It does go crazy here during World Series years but we haven't had one since '87 but this is different. This is even more intense – if only because this is so dramatic. Everyone had kinda settled into this notion, "Oh gee, well we do have an NFL team you know we didn't have one, but we've got one now. But they're terrible." And it's gone from that to just absolute euphoria. I haven't been to a game recently but people who have gone to the last games they said the Laclede's Landing area on the river was bedlam. This is essentially a baseball town, and I don't sense this season has surpassed the McGwire thing. I don't think anything ever will duplicate that. I've never seen anything like the McGwire phenomena, when McGwire hit his sixty-second homer in '98.

The morning after McGwire hit number sixty-two, I'd already thrown the paper in the recycling bin and all of a sudden my phone starts ringing. The first call was Bob Costas' secretary. She said, "Can you get us a copy of the paper? There are lines outside the paper and people are standing three blocks long." I said, "What?" Then I ran out and got the thing out of the bin because I hadn't realized. I don't think this has achieved that level yet but I don't know, it's pretty amazing.

My personal feeling is that this far exceeds McGwire. I mean Mark had hit 58 the year before so where's the surprise? But this guy, Warner, this is just an astonishing story. I don't think it's ever – I don't know that much about the history of the NFL but I don't recall anything in the history of the NFL quite like this where a team came out of nowhere with a total pretty much unknown guy. It's incredible. Then there's Vermeil, who is older now so you end up rooting for guys like that. Being around here a long time, I can say I don't think any of us – it was such a long series of humiliations for the town. First of all you lose a team, then everyone says, "Well you're in the driver's seat for an expansion team.

There's no way you guys won't get one." I'm at a Blackhawks game at Chicago Stadium and they said from the press box the second expansion team went to Jacksonville, Florida. People were saying, "Oh, my God." And the whole town was embarrassed, it really was; it was just humiliating. We were clearly the front-running city. There's no way we couldn't get an expansion team, and we didn't.

Then along came this deal with the Rams where they shook every penny out of our pockets. They emptied them. Then the Rams got off to a nice start that first year in 1995 when they played outdoors – the first five wins and from there on it was right down the tube. Not only did we not get the expansion team that everyone said we were gonna get, we paid a fortune, a kidnapping ransom, for this team that's just awful. I'm still kind of disbelieving. I still can't believe this St. Louis football team can be in the Super Bowl. 'Cause no one ever really believed in them. That's

In the 1970s a St. Louis football Cardinals fan bought an ad in the *St. Louis Post-Dispatch* offering to sell the "Official Cardinals' Playbook" with "all five plays illustrated, including the squib punt."

what happened with the Big Red (The St. Louis Football Cardinals, who moved to Arizona in 1988). All we hoped for with the Big Red was, "Gosh, can't we have a playoff game here?" It never happened.

You see Kurt Warner jerseys everywhere. I thought "13"– what kind of number is that? But he definitely is the centerpiece. The postgame stuff was pretty much all about him. That's how big he is. It's just a Disney movie – that's what it is. My nephew is here in town and works for my son and his name is Kirk Warner. He's getting calls at three, four o'clock in the morning. "I hate to bother you Kurt, but can you get me tickets?" That's just how everyone associates what's happened with Kurt Warner. I mean he is the absolute focal point of everything this season. And my poor nephew couldn't wait until February.

Warner popped up for the Billy Graham rally, and I thought, "What is he doing there?" Billy Graham had a weeklong rally at Trans World and there's Kurt Warner, and I thought, "Oh my God, he's unbelievable." And he was there several nights speaking. I don't know how long he's been religious. I can't recall an athlete who genuinely thinks like he does. I'm sure there are baseball players and others who think this way, but this guy – the first thing out of his mouth is "thank God!" This guy seems genuine.

> The only coach to win over 100 games
> in both college and the NFL is Don Coryell.

Chapter 11

Steve Sabol

Kirk Warner

Curt Warner

Melissa Heher

Suzy Abrams

Stephanie Pritchett

Tom Moses

Randy Gibson

Super Rams,
Super Bowl,
Super Man

Stephanie Pritchett and husband Jim smile at their good "Wheel of Fortune."

IF YOU RUN NFL FILMS BACKWARDS, IT LOOKS LIKE THE PLAYERS ARE HELPING EACH OTHER UP AND SHOWING THEM ON THEIR WAY
STEVE SABOL

NFL Films was established in 1964, when Ed Sabol, Steve's father, convinced then-NFL Commissioner Pete Rozelle that the league needed a motion picture company to record its history. NFL Films has mushroomed well beyond the role of mere historian. The entity has won 73 Emmys for outstanding cinematography and sound, and it represents the quintessential standard for sports filmmaking.From theme programs, such as NFL Films Presents, *to team highlight films, to emotional behind-the-scenes detailing the nuts and the bolts of HBO's* Inside the NFL, *NFL films, as an independently operated arm of the league, captures the essence of football like no other visual entity. No story of Steve Sabol could be complete without a story or two of NFL Films dealings with George Halas or Sabol's exploits on the college gridiron four decades ago.*

Kurt Warner is the most incredible story ever in the history of football – maybe in the whole history of sports. With NFL Films, it's never been about making money. That separates us from others 'cause we've been allowed that privilege. There's magic in the sport of football and we're there to reveal it, document it, and preserve it in our film. But basically we're fans at heart. NFL Films selected Kurt Warner as the 1999 NFL Player of the Year.

It is truly a heartwarming story. The videotape of his Super Bowl XXXIV performance was produced in three days and ready for distribution less than two weeks after the game. Through the end of the Super Bowl week, thirty producers combed through seven hundred and seventy miles of film from this season to put the finishing touch on the Super Bowl film. So people worldwide and for years to come will know the Kurt Warner story.

With regards to George Halas, who died back in 1993, he had a love-hate relationship with NFL Films. Halas used to sell seats on the visitors' bench at Wrigley Field. After Minnesota Vikings Coach Norm

Steve "Sudden Death" Sabol is president of NFL Films.

VanBrocklin complained to the league office, then-NFL Commissioner Rozelle asked me to shoot footage of the bench as he proceeded to investigate. But I told Rozelle, "I've already got that." So I sent Rozelle the footage and sure enough, there were those guys on the bench. Rozelle confronted Halas and found out that Halas actually sold seats on the bench. They fined Halas and when Halas found out the footage came from us, he tried to have us banned from the sidelines. He also detested the close-ups we took of people like Dick Butkus and Gale Sayers. He said, "I don't want any face shots 'cause the players will see that and want more money." It helped when we made an extra effort to include clean-cut Bears fans in the highlight films. Because back in 1967, Halas became enraged when one of our films showed a fan lunging for a ball in the stands with a pistol tucked in his belt. Halas kept saying, "Those are not Bears fans. We don't have people like that come to our games. We have good fans." But Bears fans in the '60s made the Indy 500 infield look like a parliament. They were wild. But Halas didn't want that. So the next year I went to Washington and got a close-up of Redskins fans with their camel-hair coats, pretty sweaters, and scarves. Every year I'd splice those shots into the Bears films, so until the day he died, he'd say, "See, those are Bears fans." He never knew. That was one of our running jokes at NFL films. We always had an assignment for a guy to go to Washington to shoot "Bears fans."

I can't believe you remembered the story of the "Fearless Tot from Possum Trot." What happened was I was raised in a suburb of Philadelphia called Villanova, Pennsylvania. I had great grades in prep school but I had lousy SAT so I ended up going to school in Colorado Springs at a college called Colorado College. I wanted to play football out there so one of the first things I did was change my hometown from Villanova to Coaltown Township, Pennsylvania. It was a nonexistent town but had the ring of solid football to it. Everybody knows that western Pennsylvania is where the football studs come from. I'd never seen a coal mine but if coaches thought I had been rubbing shoulders with guys like Mike Ditka and Leon Hart, they'd have to start thinking. I carried it off all freshman year and nobody caught on. Guys would come up and ask me why I hadn't gotten a big scholarship from Notre Dame or Ohio State or someplace, and I'd just say, "Aw, I was just third string."

But I didn't play much freshman year so I knew I'd have to do something to impress the coaches. So when I came back for sophomore year, I told everyone that I was from Possum Trot, Mississippi, 'cause you can't ignore anyone from a place called Possum Trot. Then I knew I had to change my name. I had an honorable name but it didn't have the ring of greatness. I wanted something real lethal like "Sudden Death." That fit my initials, too – Steven Douglas Sabol became Steve "Sudden Death" Sabol. Then in the program for the very first game, we had "Sudden Death" Sabol listed by that name. Also I bought an ad in the program that said, "Coach Jerry Carle wishes "Sudden Death" Sabol a successful season." Everybody thought the coach put the ad in there but I paid for the ad myself. Coach Carle was a regular Bear Bryant; he never smiled. The last thing he'd do would be wish me a successful season, but a lot of people took it seriously. I thought it was all pretty funny. But the coach didn't have any scholarships to give so he couldn't run off any players like me.

New York Giants owner Wellington Mara was on the Giants' bench for their first-ever game in 1925.

Unfortunately I only weighed one hundred and seventy pounds, so the nickname "Sudden Death" just didn't seem to go with my build. Nevertheless, in the final program of the season, I ran an ad that said "Coach Jerry Carle congratulates "Sudden Death" Sabol on a fantastic season."

So before my junior year, I added forty pounds – I really bulked up. Then I started sending out press agent stuff to both the local and the Denver papers. One ad told everyone "The Possum Trot Chamber of Commerce extends its wishes for a successful season to its favorite son, "Sudden Death" Sabol." Another advertisement included a picture of me in a football uniform at about the age of ten in Philadelphia where I played on a Midget League team, called the Little Quakers. Then came a hundred T-shirts made up with the drawing of a possum and the inscription "I'm a Little Possum Trotter." I gave half of them away and sold the rest for one dollar.

So with my own money, I'd paid for newspaper advertisements, colored postcards, brochures, tee shirts, lapel buttons and pencils on which were written such legends as "The Prince of Pigskin Pageantry now at the Pinnacle of his Power." And "One of the Most Mysterious, Awesome Living Beings of all Times." I sent out news releases reporting incredible accomplishments of "Sudden Death" Sabol on the football field with sidebars describing his colorful campus life. And as testament to my ability, the sports editors swallowed all this stuff hook, line, and sinker.

I sent out news releases reporting incredible accomplishments of "Sudden Death" Sabol on the football field.

Now football practice itself was tedious. It was a period of intense boredom punctuated by moments of acute fear. So I began writing the game program itself. And I did a column for the school newspaper entitled, "Here's a Lot from Possum Trot." I also was the team cheerleader, and I began plastering the walls of the locker room with posters and slogans and slipping fight songs onto the record player. Then I shipped off a press release to our rival, Concordia College, team's hometown paper. They were unbeaten at the time. The quote says, "Sudden Death says Colorado College will Crush Concordia College." Their game plan was simple. They wanted to break my neck. But I loved it. It makes the game more personal. This one big end was particularly anxious to break something. He seemed very capable of it, too. So at halftime I go up to the referee. I'm putting on my "choir boy look" and say, "Mr. Referee, Sir, that end – well I hate to say it, but he's playing sorta dirty and I wish you'd watch him."

So on the first play, I asked the quarterback to call my number on an end sweep. Sure enough this big oaf really clobbers me. I whisper in his ear, "You're nothing but chicken ____." Naturally he takes a swing and there's the referee standing right there, throwing down his flag, and yelling, "You're out of the game." We beat Concordia thirteen to nothing.

I had a good year. I was good enough for first-team All-Conference and we won four games, which is about twice what we normally won. The news was going all over the country about Steve "Sudden Death" Sabol. It was carried on the AP wires, and I got a letter from a disk jockey from, of all places, Possum Trot. There really is such a place, but it's in Tennessee, not Mississippi. That was fine by me because I always had a sneaking hunch I wanted to come from Tennessee anyway.

So I go back for my senior year but I fought hepatitis all summer so I had to drop out and go back to Philadelphia and started lifting weights to get back in shape. Back in those days, most athletes didn't lift weights. Darned if I didn't work so hard at it, I was actually named Mr. Philadelphia. Well I couldn't let that honor pass me by, so I had eight by ten photographs made showing me all aripple and holding a spear. Underneath the picture was my name and these modest words. "Acclaimed as the Greatest New Adventure Hero of the Year." That was an inspiration I got from my huge comic book collection where I have all-time favorites such as Captain America and Batman. The pictures were immediately dispatched to editors, press agents, and fans. I had the mailing addresses of influential people well catalogued from my Dad's business.

That was a good start on the year but I was worried the people back in Colorado had forgotten all about me. So I went to a printer, and I had stationery made with "Universal International" and wrote all these letters. "You have been placed on Steve Sabol's mailing list and thus will be able to follow his movie career." Then came the information that Steve Sabol had been cast as a supporting actor in Universal's forthcoming film *Black Horse Troop*, which is a name I got from a march by John Philip Sousa. The movie would star William Holden, Steve McQueen, Eva Marie Saint, and Steve Sabol. The letter was stamped "Approved for immediate release by order of Central Casting." I'd had a stamp made up with that title on it. But I didn't send the letter to the newsmen back in Colorado Springs. They were starting to get a little suspicious. So instead I sent them to friends in the Colorado Springs area who were most likely to leak the news in the right places. It worked. Local columnists fell all over themselves informing the readers that "Sudden Death" Sabol was Hollywood's newest star. I must have had a hundred calls from people wanting to know if it's true that Steve McQueen is really a jerk. But I told them, "No, he's really a great guy."

So the next summer before returning for my final year of Colorado College, I did a grand tour of Europe and in Madrid I got inspired again. El Cordobes was the biggest bullfighter in the world at that time. There were picture postcards of him all over Spain. I said, "Now that's class." So when I got back home I shelled out some more money, actually my Dad's money. I got a couple of crates of colored postcards of myself in a football uniform. At the back of the postcard, is "Steve 'Sudden Death' Sabol, all-time All-Rocky Mountain Football Great." At the bottom it says "The Prince of Pigskin Pageantry." So in the fall, I go back to Colorado College. I had a new maroon convertible; I had a five-bedroom apartment even, though I lived alone but I could think better when I'm alone. I had a picture of me signing with the Cleveland Browns for $375,000. But the topper was when Coach Carle got upset because outside Washburn Stadium I put a sign that said, "Washburn Stadium, Altitude 7,989 feet," which was exactly 2,089 feet higher than it actually was but I wanted to psyche out opposing players when they came there. So I had a plaque remade for the visiting team's dressing room that read "This Field is named in Honor of Morris Washburn who perished when his lungs exploded from a lack of oxygen during a soccer match with the University of Denver in 1901."

The Fearless Tot from Possum Trot might be the only football player in history with a better "rags to riches" story than Kurt Warner.

Inside the NFL on HBO is the longest-running series of any kind on cable television.

A ROSE BY ANY OTHER NAME STILL CAN'T GET INTO THE HALL OF FAME
KIRK WARNER

Kirk Warner is a chef at a well-known restaurant in St. Louis and has never been much of a football fan until the 1999 Rams season. He made the mistake of having his number listed in the phone book.

The day of the first game, I got a message from Kurt's grandmother, then it continued throughout the year. One woman who called at three in the morning was one of the more clear-headed of the group. She wanted to get tickets for the playoff games. She said she had kids with cancer. I couldn't help but laugh to think anyone would actually call the quarterback of the football team to get tickets to the game. I told her she had the wrong number and suggested she not try to call him right now.

Then the next night, I got a call from a lady around 4:30 in the morning: "I've been following you for two years now and...." At that point, I go "it's not me, you haven't been following me for two years." She asked me if I was the Kurt Warner of the football team and I said "No, that's not me." She said, "Well, we love you anyway. " I get a lot of fantasy football league calls. Guys hanging around in the frat house basement daring one another to make the call. You can hear a lot of laughter in the background. They all say I really wish I'd picked you for my fantasy football team but I didn't and I'm kicking myself for it now, etc.

Actually I wish I'd kept the tapes of the different calls, but I've gotten twenty-five calls throughout the season and I've answered a few. One lady was a little scary. She called bout seven times; there were six consecutive messages on my machine. Then the phone rang that evening and I happened to be home and I picked it up and she didn't believe me when I told her I wasn't the Kurt Warner from the Rams. I finally convinced her and she said she was sorry and hung up. Then she called right back and said it didn't matter and did I want to come down and meet her for a drink.

Among people I know, it's kind of a joke. But when I go down to Kinko's to get my menu paper or something, everyone kinda looks when they call out my name. As far as everything else goes, people make a wisecrack about the fact that is my name. I've never met Kurt Warner and barely knew what he looked like. I have guys in my kitchen who tell me I should change the message on my answering machine to say, "I'll be away at the World Bowl or something." I told my kitchen guys that wouldn't be very bright because if he throws an interception or does something to lose the game, someone will look up my number and find my address and come by and shoot me on one of those days when I forget to shave. But it's been an interesting season.

Johnny Lattner, the 1953 Heisman Trophy winner from Notre Dame, didn't even lead the Irish in rushing or receiving.

IRONICALLY, THE LAST TIME I WAS IN SEATTLE IT WAS RAINING. GREAT WEATHER IF YOU'RE A CROP

CURT WARNER

Curt Warner was a great running back for the Seattle Seahawks after an outstanding college career at Penn State. For the last 10 years, he's been in the car business, the last five years as owner of Curt Warner Chevrolet in Vancouver, Washington, across the bridge from Portland, Oregon.

I first heard of Kurt Warner a couple of years ago when I was flipping through the television channels and caught an Arena Football game and heard the mention of his name. It's hard to tell from television how good a player might possibly be, but I'm delighted with the success he's had and I'm more delighted that he turned out to be an outstanding MVP football player rather than a serial murderer using the same name.

Do our customers know who I am or who the Rams' Kurt Warner is? Some of them ask our salespeople if I'm gone every weekend to play for the Rams so it's interesting to know that some of our customers either aren't real big sports fans or they're very colorblind.

Tony Dungy, Tampa Bay Coach, is the last NFL player to throw and make an interception in the same NFL game. He was a defensive back and backup quarterback for the Steelers

CEREAL IS LIKE CALIFORNIANS: TAKE AWAY THE FRUITS AND THE NUTS AND ALL YOU HAVE LEFT ARE THE FLAKES
MELISSA HEHER

PBL Sports, a food company in Pittsburgh, came out in the fall of 1999 with Warner's Crunch Time Cereal, which sold very well in the Missouri-Iowa area. Here's the story of how it happened.

PLB Sports started about four years ago by creating a food product for Jaromir Jagr of the Pittsburgh Penguins. We did a peanut butter product with him for kids 'cause we thought that would be a good complement. We put a black cap on the jar of peanut butter so it would look like a hockey puck which made the product unique on the shelf. The product sold about 150,000 units in the Pittsburgh area. We thought this did really well; let's try it again with a football player here in town.

So we started a line of condiments for Jerome Bettis which included barbecue, mustard, salsa. He has a whole line of foods through a local retailer here in the Pittsburgh market and those products also sold well so we decided to carry it outside the Pittsburgh area. We went to Cleveland and did a few products with a couple of the Cleveland Indians players. From that we signed Doug Flutie, of the Buffalo Bills, in July two years ago. He was a backup quarterback. The owner of the company, Ty Ballou, liked Doug Flutie and so we approached Doug Flutie about doing a cereal product with him. He said he would only do it if he could use it as an awareness builder and to raise money for the Doug Flutie Foundation for autism. We said sure and gave him the whole side panel of the box to describe the charity and we sold, over the past two years, 1.5 million boxes. It's also sold throughout the country over the Internet so anybody who wants the box can get a box.

They are over the two-million-dollar mark for the Doug Flutie Junior Foundation for Autism and some of that money came from Flutie Flakes but also fans wrote in and donated money as well. From Flutie Flakes, the company got quite a bit of notoriety and now we have 21 athletes under contract. Because of the Doug Flutie story, we liked how Doug was. You know he wasn't really built like a football player—a little bit shorter, didn't really get a chance in the NFL, then came back and had a great season.

We had seen Kurt Warner and were watching his story in St. Louis, so about the second week in October, we contacted his agency, Bartelstein and Associates out of Chicago, and approached them about doing a cereal with Kurt Warner. They went to Kurt at the time and Kurt was interested in doing the product as long as he could also raise money for his charity, Camp Barnabas. That's the charity where his son goes to camp and what he wants to do is build more camps in Missouri where the original camp is located so that all kids can go to camp in the summer and have that opportunity. We started selling the product in mid-November in Missouri and Iowa. We've sold half a million boxes already. The product is still selling great. We sell his product line over the Internet as well and it's doing quite well all over the country. We work with a company out of Wellsville, New York. It is a not-for-profit company that hires kids and adults who are mentally or physically challenged and they do all our fulfillment; a handicapped development center.

Kurt has been great to work with, he has been a great promoter of the cereal product. He actually picked a frosted flakes product as the product he eats, and he also helped come up with the name. He and his wife, Brenda, came up with Warner's Crunch Time and they also picked the design of the cereal box. He attended the sales calls we went on to a retailer in Missouri called Schnucks, and he went in and sold the product line to that retailer. We have a contract with him to use his name and likeness and he helped us do all those things.

Profits to charity speak volumes about him. He is very selfless. With the cereal sales, he is not keeping any of the money, he is sending it all to Camp Barnabas.

IT'S A SMALL WORLD...BUT I WOULDN'T WANT TO PAINT IT. BUT I WOULD IF DISNEY STOPPED PLAYING THAT STUPID SONG.
SUZY ABRAMS

Susy Abrams is Managing Editor of Sports at Walt Disney World in Orlando, Florida. Abrams is in charge of all Disney sports publicity including the IRL race, the golf tournaments, the Wide World of Sports complex, the Atlanta Braves spring training facility, and all other individual events throughout the year. Disney World is the home of the Amateur Athletic Union. Disney World is very protective of any information regarding trips that athletes, such as usually the MVP of the Super Bowl, take to the parks, each year. They attribute everything to "Disney Magic" and to "Disney Pixie Dust."

K urt Warner has already been at Disney World but we hope he'll go to Disneyland. It's all about Disney Magic; The Magical World of Disney works it all out.

Since 1987, Phil Simms was the first. We also did Dennis Conner and the America's Cup 1987; Magic Johnson, Lakers, 1987; Frank Viola with the Minnesota Twins World Series win in 1987.

1988: Super Bowl XXII with Doug Williams; Miss America 1988; World Series Orel Hershiser; Kareem Abdul-Jabbar, Lakers.

1989: Joe Montana; Al MacInnis, Calgary Flames, NHL; Joe Dumars NBA. 1990: Joe Montana; Graduation of Jim Thompson, Temple University; Matt Kaldenberg, Phyllis McEwen Kaldenberg and Laura McEwen of Simpson College, Indianola, Iowa.

1991: O.J. Anderson, Giants and Michael Jordan, NBA Bulls.

1992: Mark Rypien of Washington Redskins.

1993: Troy Aikman, Dallas Cowboys, Patrick Roy, Montreal Canadians.

1994: Emmitt Smith, Dallas Cowboys; Nancy Kerrigan, Olympics.

1995: Jerry Rice, Steve Young.

1996: Emmitt Smith.

1997: Desmond Howard. Santa Claus.

1998: John Elway, Denver Broncos; Mark McGwire.

1999: Terrell Davis, John Elway; Women's World Cup team.

2000: Kurt Warner.

There's no commemoration at the park to show who has been selected. Transportation type varies according to year, time, and how easy it is to get them down there. It's all decided by Disney Magic. Pixie Dust.

Typically, it would have to be someone that made a major impact. The Women's World Cup Team was historic. Mark McGwire – historic home-run record.

After the 1987 Super Bowl, quarterback Phil Simms was the first to say, "I'm going to Disneyland."

KEEP THE VOWELS COMING, VANNA...
'CAUSE YOU ONLY LIVE ONCE UNLESS
YOU'RE SHIRLEY MACLAINE
STEPHANIE PRITCHETT

Stephanie of Rolla, Missouri, reached a dream of many people in 1999 when she not only made the Wheel of Fortune *TV show, but she was a partner with Kurt Warner. Stephanie resides in Rolla with her husband, Jim. She is the head volleyball coach at Rolla High School and Jim is the head basketball coach.*

There were some auditions, more like a signup, for *Wheel of Fortune*, in Springfield, Missouri, in October 1999. About six thousand people signed up. Basically, they did a promotion through KY3 television in Springfield, about two hours from here. We signed up at Battlefield Mall there that day and we just waited. We were supposed to find out in a couple of weeks if our names had been drawn. We were told they would draw one hundred to one hundred fifty names out of all the people that had been there the night before and that day. I think they drew two hundred names, so my name got drawn.

Then we had to go back in the middle of November and go through an audition. We were divided into two groups – one hundred in the morning and one hundred in the afternoon. When we were there, they kept saying, "If you are an NFL fan or soap opera fan, write it down on your application." I didn't write anything down. I had been watching Kurt Warner. I'd seen him in a couple of interviews and thought he was really neat. Instead of being gung-ho for the Rams at that point, I just really liked him. But I still didn't write anything down. They narrowed it down to twenty people from that hundred. Basically, we had gone through like mock puzzles where at different times, different people stood up and they just kinda looked at how you presented yourself and how you reacted to things and just overall what you looked like. Then we took a puzzle test; you had to get as many puzzles as you could in five minutes. After that is when they whittled it down to twenty people. At that point they took a Polaroid picture of everybody up close and stapled it to your application. Then you talked about yourself for a couple of minutes – where you're from, what you did, just a little bit about "Wheel" or whatever you wanted to talk about for a couple of minutes just so they could kinda get to know you.

When I was talking, I said, "I am a football fan. I like football a lot. We watch it all the time, and we watch the Chiefs mainly but we've been watching the Rams. If I had to pick somebody to be on a show with, I would have to pick Kurt Warner because I just think he's really cool." I think I just said the right thing because they probably already had him picked. They told us we wouldn't find out for three weeks or so if we were even gonna be in the contestant pool. Right in the middle of October was when we first signed up, November 15 was the interviews and the Polaroid. I just said that it would be cool to go on with the NFL players. There wasn't a limit of how many would be picked; if everybody was good enough, out of that twenty, they'd pick everybody. They'd call you in two and a half weeks or so before your show aired. They would send a letter in a couple of weeks saying you were in the contestant pool so you could know that you would be called. They told us we probably wouldn't even get on until maybe up to a year or more because there are so many contestants for the shows so I wasn't expecting anything for a long time. I just thought, "Well, maybe in the next few months, I'll get a phone call."

In two days they called me and said, "We want you to come out and be on Wheel of Fortune and Kurt Warner's gonna be your partner." I was like, "Huh-uh, now who is this?" "This is so and so from *Wheel of Fortune*." I said, "No it's not. This is one of my husband's friends. You're just giving me a hard time." He goes, "No really." And he kept talking and about halfway through the phone call I said, "I'm really sorry, I'm gonna have to write a bunch of stuff down because I really thought you were just joking with me and I really didn't expect it this soon." He said, "Well, wait a minute I'll just read to you off your application." So he started reading down my application, and I said, "Now I really believe you." It's just amazing. It must have been a full minute or two to believe that it wasn't one of my husband's friends. By that time, when I realized I actually was going to be on the show, and be on with Kurt Warner, I really started listening intently. I was very excited but I thought, "I can't miss anything," because I just thought I'm gonna screw something up. My problem was when they called me they said we want you to come in two and a half weeks. I said, "I'm eight months pregnant. What do you think about that?" They said, "We know you are." I said, "Well, I'm gonna have to talk to my doctor because I don't know what he'll say about flying. I've never been in that situation so I don't know." I was going to the doctor the next day, so he said for me just to call him back. It was no problem. My doctor was like "You're fine, no problem at all." So the tape date was December 7. I was due January 7 so I thought, well, I was right on time or a little bit late with my first child so I wasn't really worried about it. And I felt fine. So we just started making plans from there. The guy from the *Wheel* told me some things like this is where people usually stay, and he told me the rate that they usually give and he gave me the phone number for the hotel. The downer to this *Wheel of Fortune* thing is when you go you have to pay for everything – airfare, hotel, the whole deal. You know when you go, if you don't win any money, that's too bad. You've had the experience of being on the show, I guess. So I knew that. We'd already decided, of course, that if I got called, I'd go.

> **My husband, Jim, was right in the middle of his season and that was tough because he had to decide whether he was gonna miss a game to go.**

My husband, Jim, was right in the middle of his season and that was tough because he had to decide whether he was gonna miss a game to go. The game was with St. James, which is about eight miles up the road and is a huge rivalry and he had to decide whether he needed to not be there for a few days. He made his decision pretty quickly; he wasn't going to miss seeing me on the show so we went together. People at his school were very cooperative and basically gave him the idea that this was a once-in-a-lifetime thing.

Actually, KY3 out of Springfield, when they heard that I was gonna be on, sent a guy named Ed Fillmer out to talk to me. So he came to my house and interviewed me about being on with Kurt Warner and just about the whole process. Then he did a couple of video stories on Kurt Warner, then he went to Los Angeles and taped what he could while we were there. He did a whole "follow you there and back" story on it and then when we did the "watch party," we had a bunch of people over to watch the show with us. We had a party while we watched it, and all my friends got to make fun of me and stuff like that. He came out and did a live interview with me and then they did a ten p.m. follow-up.

In California, we did some sightseeing. The next day, Tuesday, was *Wheel of Fortune*. And because it's NFL Week, we had to be there like 6:45 in the morning. Usually they start at around nine in the morning, when they don't have people flying in, I guess. The athletes were in season so

I guess they wanted to get them back as quickly as they could. Tuesday is basically an NFL off-day for them. So we took a shuttle over to the Sony Picture Studios.

Basically, it's just you and the other contestants because they don't let you have contact with anybody else until all the taping is over. We were really excited. We started meeting the other contestants and they were telling us who they were with and everything and it's pretty exciting because everybody is excited about being with their football players. We got there, and they went through some paperwork with us on rules and regulations. We didn't get to meet any of the football players then because they weren't there yet. They were coming later than we were. They had them in a different room, going over different stuff with them and getting their charities all worked out. So we did a few little practice things. There were sixteen contestants that day. One is an alternate and knows they are an alternate before they come. They are promised to be on another show by a certain date. The other fifteen of us were assigned to what show we would be on, then we drew numbers to see which position we'd be in on the stage. Then we went out and we spun the wheel to kind of familiarize ourselves with everything. The people who were helping us were super nice and they were explaining to us all the different things and where to look for the letter board and those kinds of things. We went back in and they did a few other things with us.

Actually I guess, the first time we were out there, some of the players came down. So that was about nine or nine thirty in the morning and Kurt was there at that point. He pretty much already knew who his partner was because I guess they had told him his partner was the one who was pregnant. I was the only one there that was pregnant so they didn't have to introduce us. Actually we were standing there and they said if you know who your partner is, go over and talk to them. So I'm like okay, so I just walked over to him and say "Hi Kurt, I'm Stephanie, and I'm your partner." I just introduced myself and he introduced himself and we just started chatting from there. I told him I really admired him and his witness and how neat that I just thought he was as far as his example for kids As coaches, my husband and I have a lot of contact with kids who need positive role models and when they see those people in such public places, and such an incredible story as his, then it's just encouraging to a lot of those kids. We talked about that for a while and then later on everybody practiced with their partners spinning the wheel and calling out letters and solving some puzzles. They had some mock puzzles up there and everybody went through them. He told me, "I'll spin the wheel the whole time and you call out all the letters." He said,

"Listen, I'm not gonna say anything. You know what you're doing." We would stand back there and he would say, "Oh, I know what it is" and he'd be solving it. I said, "You'd better tell me something – if you know what it is, you'd better be telling me what it is." This was when we were practicing and other people were spinning the wheel. We were kinda standing behind them. If he knew what it was, he'd say, "Okay." Or I'd say it, you know. I said, "Listen, if you know what it is you better be telling me what it is."

He's almost exactly the same size as my husband so I knew what to expect when I went in. He's just built different from my husband; he's 6'2" or so and a little bit thicker than my husband. He was just incredibly nice. While we were up there practicing he had on like a beige suit with a black turtleneck underneath it, and I had a purple shirt on and all of a sudden he said, "You know I've got a purple shirt. I could go change into it and then we could match." I was like, "Really!" He turned around and told the girl there that he was going to change his shirt. She was like, "Yeah," 'cause we were just practicing stuff then so he went and changed and he put on a purple turtleneck to match so that we would have the same colors on while we were out there.

He's just nice. His kids were there. His wife was not there because she was home with the baby but his other two children were there and they got to go down on stage and do some things. His little girl got her hair done by the makeup people. Everybody there was just super, super nice. After that we went back up in the stands and we had to wait; we were on the second show. They taped the first show before us. We were sitting in a place where all the contestants sit. It's in front of all the family members and friends. You can't even look at them. You can't turn around and look at your family members; you can't even talk

> **You can't have contact with anybody except the people who run the show and the other contestants.**

to them – nothing – because they want to make sure there's no cheating whatsoever of any kind. You can't have contact with anybody except the people who run the show and the other contestants. We were sitting there and I think actually the football players were back in the little room they had been in earlier. So we watched the first show. Then we had makeup touchup before our show was taped.

Then it was our turn. We were the first couple – standing right by Pat. I was not nervous at all – it was so exciting just to be there and so much fun and Kurt was very nice. We were introduced and we got to introduce our players. Then we got to spin and I can't remember all the little details of all the games, but we solved all four puzzles, none of the other people got any. You feel real bad because those people, you meet them through the day and talk to them, so you want everybody to win something because they had to pay their way, too. But you can't throw a game just because you want somebody else to win something. We got going at them; Kurt would hit "lose a turn" and he'd turn around and apologize to me. I'm like it's really okay. It came back around to us, and we would talk back and forth. The first round was a puzzler round, and I solved the puzzle and then I solved the puzzler so we got like four thousand dollars on that round. The second round, we both knew it; we had been talking back and forth so I solved that one. I think we got five thousand something for that one. The third round we both knew, too, and I think we got four thousand for that round.

So now we got to the fourth round, which ended up being the final round 'cause time was running out. Pat Sajak had to spin and he hit the five thousand dollar mark. We wished it would have been one thousand dollars because at that time we had eleven thousand dollars so this meant that someone could hit two letters and beat us 'cause there was also a thousand dollar bonus per letter. So actually every letter was worth six thousand dollars. So we didn't know if it was good or bad. We started. I guessed an N; there was no N. The next lady guessed an S, and got twelve thousand dollars but she couldn't solve the puzzle. The next lady guessed and got six thousand dollars but she couldn't solve either. It was a three-word puzzle and the category was "Around the House." At that time there were only three letters up on the board. After the second lady had guessed, Kurt leaned over and said I know it. I was like "Oh, my gosh!" He said, "It's 'chest of drawers.'"

Now it's time for the bonus round, my husband came down. He had told me earlier. "Now you have to win the bonus round because that's the only way I'm gonna get to meet Kurt Warner." So he came down, we had to turn and face the back wall. He had to turn, too, 'cause they wouldn't let us make eye contact or anything. So we turned back around and they put our category up there. It was Event, seven letters, one word, and it had the first and last letters – R and N. Pat was joking around with me, and I said to him, "Kurt knows what these puzzles are; he's just not saying anything." Sajak goes, "We're gonna make sure that people know that." When we got down there, Pat said to Kurt, "Now Stephanie told me that you're telling her stuff." He goes, "Well I'm just trying to do my little part," and kinda smiled. So I guessed an M, a P, a C, and an I.

There wasn't any of those up there. You get fifteen seconds or something, and we just stood there the whole time. I just was like, "I have no clue." We kept looking over to the letter board to try to give us some ideas; it could have been anything. We both had thought of reunion but I knew it couldn't be reunion because of the letters that were already up there, and he said it kinda right after the buzzer sounded but it couldn't be that. So then Pat said it's not much of an event, but it's "rubdown." The whole place just went "o-o-o-h!" And all my friends, it's hilarious because I wouldn't tell anybody what any of the puzzles were, because when they saw the show, I wanted them to have to solve them. So the last puzzle everybody was calling me, "I can't believe that's an event. That is not an event. I would just be hacked...." Well you know, I won $23,000 so I'm not too hacked.

Had we solved the bonus round we would have won a golf trip package to Hawaii for like seven days or something. It wasn't that big a deal because we would have had to pay taxes on it, and it was a trip we might not have even been able to take because of our schedules and we don't play golf, but it would have given Kurt 17 or 18 thousand more dollars for Camp Barnabas, the charity of his choice. If it had been one of the other prizes, like a Tahoe trip worth like $40,000, that would have been fine, or the $25,000 would have been great. We weren't too upset. It was just our competitiveness. We wanted do it all – I wanted to solve all the puzzles. Just not knowing that one just kinda drives you crazy.

I felt so sorry for the other people. I was like maybe I ought to write them a check or something for five hundred dollars to cover their expenses. Cause like I said, we had talked to them all day and I just hated that they didn't win anything. Some other players were Marvin Harrison from the Colts, Tony Brackens of the Jaguars, Rocket Ismail of the Cowboys. After our show we had gone back to a room for a bunch of interviews. It was kinda dark because they had brighter lights shining on certain people. There was this guy standing there. He gives me a high five and says, "Man, you're awesome, that's so cool." I'm like, I had to look at his name tag cause I could hardly see him – just his hair. I said, "Thanks." That was Rocket. He was really nice. I did talk to him and a little bit to the other two who were on our show. Others I saw but didn't get to talk to were Dick Butkus, Kevin Greene, Franco Harris, Jon Kitna from the Seahawks, a kicker from the Broncos, Jason Elam.

My husband Jim did not get to meet Kurt. Only if you win will they let your spouse come down on the stage to be with you. So we didn't win, and they ushered him right back up in the stands. Then, of course, Kurt had to leave so he didn't get to meet him after. I think his plane left at three, so he left after all the interviews and stuff. We just said goodbye to each other and at that point I said, "I didn't get your autograph; I didn't get anything." He said, "Well send me a letter." And so we did send him a tape of all the KY3 coverage up to that point that we had just taped off the VCR and put *Wheel of Fortune* real big on it so maybe he'd see that one and be able to open it. But like he said, he hadn't opened any of his mail, and that was the beginning of December so I have no idea whether he's even seen any of our stuff yet. So KY3 ended up sending him a copy of all the stuff too so he has a clean copy of all of it. So he will get to see the interviews they did with me and the interview they did with him and they highlighted Camp Barnabas in the interviews they did with him. So he had to leave on a three o'clock flight after we did all our interviews and everything. The one thing we did have to do, that nobody will ever see, that was kinda funny the big winner for the week. Whoever won the most for all five shows, got a super package with like a trip to the Super Bowl, tickets to a party with the players and like this big Sega video package of game sets with several sports games, expensive jackets from players, etc., and all this stuff. We were in the running for that until the next show – a girl won like $27,000 in the next show.

They took promo shots of everyone for their station affiliates where you were from and then they also needed shots for whoever the big winner turned out to be. There was this big package so they wanted to get a celebration between the two people. They did it for everybody in case you won. If you won, they put that on. Kurt and I did the Bob and Weave, the dance that Rams linemen do in the end zone after a touchdown. Here I am eight months pregnant, and didn't even know what I was doing, so we're doing the Bob and Weave and just laughing. I didn't know whether he was any good or not; only since then have I really paid attention to how the Rams really do it so I knew what it was. Now I'm like, "Oh, I should have done it like that." They never had to show that 'cause we didn't win.

Before I left home to go to California to tape the show, I was pretty much like, **"I'm going on 'Wheel of Fortune!' with Kurt Warner!"** Everybody's all jealous. They said they wanted to give me a jersey or whatever for him to sign. I said, "Listen, I am not going to have time to take all your stuff and get autographs." The way they had it set up, I didn't even have a chance to get myself anything. There was no way I would have been able to get them anything. KY3 did a story – that was on Tuesday – on Wednesday they did a story about me actually going out there. That's when they put my interview on. Well, at the end of that story, the news anchor said, "I have the results in from this; she won – and he said like $26,000. Well, they had told me that they were gonna tell people how much I won. I told them all, "I wish you wouldn't tell them anything because I want them to be surprised when they see it." Well they said $26,000 which was an overestimation there. So then everybody was, "We heard you won $26,000."

I was pretty much inundated from then on out and I told people, "I feel sorry for people like Kurt Warner or anyone who is a major celebrity because you know they have to just be completely bugged by people all the time for autographs or just to have a little piece of Kurt Warner." Because even in my town, Rolla has about 15,000 people, plus then my parents told everybody in the world, Jim's parents told everybody in the world. After that point, I'm a big celebrity in Rolla. I was going, "Guys, I was just on one little game show. The most fun thing was being on with Kurt Warner." But people knew then, and our sportswriter put a couple of little things in the paper about "Santa was good to the Pritchetts."

Kurt was just like a lot of my friends. I have a lot of great friends, and their lives are all very focused and their lives are committed to Christ and when I met him, it was like, "We could have been friends." The funny thing about it is I played volleyball at Southwest Missouri State University in Springfield (SMS), and he played football at Northern Iowa, and they're in the same conference. So our biggest rival every year was Northern Iowa. And so we talked for a little while about Northern Iowa. He knew the volleyball coach at UNI. I was just asking if he was still there and things like that. I'm two years older than him and we were in college at the same time. It's funny because he could have been somebody I went to school with that made it big in the NFL. He's just so down to earth and it was fun, just a neat experience. Someone that you can look at and go, "Man this guy is an incredible quarterback and I know him."

I talked to some of the kids at school before I left. They said, "He's really good, he's really cool." I haven't had a chance to talk to a lot of them because I haven't been back at school since I had my baby January 9 and his name is Joshua. At the January 25 party at our house, at our church we have a praise band and I sing in that so I had all of them over plus our pastor and his wife and it was pretty fun. I know some pretty crazy people.

What I think is neat about Kurt and the whole situation, too is that I saw incredible coverage of a lot of other positive and Christian athletes this year than I've ever seen before. It seemed like maybe it was just a coincidence, but it all started to center around Kurt. When his story came out, it just seemed like there was a lot more media attention drawn to athletes of that caliber. The *St. Louis Post-Dispatch* had a story about Marshall Faulk and Isaac Bruce and some other Christian players on the team, so I just think he's where he's at for a reason. I just think it's awesome.

I told my husband a couple of weeks ago, "I admire Kurt so much." Because he could let all this go to his head. He's had the most incredible season probably that anybody's ever had – coming from nothing to everything. And he still acts like it's no big deal that's; the way it's supposed to be. Every time he turns around he gives glory to God. It's not like he can't believe it. It's just been so neat and so uplifting and I am just so excited that I can even be a part of it – just to say that I actually met this guy and talked to him for a few hours and we won twenty three thousand dollars. I mean if he hadn't gone through anything, if he had just stepped out of college as one of the best quarterback in the United States and comes and plays and is one of the best quarterbacks in the United States in professional football, maybe you could say something a little different but I mean he's gone through everything. His faith has held him up in a lot of bad times, a lot of hard times, not just with football but with his family and then I just don't see that. His fame and glory is really grounded by a lot of other things that have happened before this one year by Kurt Warner, regardless.

The Cinderella story that it is – I was amazed to listen to Boomer Esiason on the Super Bowl, just a lot of those announcers are enamored by him. The first couple of weeks these guys were "Well this guy's doing really good." Then he just never stopped, never stopped, never stopped, and by the end of the season it's like, "This guy is so for real." And they were saying what a Cinderella story it is and I just think people like the assistant coach for my husband at first he was like Trent Green would prob-

More NFL games have been played at Wrigley Field than at any other stadium in the country. Mile High Stadium in Denver is in second place.

ably be doing the same thing, and what are they gonna do next year, are they gonna have to trade Warner, what are they gonna do? And of course the whole time I'm going, "No way, they're keeping him." By halfway through the season and getting toward the end of the season, he was saying, "There's no way they can trade Warner." I'm like, "No kidding." First of all they'd have a mutiny in St. Louis if that would happen. That was before he was named MVP and all that kind of stuff. I think people are just loving the story anyway just because it is such a "come-from-nothing and work-your-tail-off" and so, of course, I think this book will be great for that whole aspect of it. I think people who know about his faith are gonna buy the book just for that. And people who don't know about it aren't gonna be put off by it because it's so true.

Kids notwithstanding, sports people in general, it doesn't matter, are searching for something like that. It's so incredible. You can see all kinds of examples of everything else in the world anytime you look outside. Every time you watch a football game you're gonna see the guy that's losing his temper and cussing somebody out or doing whatever and I think it's refreshing for a lot of people to see the kind of example that Kurt sets. I think people are searching to see what makes him different than these other guys who are out here doing this or that. I think it's great, and I think it's gonna be a good book.

I don't know when I will get my money from *Wheel of Fortune*. They said it would be two weeks to four months after the show aired and it's been less than a month. So I'm just waiting patiently for the check to come in. We're gonna buy a new computer and get set up on the Internet 'cause we don't have that. I stay home with our kids so we live on my husband's income basically. Our computer's really old so we'll get a computer with Internet. From there, I think we decided I'm gonna buy some new clothes and probably put the rest of it in savings until we can decide what the best thing to do with it is. I know that the first ten per cent, anyway, off the top will go to our church and then other than that it's just gonna.....we have some people we support in different ministries that we decided we'd send a little bit of extra money to. Other than that, it's just deciding where we need to use it the most.

> The Rose Bowl parade originally had nothing to do with the Rose Bowl football game. It was a celebration in Pasadena for the ripening of the oranges.

FURTHERMORE, I THINK THE WASHINGTON GENERALS ARE DUE
TOM MOSES

Tom Moses is a day trader from Tempe, Arizona, and a lifelong Rams fan.
He watches the Rams at Ray O'Sullivan's Bar in Mesa, Arizona.

Kurt Warner's aunt was always there at O'Sullivans. Channel 15, the Phoenix ABC affiliate for the Super Bowl, came in and did a piece on her and they also came to me and said we want to do a piece on you. I'm a big Rams fan – have been a Rams fan forever. Before the season began, I put $100 on the Rams to win the Super Bowl at odds of two hundred to one.

I bought the ticket the day Trent Green went down. I was in Las Vegas at the Imperial and later that day I heard that Trent Green had gone down. I thought Bum Dog! I didn't even know who Kurt Warner was – knew he was on the roster. I put down a hundred bucks on the Rams, like I always have done. Every year I put a hundred dollars down on the Rams to win the Super Bowl – whatever the odds are. I started that back when Jim Everett got happy feet and just played the ticket. And every year I throw away the ticket about the end of September!

This was the greatest football season I've ever had – absolutely the greatest football season ever. I'm a Rams fan. I've lived with the worst record in the decade so this was the greatest football season I've ever had. Kurt Warner, I got to say, he's my hero. He is.

I hedged my bet – I feel bad about it but I hedged the bet. I had two hundred to one odds and knew if the Rams were gonna win, I would win twenty thousand dollars. The day before the Super Bowl, I went to Las Vegas and put three thousand three hundred dollars on Tennessee, plus seven points, to hedge my bet. So whoever won, I was either gonna win $3,000 or $16,600 on a hundred dollar bet. My friend, Greg, gave me the idea to do that. On Thursday we were at the Phoenix Open and he said, "You know what, if the Rams win you win $20,000 for your hundred dollars, but if you also bet on the Titans, you're guaranteed to win." Actually people were getting up a collection to give me $10,000.00 to go up and put $10,000.00 on it. If I had put $10,000 on it, I was assured of winning ten thousand either way. And the weird part is I was gonna take my own ten thousand but when I went down to get the ten thousand, Charles Schwab's office was closed because they were moving the Charles Schwab's office from Mesa out to Superstition Springs so I couldn't get the ten thousand myself. Anyway I hedged, I put $3,000 on Tennessee to win plus seven, and that pushed. I got my three grand back, and I collected the $20,000.

I've just been throwing it away. Ninety per cent I'll spend on wine, women, and song and the other ten per cent I'll waste. I'm a really happy guy.

I watched the Super Bowl at O'Sullivans, because on the very first Sunday of the NFL season, I came in there, and they wouldn't let me watch the Rams games on any of the big-screen TVs. They made me watch it on one little TV in the corner. I said, "Come on Ray." But they wouldn't put it on. So me and three Ram guys watched the game on one little corner TV. By the end of the season, we had sixty people in here and at the conclusion of the Super Bowl, we smashed the little TV that Ray made us use to watch the Ram games earlier in the season.

In the 1979 baseball draft, the Kansas City Royals drafted high school baseball standouts Dan Marino and John Elway

Women buy 70 percent of all NFL merchandise and 44 percent of all major-league baseball merchandise.

I CALLED THE CLINIC ABOUT MY CASE AND THEY SAID THAT I'M OVER MY SHYNESS
RANDY GIBSON

The 1999 NFL season was a dream come true for Randy Gibson, who watched most Rams games at Paddy O'Rourke's bar in Cedar Rapids, Iowa.

I have been a Rams fan since I was a kid – all my life. I'll be 38 soon so I was an L.A. Rams fan and still have some shirts that say "L.A. Rams" on them. What's funny is, I was born and raised in Cedar Rapids. So to win the Super Bowl with a quarterback from Cedar Rapids – you can imagine it's ironic.

There were some Rams fans in Cedar Rapids before Kurt Warner played for them, but you never ran into them. We have the Bears, the Packers, the Vikings, the Chiefs – I mean the whole nine yards. Obviously, once the Rams started doing well, they all came out. But to watch the games there in the back room was the most incredible season I've ever been through. We watched the first two at another bar, then all the rest at O'Rourke's.

It was incredible. A year ago, when Kurt Warner made the Rams as a backup quarterback, I was excited about it. I watched him play Arena Football in Des Moines. I've got some years on Kurt, but just the fact that he's a Cedar Rapids boy that had even made the team. We both went to Regis High School, but nine years apart. There were two high schools in town, but they have now blended into one, Xavier. I thought he's going to be the backup – that was great! Then Trent Green gets hurt and Boom – here he comes. I'll tell you what – I had all the confidence in the world in him because I had seen him play and I knew that if he had his chance he would make it go. So where they ended up going is incredible!

When his Mom didn't actually go to the games, she would come down to the bar and watch it with us. She's a super lady, and I met a lot of great, great people who were there to watch Kurt Warner play football. They were there for that simple fact, which was fine. And it made my season that much better because I had all these people who wanted to watch the Rams play football.

When they scored a touchdown, I would run through the bar and high five everybody from the back room to the front room, that sort of thing. I did a lot of high fives. I actually went to St. Louis the weekend after Thanksgiving and watched them play the Saints. The first half wasn't so good and I was a little nervous.

Kurt Warner is not just a flash in the pan, so to speak. He's for real. I guarantee you, he's for real. It's incredible! It's awesome! I don't know what else to say if you are a die-hard, since you were a kid, Rams fan. I remember the 1980 Super Bowl, with the Steelers, we were ahead at halftime and lost 31 to 19. After all these years, could it happen again? Can it happen again? And for it to happen, the way it happened, and I'm from Cedar Rapids and quarterback that took them all the way there is from Cedar Rapids, it's simply incredible. I don't know how else to describe it.

I've got friends here, and I got dogged for years for being a Rams fan. Now we win the Super Bowl with a quarterback who's from Cedar Rapids. It's simply incredible. I'm still on that cloud nine. I don't want to sound like I'm at a loss for words but I have no idea what to say. It's crazy! It's awesome!

The Los Angeles Rams were the first NFL team to wear helmets with a logo. The logo was designed by a player, Fred Gehrke. The Cleveland Browns are the only team with no logo.

Chapter 12

Mike Monson

Paul Charchian

Matt Pitzer

Scott Kelnhoffer

Jeff Rosenberg

Ya Gotta
Have a Hobby

IT'S ALL IN THE CARDS. AT LEAST IT WAS IN 1982.
MIKE MONSON, Pacific Trading Cards, Inc.

W hat happened was well before the preseason even started. We were putting together what's typically our most popular football card set. It's called 1999 Pacific Football. We wanted to include as many NFL players as we could. We wanted to include as many of them as had never appeared on a card as we could and it just so happened there was a player named Kurt Warner who none of us were real familiar with but we realized that we had couple of photographs of him available. We realized he had never been on a card before. There were 450 cards in the set. We said, "Okay, we're gonna give one of the spots to this guy named Kurt Warner. This was well before the season started – probably late June. Preseason starts, Ram starter gets injured. We thought, "Hey this guy Warner's gonna play. We'll see what he's all about." Sure enough he starts, and they start winning – I think six straight. Pretty soon they are six and zero and people are starting to say, "Wow, what about this guy's card?" After a couple of months people realized he only has one NFL football card – a single football card. Here this guy's six and zero and it's his first time ever to appear on a card. Pretty soon people start going crazy for it.

In June when the set was first released, Kurt Warner's card was considered a common card. A common card sells for fifteen cents – five to fifteen cents is probably more accurate. As he started winning, people pretty soon started paying attention to his cards. Card collectors said, "We need to start finding some of this guy's cards." Pretty soon it went to a couple of dollars – then on and on and on. By the time they reached the playoffs, people are paying an average of forty-five to fifty dollars a card. For about five months, it was his only card on the market. It takes so long once you decide to put a player in a set – from inception to the time it's actually shipped and the collectors can open the package – you figure it takes four or five months. So we were able to enjoy a four- or five-month period where our Kurt Warner rookie card was the only one on the market. The interesting thing about this card is you've got people wanting it 'cause Kurt Warner was an incredible NFL quarterback. It didn't have an autograph on it, it didn't have anything else, it was just a regular main set football card. It's a very pure thing – they didn't want it 'cause they were speculating his autograph might go up in value. It doesn't feature an autograph. By the time the playoffs rolled around, other companies had been able to produce some Kurt Warner cards, but the thing that was really interesting was that this Pacific rookie card was so ingrained in collectors and football fans minds, it WAS his only rookie card. To this day it continues to be his only card that really is important to collectors. We just got back from the Super Bowl Card Show where everybody reminded us of that fact, which was terrific, it was really exciting. Even *USA Today* did a story on it. It was pretty exciting – lots of television coverage in the St. Louis area. Pretty neat. In fact, even Kurt was kind enough to do some interviews with trading card magazines to talk about his card.

He's real humble and real down to earth about it and about all his success. The thing that is just so "over-the-top" about Kurt 's rookie card. In fact, a few minutes ago I went on eBay just to check the status of what his card is doing on the secondary market 'cause it's just fascinating.

The thing that's amazing is that a couple of months ago, it was a five- or fifteen-cent card.

The PSA grading process is what they've done with coins for years. When someone goes to sell a card or, especially these days with the Internet, there's a secondary and impartial party, a company called the PSA, who takes a card and puts it under the microscope. Okay, out of a ten which would be perfect, this one's a nine or nine and a half or this is a ten or a one, ten being best. The Pacific Kurt Warner rookie cards that people have had graded by the PSA Co. that have been ten out of ten have just been astonishing. I just printed out some information off eBay today that gives you the best mirror of what collectors are paying at this very moment for an item. There's a PSA 10 which means it is considered a perfect specimen that went for $670. The thing that's amazing is that a couple of months ago, it was a five- or fifteen-cent card. When you do the math and figure out how many times this card has increased in value on the secondary market, it's astonishing. Then he was named League MVP, and then named the Super Bowl MVP. The guy has just kept his poise the entire time. He's been super humble – very likeable. And he's also very much a winner – he's very confident. I can't remember a more popular rookie card in the last decade – whether it's football, baseball or hockey or otherwise. I think over time, Ken Griffey Jr.'s rookie card is the only one I can compare it to. That's a phenomenal comparison – Ken Griffey Jr. is one of the biggest sports names in the world. Here's Kurt Warner after one year – his rookie card has been as popular as anything I have seen in the last ten years.

It's called a rookie card because his first year, in 1998, he did not have any cards produced. 1999 was not his rookie football season, but it is his rookie card. It's his first NFL card.

Media calls have been incredible. It's been an incredible journey for us, as well. Typically, when we feel like we've done something innovative or something special the world needs to know about, I'll call them and try to inform them and say, "This is something worth covering – worth your time." I've been receiving calls from *USA Today*, HBO Sports, name the media outlet in St. Louis and I've talked to them about this card. It's been unbelievable. It's been unbelievable. I've received...it's hard for me to put into words how much interest there has been in this. It's unprecedented for Pacific Trading Cards.

About the second week, when the Rams went 2 and 0, we realized we had the only card. We realized that the program that we have been committed to since we started making NFL cards in 1991 was working, that's what we realized. It has always been the case with Pacific Trading Cards that we were going to include as many NFL players as we could in our product. We always have included players that had not had the opportunity to appear on cards before. For example, Jon Kitna, the Seattle Seahawks quarterback – only rookie card in 1997

Here the Rams had gone 2 and 0, and people started saying, "Hey, did you guys make a card of Kurt Warner?" And sure enough, we did! We also looked into what else was out there and found there's nothing else out there. This is amazing. This is interesting. He's 2 and 0! Let's see what happens. By the time the Rams went 6 and 0 we were so firmly established as the company to produce his only card, we knew no matter what came after us, we had really set ourselves apart.

I don't know if this will cause companies to begin taking pictures of every guy who wears a uniform. There are only so many cards in every set, so you might do your best to include a whole bunch of guys who haven't been on a card before. But there's always going to be – a little bit of luck is involved too, but it was mostly a continuation of what we've been doing in the past which is including a Jon Kitna or Charlie Batch. Kurt Warner falls into that category, too. Had photos available and said, "Yeah, let's do it," and you never know. Because what we always say when we put these guys in, "Yeah, let's get him in, that'll be great. 'Cause he's never had a card before." But it wasn't until about two weeks into the season, we realized we really do have the only card on this guy on the market. Unbelievable! It has meant a lot to our company. It's not just Kurt Warner's card. It's more than that. It's a number of factors that work in unison to create the interest in this card. You take the fact that there are very few in circulation and it isn't easy to get your hands on one because you have to do your homework, find one, and pay top dollar when you do find one. Then you have Kurt Warner performing at MVP level – both regular-season and at the Super Bowl, and he started in the Pro Bowl. You have that working. The third factor is Kurt Warner off the field. Kurt Warner is probably the finest example of a pro athlete – what you would want a pro athlete to be off the field. He is the ultimate gentleman, family man, father, husband. He's likeable, he's honest, confident, survivor, all the intangibles you cannot coach somebody to have off the field. He is the most respectable decent human being that the sports world has had to view off the field in a long time. At least I think he is. The fact that this company had his only rookie card just makes it that much more special to us, but even that aside, I think it's one of the greatest – if not the greatest – sports story ever.

It was tremendous in Atlanta at the Super Bowl where we set up our corporate booth at the NFL Experience Card Show. They give us booth space. Just about everybody there had on Titans uniform stuff and Rams outfits. Whether they were rooting for the Rams or the Titans, of all the fans that approached our booth to view our cards, at least half of them said, "Boy you guys did that Kurt Warner right this year, didn't you?" At least half the people mentioned it to us. It's very difficult to have it be so widely known in the trade that you have done this or that. There's so many different brands and lots of manufacturers, so how do you stand out above all the rest where most people recognize you as the company who did this or did that? Only with this spectacular story could something like that happen.

So we love Kurt Warner. Aside from his card we are just big fans of him on the field and, as a person, off the field, too. We could use many more like him as fans and as sports card collectors. It's exciting to know that such a person can succeed at the absolute highest level and dominate the entire league but he's never out there pounding his chest and things like that. He's so poised and Kurt Warner's confidence is so evident on his face even in the Super Bowl when the Titans were making that run in the second half. Kurt Warner's facial expression never changed. You can see the confidence. He wasn't yelling or screaming when he scored or when the Titans were making that run and it looked like the momentum was changing; still the same guy. He stayed healthy the whole year, which is uncommon as well. It just seems like everything he touches turns to gold – finally. I couldn't be happier. We could use him in every sport. He's been a real pleasure. We've had a very special player come to the forefront. I don't know that we'll ever see another one like him.

Quarterback Brad Johnson, who started more games at Florida State in basketball than he did in football, is the only NFL quarterback in history to complete a touchdown pass to himself.

I LIVE IN THE TWIN CITIES, BUT IF I MOVED TO THE QUAD CITIES, I'D BE TWICE AS WELL OFF.
PAUL CHARCHIAN

Publisher, Fantasy Football Weekly *magazine, the best-selling fantasy sports title, headquartered in Minnetonka, Minnesota.*

We hold a fantasy football convention every August. The key note speaker is Chris Mortensen of ESPN. The Trent Green injury happened that same weekend of our fantasy football expo held in the Twin Cities, the biggest fantasy sports event in the country. There are more fantasy players in that place than at any other time of the year. It was a Saturday night that Trent Green went down for the year. Most of us knew Kurt Warner by name but that was it. I remember on Sunday morning, Chris Mortensen was our first speaker and he started to talk a little bit about Kurt Warner. Basically, he said we don't have anything on this guy and it probably means that what would look like a successful season or maybe a rebound season for the Rams is probably over. We assumed they had to go look elsewhere for a different quarterback. Mortensen listed off some names, Mark Rypien and Jeff Hostetler came to mind, and I think some others, transient quarterbacks. Nobody really had any faith, obviously, in Kurt Warner. Nobody could have possibly known. Even for somebody of Chris Mortensen's stature, at the time of the injury, nobody saw it coming. I think people assumed that the team would have to go elsewhere for a new starting quarterback. I can recall from a fantasy perspective that even after Warner had a great first week of the season, there were still a lot of doubters. In fact, within our own league here, made up entirely of fantasy football editors, reporter, writers, we have a bidding process by which you pick people up. Everybody vies for different people. In week two, when one of our editors picked up Kurt Warner, when he found out he actually had the high bid on him, he was so upset that he had gotten stuck with Kurt Warner at this high bid, he spent two days complaining and groaning and moaning because he had just spent too much money on Kurt Warner.

We heard a lot of stories. Almost nobody drafted Kurt Warner. He'd had a reasonably good preseason, but he was almost undrafted in all but the biggest of the leagues. Everybody had stories about how they traded for him early on. How did you win your league? "I picked up Kurt Warner in week one." "Or, I picked up Kurt Warner in week two." "Or I traded for Kurt Warner before he really took off." It was a real strange football season. He was easily the strangest part of it. He was the guy that turned bad teams into good teams.

The guy in our office who had complained so bitterly about having gotten "stuck with Kurt Warner" ended up having his best season ever! Obviously two or three weeks later we ended up razzing him for even having the nerve to be upset about having paid what ended up being so little in our auction system for Kurt Warner. Fantasy Football is all about bragging rights. So for the rest of the season, we had to hear about "how only he knew to bid, in our case, thirty mythical dollars" on Kurt Warner. Even though it was the same thirty mythical dollars he was hitting himself for having spent within a day of having found out he got him. He was in a blind pool – a blind bidding process for determining free agents. I don't know for sure why he bid as much as he did, that's the way it works. When you get anxious and you need a quarterback, you know. In fact, he had Vinnie Testaverde, the Jets quarterback who went out in the first game of the season. Vinnie was not an injury-prone quarterback prior to this so all of a sudden he didn't have an adequate backup so he was really just picking Kurt Warner up out of desperation. Look what happened.

We've just completed year seven; this is year eight for the magazine. I've been playing for many more years than that. Boy, certainly from the perspective of there's never been a Kurt Warner – in early August, nobody knew his name and he went out and threw forty touchdowns – there's never, ever been anything close to what he's done. No player has ever exceeded the possibility, even the forecast of what he could have

Fantasy leagues are often called rotisserie leagues.
Rotisserie was the name of the restaurant in
New York City where Daniel Okrent and friends
dreamed up the concept during a luncheon meeting in the '70s.

achieved, more than he has. In terms of a statistical sense, and obviously as it turns out in almost every sense of what you could look at. There have obviously been players who have had better seasons, but you knew going in the possibility was there. So as far as I'm concerned, his story is probably the most interesting and compelling fantasy football story that we've ever covered here.

Some other significant events come to mind. Dan Marino's second season, he'd already had a very successful rookie year, but he had an enormous second season. I think he threw forty-eight touchdowns. I'm not a very good historical stat guy. Emmitt Smith had a 26-touchdown season, which for a running back, is insane. Jerry Rice's consistency over his career. But this, as a single season event, ranks certainly among the top three or so stories in the history of the league as far as I'm concerned. Going back as far as fantasy football has really been played, going back 20 years, I don't know of anything else like this.

How did this publication start? I'm from Minneapolis and went to school at the University of Minnesota, and had a journalism degree which was going unused, and I've always been a fantasy football player. A friend and I thought we were missing a chance here. We felt there was a need for the magazine. We knew we would buy it if one was out there. So we put out the first weekly fantasy football magazine and remain the only weekly fantasy football magazine that has since spawned a television show, radio show, and Web site. We just finished a poll showing thirty million fantasy players in America, 70 per cent of which play football – twenty-one million – that's a lot of people playing. We're just providing a service to those people, and thankfully the market's there. We used Warner only once on the cover of our magazine. If we could have gotten away with it, I'd have wanted him three times. On the cover this preseason, we're gonna use Edgerrin James, in part because of the amount of exposure Kurt Warner got for the Super Bowl. I don't want to say he's passe after one season – the exposure level is so high – throwing an Edgerrin James cover out will seem a little bit more different to our guys. Steve Sabol said Warner is the greatest story in the history of football, and coming from him that's really significant. I've only been doing this for eight years, but have obviously been a fan all my life, and I can't remember anything like this.

I CAN'T JOIN A ROTISSERIE LEAGUE BECAUSE I'M ALLERGIC TO CHICKEN
MATT PITZER

Matt Pitzer is in charge of all fantasy sports leagues for Sporting News. *He also has been a fantasy football writer for two of his three years at the* Sporting News.

From a fantasy perspective, the first couple of weeks were prob ably similar to what most fans around the league were thinking. Warner put up a couple of good games to start the year and it was kinda like, "Well, this guy's doing good but it's probably just a fluke and he'll crash back down to reality here pretty soon." And he wound up just being a phenomenal success week in and week out. He was one of those guys for Fantasy Football you could count on every week for three hundred yards, two or three touchdowns and players like that are very rare. I think of Terrell Davis the last couple of years and Warner this year. There are usually only one or two guys like that in the league every year who can carry your fantasy team week in and week out and he wound up being that man. The amazing thing about it is that he probably was not drafted in most leagues. We are talking about the Rams here so fantasy players weren't all too excited about them before the season when they were drafting their teams. Trent Green had generated some excitement just because of the way he was playing preseason. Isaac Bruce was playing well.

Maybe the Rams offense would be better so maybe Trent Green would be worth a shot. When he goes down, forget about Kurt Warner. Let's go find a quarterback somewhere else. To the fantasy players who had Trent Green, the logical replacement for Trent Green was not Kurt Warner. So you got a couple of weeks into the season and Kurt started picking up some good stats. They were all scrambling to pick him off the waiver wire, which makes his story even that much more phenomenal. A guy like that who produces like he does should be the first guy picked in the draft, not some guy to be picked off waivers the third week. The difference between the Cleveland Browns not picking him up in the expansion draft and the fantasy players is that, for the most part, fantasy players don't have the opportunity to actually see him practice.

We sponsor a fantasy game which our users can sign up and pay to play. Most of the major media companies decide to do that, ESPN.com , CBS Sportsline, CNNSI, Fox Sports. They all have similar type games where you sign up and pay to play. During the week I write about who I think will do well in the coming week. On Sunday I write a recap of that week's action.

The quarterback might get one point for every fifty yards passing, five point bonus for every one hundred yards; a running back might get one point for every ten yards rushing and a five-point bonus if he gets one hundred yards. Field-goal kickers get three points for a field goal and one for an extra point. You draft a defensive team and then you get points based on their production from their defense and their special teams. If the defense picks up a fumble and runs it in they get six points for that score. A safety is two points. If they shut a team out you get points for that. Typical starting lineup is a quarterback, two running backs, two wide receivers, a tight end, kicker, and defense/special team.

Say you have Kurt Warner and Troy Aikman, you don't even think about it, you play Kurt Warner every week.

And you have backups at all those positions on the bench. So if you don't have an obvious starter every week you make a decision each week on who to start based on how you think those players will do in their games the upcoming Sunday. When you have a guy like Kurt Warner, you don't even think about whether you should start him. Say you have Kurt Warner and Troy Aikman, you don't even think about it, you play Kurt Warner every week.

The way Fantasy Football works is that a group gets together, 10 or 12. They draft their own fake team comprised of real NFL players; you track their statistical performance throughout the entire season. Most weeks, not all, most have it set up so each participant is actually playing somebody else in the league—actually playing. So for any particular Sunday, if my guys add up to better numbers than your guys then I win the game that week. The primary way to count points is through touchdowns. There are many different variations. An example is six points for touchdown scores—passing, rushing, receiving—all worth six points.

I imagine Kurt Warner was on our list of players at the start of the season. I rank the top one hundred players regardless of position and I know for certain he was not on that list. Among my quarterbacks I had Kurt Warner thirtieth behind Billy Joe Hobert and Doug Pederson after Green got hurt. Before Green got hurt, Warner was not ranked at all – nobody even thought about him. Now the season starts, he started putting up pretty good stats right from the beginning.

If you look at Warner, the first game in Baltimore – three touchdowns, three hundred nine yards passing, so I remember the atmosphere around here was kinda like, "Well, but it was against Baltimore" and nobody really thought too much about it. The following week they beat Atlanta 35-7. Warner threw another three touchdowns and ran for one. Now you're talking seven touchdowns in two weeks and that got Fantasy people to notice. It's still hard to be convinced because Atlanta stumbled out of the gate so badly this year. The next game they beat Cincinnati so you've got three games against not-so-great teams and they put up a lot of points each game and Warner was throwing the ball great. But it was still, "Well, they're not really playing anybody." But by the second and third weeks there was somebody in almost every fantasy league whose quarterback hadn't really been doing well. They needed somebody and Warner was probably one of the five or six available starting quarterbacks out there that they could just pick up off the waiver wire. During a season if a player gets hurt or if you are unhappy with how one of the guys on your fantasy team is playing, in most leagues you can pick up any player who had not been drafted and so Warner was one of those guys. By the second or third week, he was being picked up in those drafts. I had people write to me, even after the Baltimore game, "What do you think of this Warner guy? Is he for real?"

And at that point it was really hard to say, "Well yeah, Kurt Warner's for real. Go grab him quick as you can," because so many guys have one or two great games in the season. It's that consistency over the entire sea-

Troy Aikman wrote a book which had nothing to do with football. It was a kids' book called *Things Change*, and it sold an astonishing 200,000 copies.

son that you need. The defining game was that October 10 game against San Francisco when he had five touchdowns. I think that legitimized him across the board with football fans, fantasy players, and nonfantasy players. But by that game it was probably too late to go out and pick up Kurt Warner for their teams, he was already gone by then. I'd not seen before anyone put out his production as opposed to everybody's expectations for him. The expectations for him were zilch, and he has one of the great seasons in NFL history. Before the season I rank players, based on projected draft order. For football, it has been my experience, the majority of leagues just draft, not buy, players. So I actually do not deal much with the auction-type leagues in my commentary. For next season I haven't really thought too much about the rankings, but barring something crazy happening in the off-season, you would have to consider him to be the top quarterback out there and one of the top players if not THE first player overall.

Living in St. Louis, it was just really amazing. Every week it was just what's this guy gonna do this week and how long can this ride go on and how much crazier can the story get? At first, when Trent Green got hurt, it was the end of the world. Rams fans were hanging their heads in total dejection because they finally thought they had a quarterback in Trent Green. Then he gets hurt—well here we go again, same old Rams, another four and twelve season. So to not only see and get caught up in the emotion of the story of a guy like Kurt Warner, but the entire team from being so bad to Super Bowl champions. I mean he took that story, which was originally about him and his excellent play this year and made it first, a teamwide story of the Rams doing well, and then a citywide story with everybody in town getting behind the Rams and eventually the playoffs where it became a national story.

The B.C. character in *Doonesbury* is named after former Yale and Cleveland Browns quarterback Brian Dowling. The title character in the current sports comic strip *Gil Thorp* is named for Gil Hodges and Jim Thorpe.

WHERE CAN I FIND PETE ROSE CARDS WITH THE PULL-TABS ON THE BACK?
SCOTT KELNHOFER

Scott is one of the assistant editors, working as editor on a publication called Card Trade, *which is a trade journal for the industry, mostly for the shop owners, wholesalers, and manufacturers. The company is based in Iola, Wisconsin.*

K urt Warner was an interesting player in the NFL in the trading card standpoint for a number of reasons. The market, especially in the last two or three years, has really been a market that has thrived on speculation of rookie players. To go back a little bit into the peak of the collecting hobby, late '80s and early '90s, the rookie card hype was one of the reasons the industry at one point back in 1992 got to over a billion dollars a year in retail sales. A lot of that was caused by people who were buying up huge lots of individual player rookie cards with the hopes that if they bought them all at a penny or two cents each, five-ten years later they could turn around and sell them for a dollar, two dollars, five dollars, ten dollars, whatever the market would get up to. They weren't just buying one or two Ken Griffey Jr. '89 rookie cards. They were buying five hundred-card lots, one thousand-card lots, two thousand card-lots at thcsc initial priccs and hoping that a "three-home-run performance" or "rookie-of-the-year candidate," "rookie-of-the-year award" would drive the price up to seventy five cents or one dollar per card. It became really like penny stocks at that time. The market got away from that a little bit in the mid-'90s because it became apparent that you might have 2500 cards of Ken Griffey Jr. that you could sell, but you could also have 2500 cards of Jerome Walton that you couldn't sell. It became apparent that the real liquidity of many of these cards was minimal so people just got out of the market. As interest in rookies faded, the interest in the sports card market faded and that, combined with the baseball strike in '94 and other stuff, took our industry down to a fifty per cent drop in sales in a four-year time period.

What happened then, about 1997 or '98, companies were looking for ways to create excitement again in the rookies and really get avid rookie card collectors back in the sport. One of the ways of doing that was

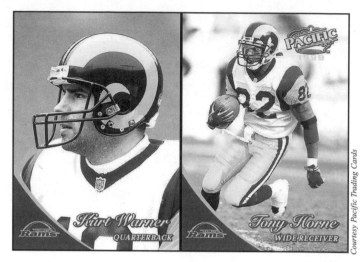

Kurt Warner was featured along with Tony Horne on this Pacific Trading Cards product.

Courtesy Pacific Trading Cards

"short printing" the rookie cards. Their cards would still be part of the regular set but their cards would be found in numbers smaller than the other cards in the base set. So you could have a short printing of rookie cards including Peyton Manning and his card would be found at a rate of one in five times harder to get than the standard player card in the set. That has really worked. It has created interest again in rookies. It has created an interest again in trying to add value to the base sets. Because for a number of years there, as the market was an exclusive interest in rookie cards, a lot of collectors put their resources into trying to collect limited-edition insert cards which are not part of the base set. It may be a card that's only found one in every one hundred-two hundred packs and are part of a little subset that's a little bit larger set. What was happening was people were opening up packs, looking for insert cards and if they didn't find them, a lot of people just throw away the cards they did have, and they didn't have an interest in them. They weren't trying to build a set they were just interested in these rare high-ticket, sometimes-valuable cards.

So what Warner did was that he brought an interest back again into the players who weren't the preseason hyped-up, expected-to-be "super stars." Tim Couch and Ricky Williams cards were red hot, and—April and May already—they hadn't stepped on the field yet, because of the interest in them beforehand. Nobody heard of Kurt Warner until obviously he got called into action the first week of the season. As a result, most of the card companies had also overlooked him with the exception of one, Pacific Trading Cards based in the Seattle area. They had included him in their 1999 Pacific Football product. In fact they pictured him on a card jointly with Tony Horne, the kick returner – on the same card together. Kind of like a throwback to the old Topps cards that paired baseball rookie prospects where you have more than one player on it. He shares this card and nobody thought anything of it really. In collecting terms, it was just another common card and was probably worth 25 cents on its release. It was just considered one more card in their set. But as the season went on and it became apparent that he was throwing touchdowns at an incredible rate, and it became apparent that this was his only card that had been produced to date, collectors suddenly began looking for this one card. Even though now companies are putting out products with Warner in it, the production window on training card sets for football is very small because it is a shorter season than other sports. You go to press with a product in late September for November release, it's kind of hard to project everyone who could possibly be a breakout player at the start of the season. By the time products are coming out in December and January, Warner was a part of some of those products but for much of the season most of the interest in him was strictly limited to this one trading card. So what started as a 25-cent card, by the time Monday, the day after the Super Bowl ended, the value of the card was about thirty-five dollars. If you go back to the old mentality of ten years ago, if you had purchased one hundred Kurt Warner cards at 35 cents each, and sold them today at thirty-five dollars each, you've done okay—a profit of $3,465 on a $35 investment.

So what started as a 25-cent card, by the time Monday, the day after the Super Bowl ended, the value of the card was about thirty-five dollars.

But I think what was just nice about the Kurt Warner situation is that, for the most part, in the sports collectibles industry, the interest in rookies is so high that everyone turns their attention to who is gonna be the next impact rookie. We can look ahead to the football draft this year and the interest is already there. Peter Warrick and Ron Dayne and a number of other players who are going to be first- round draft picks. Once in a while that player no one thought much of becomes a star. Terrell Davis is a perfect example and that creates a search, a hunt. "I've got to get something with him on it! I've got to get something he's signed! I've got to get something depicting him!" And it drives traffic into sports collectible stores and it creates instant demand for something that's not available. That thrill of the chase, that search, that finding something unique is something that's inherently fun to any collector whether it's coins of trading cards. So when you get a player that busts out on the scene, kind of out of nowhere, it can really set the industry on its ear a little bit and I think Warner has done that to a large extent this year.

In 1998 nothing was produced on Kurt Warner prior to the Pacific card. A third-string, or reserve, quarterback doesn't usually get cards produced on them. I guess during the days he played Arena Football in Iowa, Taco Johns, a local chain, produced a set of cards just of the team and he was on a couple of those. But nationally he was not on any. It's not unusual in the football card market for a second- or third-string quarterback not to be pictured on the trading card product because generally the card sets are about 150 players maybe 200 at most and they just generally don't go that deep into the roster unless it's a recognized name. Sometimes photo availability is a factor. If they go to press for a product to be released in September, October, they may still get a photo out of a training camp or of a preseason game if it's a real noteworthy player or someone who's changed uniforms, but they're not necessarily focusing a lot of efforts on these reserves. They might even just take a picture of him, in case someone gets hurt and they become a starter later in the year. With Warner's case, I don't know that anyone thought much about that other than Pacific. I think they have a larger set – maybe 300 cards and they get more players in there.

Three years from now if you look back the feeling won't necessarily be, "Well that Pacific card came out before all the others." It's possible that someone will produce a card that is scarcer and may eventually be considered slightly more valuable. But during this season, that Pacific card was the one collectors were chasing. For a while it was the only one and was still considered the first one. But as the years go by generally any card released during that season would be his rookie card. So anyone who put out a 1999 licensed product that had Kurt Warner in it, those would all be considered rookie cards. But this one, at least for the time being, is the one people are chasing because it is the first one that was there. If you were lucky enough to still get it at thirty cents, sixty cents, dollar fifty, two fifty, anywhere in that early progression, it's certainly one you're happy to watch the activity on in the price guides.

The Taco Johns card was not known to me; I have just heard about it. Regional issues do not tend to gain a lot of national prominence. They are not considered true rookie cards because they are not available to collectors nationwide. It's an unwritten rule in the hobby that a regional issue is not considered a true rookie card. That does not mean there won't be interest in it. The problem that you also have with regional issues is that they are very easy to counterfeit. They are also very easy to go back to press on. We have had instances in the past, I'm not saying this will or would happen with the Taco Johns thing, but it's not out of the realm of possibility. We've had things happen in the past where a company had done a regional release of a product, especially in the minor leagues, that had a player nobody had ever heard of at the time. Four or five years later he's starting in the major leagues and all of a sudden five-six thousand more of these sets show up. They're not necessarily licensed

The key players on a Super Bowl Championship team will have more interest shown in their cards.

by any professional sports league that monitors its print runs so there's just a lot of red flags that come up with regional issues. But I wouldn't be surprised to see interest on eBay hyping that regional card as the "first true Kurt Warner card, etc., etc." But even if there were only five hundred produced, there would be more collector value seen in a Pacific rookie card of which there may have been ten thousand available than there would in something that has only if it's a regional issue.

The key players on a Super Bowl Championship team will have more interest shown in their cards. Isaac Bruce, Marshall Faulk, and others have seen increased interest in their cards and generally it's stuff going back to their rookie seasons. The emphasis for today by card companies is to get as many of the skill position players in or a few of the impact defensive players. There was a philosophy at one time when the card sets were four hundred or five hundred cards each, that if you had (there was even a licensing rule at the time) to put the quarterbacks in there, you also had to include the center, the punter, right tackle, etc. The players association wanted everybody to get their "day in the sun" so to speak. The market just has no interest in cards of centers, right tackles and punters and so the philosophy in place now is you try to get a representation of every team that's out there but let's focus on the high-profile players. The other guys will still get their cut of the royalties from the overall licensing sales of cards, but let's focus on the most collectible players which tend to be quarterbacks, running backs, receivers, anyone who theoretically can score a touchdown—with a few defensive players who make impacts on their team. We are now dealing with card sets of one hundred fifty to two hundred cards, you just don't focus on a lot of those role-type players.

What you see now is interest in players like Warner, for autograph signings; Marshall Faulk, for autograph signings. Ten years ago what that would mean is that promoters of collectible shows would call up athletes or their agents and say, "We're having a card show in Louisville this weekend. We'll fly in Kurt Warner and pay him $10,000 for the weekend to come in and sign autographs for three hours." Often that's the way things were. But generally, the athletes are making so much money today, that even to get paid $50,000 for three hours of autograph signing, a lot of times it's just not worth their time and effort.

What's happening is we're seeing a lot of athletes now work with autograph companies who will sign a guy like Kurt to sign a thousand items in a private signing. That company will then act as a wholesaler and sell them to sports collectible stores, distributors, whatever; kind of act as a middle man and let those people get the product out. So I know Warner has signed at least one autograph deal so far – I think with TriStar Productions out of Houston. They had a show in St. Louis and brought him in. Then they said, "How about if we do some private signings with you and we'll offer your merchandise for sale around the country?" I think they had one signing session with him at some point after the regular season and have another one scheduled this month. I don't know how long their deal with him lasts but I know they were the first to lock him in to an exclusive autograph deal. If you want to have him for a signing, you have to go through them and they're the ones who have coordinated that so far.

Do you confuse Miami (Ohio) with Miami (Florida)?
Miami of Ohio was a school before Florida was a state.

I DON'T WANT TO DEPLETE YOUR INVENTORY SO I'LL JUST TAKE TWO MILLION PETE ROSE AUTOGRAPHS
JEFF ROSENBERG
TRI-STAR PRODUCTIONS, Houston, Texas

We're a large producer of sports collectible trade shows and produce autograph memorabilia, and we had a trade show in November of 1999 in St. Louis and wanted Kurt to be there but because of his practice schedule and playing schedule he wasn't able to make it. So we scheduled an autograph signing with him on a Friday, November 4 or 5. He couldn't come to the show so we just did a signing in a hotel and took orders from people and our customers. I actually attended the signing, and just really liked this guy – just one of those guys you could tell by meeting him he was a class act.

I really saw what kind of person he was and he fit the kind of profile we like to deal with, especially when we do it on an exclusive basis. At that time the Rams and Kurt were doing very well, but I'm still not sure a lot of the country were believers. But certainly Kurt was a believer in himself and that came out. He had a lot of self-confidence. I guess it was early December. We decided this is the type of guy we would like to do some things with and have at some of our card shows and do some autograph signings. In our industry, we find a lot of agents don't want to deal with a multitude of people. They kind of like one-stop shopping when they find someone they can trust. Some of those issues started coming out with his agent, and we decided it was certainly a fairly nice gamble for us at the time because who knew he would get where he is. So we decided to sort of partner and handle all of his autographs and make a commitment to do that. It looks like it's gonna work out pretty well.

We've been around – this is our fourteenth year in business. We started in 1987 putting on sports collectible shows in Houston, Texas. In fact the first autograph guest we ever had at a show was Mark McGwire, so we started on a pretty good roll. It was in November during the baseball off-season and we lived in Houston. We bought and traded baseball memorabilia at the time he came to Houston for us. At that time most of the people who came were people like Hank Aaron, Willie Mays, from that generation. I'm not from that generation and wasn't fortunate enough to get to see those guys play – too young. Mark McGwire was somebody who really attracted us, he was Rookie of the Year that year in 1987.

Mark was great; it was his rookie year – he had hit 49 home runs that season – very young guy. He signed the night before somewhere in Wisconsin and it had been below zero, freezing cold, snowing. He couldn't believe people had been waiting all night to meet him and get his autograph. Sure enough, the same thing happened Saturday night where he did an autograph signing show in Florida. Late Saturday night he came into Houston and people were camping out to meet him. On Sunday we had a line down a corridor of the hotel where we were and down a freeway street. He was a real pleasant guy to work with, very focused, similar to Warner and very confident in his abilities in himself. You don't see that a lot in young rookies. He saw himself going places. I feel like that with Warner. He just never had the opportunity and now once given the opportunity, boy, he has obviously thrived.

McGwire was our first in '87. We actually were in Houston and our next show we had Willie Mays and Don Drysdale. We charged six dollars an autograph and I think that's what we paid McGwire. There were one thousand autographs, one per person, and those sold out as fast as we could sell them. The first area outside of Houston was St. Louis in November of 1991 at the Cervantes Convention Center, now the America Center, which is actually attached to the TWA Dome where Kurt Warner plays. At that show we had Mickey Mantle and Ted Williams. I think they got twenty-five dollars per autograph. They were a big draw. Nine years ago, we had some of the players who were Blues at the time: Adam Oates, and a couple of their other players. We ended up going other places, Phoenix, Kansas City, and San Francisco and southern California, Milwaukee – about fourteen shows per year.

Early in the 1999 NFL season we were taking about "What do you think of this Kurt Warner?" I said, "I've been watching him and, man, they

> Cleveland Browns quarterback Tim Couch led the state of Kentucky in basketball scoring his junior year in high school.

look good. But, you know – they're the Rams! How are they gonna do?" As a Titan fan being here in Houston, I don't think people thought they were for real either. I did, so I said, "You know they have quite an offense. Who knows? The way the NFL is parity these days, anyone can win this thing." So we said, "Well, we'll try to have him in our show in St Louis."

We got in touch with him through his agent, and have personal relationships with them so we can contact the players. What we've read in the press: He's so religious. Several things were coming out – about this wonderkind kind of guy from bagging groceries to Arena Football League to NFL Europe. How's he's persevered and what type of person he is, he'd already made a statement. I believe that I had read somewhere, "Even if the Rams were gonna renegotiate, he wasn't interested in the money, he would give it to charity, he was there to play and to win – that kind of thing." Things you just don't hear out of the mouths of anyone, much less athletes, or anybody else in society, frankly. You could just kinda tell there was more to this guy than the average person, and certainly average athlete.

However, there are people who have won those trophies that people aren't interested in from a marketing standpoint because their conduct off the field is not like Kurt's, let's just say.

In the course of conversation with his agent, we both came to that kind of agreement whereby we have an exclusive with him. From our side of the business, it's good exposure – people know who he is. The hard core football fans knew Kurt Warner, but the average person on the street had no idea who Kurt Warner was. You know now he's in People magazine, and all the different newspapers, and going to Disney World, and that kind of thing. So it really puts him at another level where his name is talked about with the Joe Montanas, 'cause he broke his passing record, and the John Elways and the Favres. Still he has a lot to prove to become those type of players; those are people who did it consistently – the mark of a true champion. He's certainly not in that league and at that level but he has had a lot of notoriety at this point. We were very pleased. It certainly doesn't hurt what we were doing when he started to have success. You are dealing with the right person. However, there are people who have won those trophies that people aren't interested in from a marketing standpoint because their conduct off the field is not like Kurt's, let's just say. So it's more than just the awards, it's how he has handled himself off the field as well.

His endorsement future? It's gonna all depend obviously on how he performs on the field. It will be a hectic off-season for him but a very good one from a marketing standpoint, obviously, because he is such a great story. But you know, come August, September next year, it starts all over again. Everybody's coming at you. Last year it was Elway, this year it's Warner, and he's gonna have to keep doing it. Because now the expectation level is gonna be very high for him and he's gonna have to produce. He's just gonna have to work hard and keeps doing the things he's doing, there's certainly no reason to think things won't keep happening.

The late Jack Kent Cooke is the only owner who won both a Super Bowl title and an NBA title.

Chapter 13

Sister Mary Laurent

Cindy Teas

The Gold and Blue Brother... On a Mission from God

Paul and Cindy Teas, founders of Camp Barnabas

SHE SAID SHE WAS A NUN...YET SHE DIDN'T HAVE A GUITAR. AND GAMBLING WAS HER HABIT
SISTER MARY LAURENT

Sister Mary Laurent is a nun with the Order of the Sisters of St. Joseph based in St. Louis. The order received national notoriety previous to the Super Bowl when ESPN did a story on the Super Bowl pool of the nuns in the convent.

For the Super Bowl, we had two – a big sheet with all the numbers – of those filled – two complete pools. The wagers were only fifty cents and they drew every quarter so the winners would win twelve fifty – big deal. Naturally we, like everybody else in St. Louis, were all big Kurt Warner fans. It was all such a surprise, a very happy one, particularly after watching a year ago, and the year before that. There were eight winners in our Super Bowl pool, each winning twelve dollars and fifty cents, and I don't know how the "big winners" spent their money. We all know money doesn't grow on trees, and we all have budgets to get our toothpaste and such things. Winners were determined by drawings. I don't know how many took part in the pool because the big rollers took two chances. We had something going.

An ESPN person called one of our sisters on the Friday before the Super Bowl and asked if our community was doing anything like that. She said, "Well, of course." So they came and spent practically the whole day. They showed up when we were having nine thirty mass and took some films. Last June we had a golf tournament and one of the auction items was a Super Bowl party for thirty people. The food is all prepared at the kitchen at our Mother House and some of us went down to pick up the food and so they photographed us loading the cars. They stayed around and got more information. I happened to be one of the "toters" so I wasn't there the rest of the day.

They had a big Super Bowl dinner party at four o'clock, 'cause the game was going to start at five eighteen our time. The ESPN people came for the four o'clock, and stayed and watched the game there. And also watched the sisters watching the game. A number of our friends

Sister Mary Ann Nestel with an autographed Kurt Warner jersey

saw it, and even people out of town called to say, "Hey, that was neat." Any reactions that we got were very favorable. The sisters in the convent are very happy to know that Kurt recognizes he gets his talent from somewhere else – that God has something to do with it. Plus, it's rather heartening to hear a public figure like that who is willing to give God the credit.

Warner did leave the church – what is he, a born-again Christian? I know a number of people do have circumstances and decide the Catholic Church is really not for them so we presume that something like that happened. But regardless, certainly his holding on to all the moral values and spiritual values we hope he learned when he was younger is wonderful to see.

In most states, sports betting pools are legal as long as "the house" – or person running the pool – doesn't benefit.

EVERY FALL MILLIONS OF PEOPLE GO TO THE OZARKS TO WATCH THE LEAVES CHANGE COLORS. I STAY HOME, DON'T WATER MY PLANTS. SAME THING, LESS COST

CINDY TEAS

Cindy Teas, along with her husband Paul, runs Camp Barnabas, a camp for children with disabilities or special needs, in Purdy, Missouri, about four hours southwest of St. Louis. She once ran in far different circles than her current commitment to God's work. She grew up in suburban Dallas, Texas, where she knew many of the Dallas Cowboys in the early '70s and for several years dated Don Talbert, a Cowboy, who, along with his brother Diron, were known as the legendary Varmint brothers. In talking with Cindy, it was kind of like finding out that Mother Teresa was once good friends with Joe Namath. Camp Barnabas is just a wonderful, wonderful camp for young people and one that Kurt Warner has been very instrumental in helping grow.

T he story of our camp is such a God thing. We weren't two people with a lot of money; we weren't two people with a lot of knowledge. We were just two people who had a passion to help kids with special needs. To know the Lord and God took that passion and has just blessed it and every place we turned he opened a door when we thought it was closed. People ask how we did it, and we say "We didn't, God did it. Let me tell you the story because we couldn't have done it. We did not have the resources." Like Paul Newman has a camp. Well, my gosh, Paul Newman has enough money to do the camp himself plus enough connections. We were just two simple people working on a camp salary for a ministry ourselves. God said don't be afraid. If I call you to do something, I'll equip you. We've had it five years this month.

A friend of ours, Don, who volunteers at our camp was a piano teacher for the Warner's son and he said, "You've got to send your son to that camp." So Kurt called and said Don had told them about the camp and he'd like to know more about it. We're very interested in it because we want our child to have a Christian experience. And that's where it started. We are a Christian camp which specializes in serving special needs children and their families. We're thirty miles west of Springfield, Missouri. This was in February of 1999. At that time we had not heard of Kurt Warner.

We went to St. Louis and met with Kurt and his wife, Brenda, in their home. They were just down-to-earth, neat people. He said, "I'm going to be interviewed on the Leeza Gibbons show and from everything you've told me (we'd given them a video), and based on Don's recommendation, I think we are on the same page. We want the quality of life for our child, and obviously quality of life includes God as the primary focus. Your focus is special needs children and making the quality of their life better by introducing them to Jesus so I'd like to have your permission to talk about you on the *Leeza* show." We were like, "YES, we'd love it!"

She interviewed several quarterbacks who have specials needs children. It was kind of unusual. Kurt and Brenda, Doug Flutie and two others whose children have a terminal illness were on with their wives. Kurt asked permission to talk about us on the show when they asked, "What is your favorite charity?" We said we were honored; it would be great! That was the beginning of our relationship.

They were new to the St. Louis area, had been there less than a year. Brenda mentioned their struggles in finding a good Bible study group and a good church to go to so I called some friends and got them to invite her. We started building a friendship and relationship through that process. Then I invited her – she's a nurse – to come to camp as a camp nurse. I said, "Why don't you come as a camp nurse while Kurt is away at training camp? You wouldn't be alone with the kids and you would be able to be serving the Lord." She thought that was great and said she would love to do that. She came and worked a week at our camp as a volunteer nurse. It was really neat.

Kurt was away at training camp. He would call her each evening and she would share her prayer requests – you know the struggles he was having

During Super Bowl III, the Jets' amazing upset of the Baltimore Colts, Joe Namath did not attempt a pass in the fourth quarter.

in camp. She told us when she left it was really neat. She said, "God has a plan for Kurt and I'm so proud he hasn't given up on himself and he knows that and trusts the Lord's plan." Then look what happened.

They are every bit as nice a people as the media portrays them. Just as down to earth and he loves his children and wants to see that they know the Lord and that their life has quality to it. He loves football. The greatest statement he ever made to us is that, "I just want to play football; I don't care how much they pay me. I just love to play. I don't want to sit on the bench." That's how it should be.

My husband and teenage son are great football fans but I was one of those people who read a book while the game was on and looked out of the corner of my eye. But once you know someone personally that plays, it totally changes. You have a vested interest in their well-being and then to know that he could make a Godly example of himself, he could show young men that God does bless the lives of those who put their faith in him and follow his plan. We have such poor examples in a lot of the athletes. As the mom of teenagers, I'm going "Go Kurt!" because he's bold in his faith. We were talking to him after about his third or fourth interview with people early in the season when he first started doing well. He said, "You know it made me angry because I said a lot of stuff about the reason I felt I'd been moved into this position is that God honored my patience and my perseverance and they always cut that part out." That's the only time I've ever seen him act even a little bit angry. He said, "I just wanted to give God the glory for it; this is not about me. This is about the Lord." And it's so genuine. And it's like I told someone else who interviewed us, you've got to remember that Kurt was a Christian first and then he became the Most Valuable Player in the NFL. He didn't become the Most Valuable Player and then decide, "Well, it would look good if I was a Christian." He was a Christian first and walked in faith first.

I had always watched the Super Bowl before but kinda out of the corner of my eye while I was doing something else. I cannot tell you how excited I was. We were glued to it, and cheering. You'd have thought we were at the game. Kurt is so down to earth.

This is what a simple, good old Iowa boy he is. Our own son has had some struggles, got injured, had a hard year. He's a freshman in high school, playing on a small-town team. One day Kurt called us to discuss

> **Once you know someone personally that plays, it totally changes.**

fund raising, and I said, "Oh, I've got to go. My son has a football game, and I've got to get there. " He asked when he played and I said oh it's two hours, but it takes us an hour and a half to get there. He said, "Has his bus left?" I said, "I don't think so; it should in the next few minutes." He said, "Okay, I'm gonna call him and encourage him." And he did. When my son got home, he couldn't even come down out of the clouds. "Kurt called and encouraged me," and it meant so much to him. He told him, "If God had given him a passion for football to know it was from Him and to trust Him with it for whatever direction it was going." That was so incredible!

Then PBL Sports in Pittsburgh contacted Kurt and asked if they could do the cereal for him. He said yes if they could donate the proceeds to his favorite charity, Camp Barnabas. They said sure, and not only that we'll give them a side panel. This was from a guy who was making minimum wage in the NFL. Then when he first moved into first string, one of the first things he did was call us and said I'd like for you both to get on the phone. So my husband and I were both on the phone with Kurt and Brenda. He said, "Brenda and I were talking last night. They are going to start negotiating a new contract, and I want you to know we are both so comfortable and we have such a good life, and God has blessed us so much and we would like to share the blessings. When the contract comes through we would like to share these blessings primarily with Camp Barnabas and with our church and we wanted you all to know that and not hear it through the media. We wanted you to hear it through us first and that's our commitment. We want more Camp Barnabases; we want Camp Barnabas to succeed and we know that what you are doing for the Lord is right and we want to assist you with the blessings we have financially." I can't tell you how much that means to us. It takes more than Kurt Warner. It takes a lot of money to do summer camp.

Just having, it sounds trite, it come from someone who is not as neat a Christian man – sure we would need the money and would want it, but we want it to be the money the Lord wants us to have and that felt so right. We hung up the phone and it was indescribable. God has been so good.

After Zack left last summer we kept in touch. We still are amazed with the cereal and the pictures that are on the box. I sent all the kids whose pictures were on the box a box of the cereal and said, "You've been found. You're a star now." The parents comment saying, "Oh my gosh, this is so cool." It means so much to them to be special. What's really neat is there is a little girl in a wheelchair on the side of the cereal and she found the Lord at camp her first year. And she now is a junior counselor and it meant so much to her. She said, "It's just amazing what God has done for me." So it's just neat to see how the blessings are spread around to all the kids.

I think the Kurt-Brenda story is .... I said to Brenda last summer before he was well-known, "When your baby was injured and then your husband left you did you just feel like your life has collapsed around you?" She said, "I would have except for my faith. I realized one day that I had nothing to rely on but God and when you're at that point, you totally rely on Him and just surrender it all. From that point on, I knew that Zachary would be okay and I'd be okay – that God had a plan and a purpose for all this that was happening in our lives. Then a few years later, enter Kurt. He's one of the most kind people, who loved my children before he loved me." So their story is such a Cinderella story in itself. Then when I look at our camp, it's such a Cinderella story. In America it used to be: Get rich; everybody could make it. It gets harder. It's usually those who have who do better. To see two simple people who have the guts to try something and to stick their necks out make it just tells me it's totally the Lord. When the Lord wants it to happen, it does.

> **I realized one day that I had nothing to rely on but God and when you're at that point, you totally rely on Him and just surrender it all.**

Paul and I went to two of the St. Louis games. I'd been to pro games several years ago when Mike Ditka played for the Dallas Cowboys. I became good friends with one of the Cowboys, Donny Talbert, and went to a lot of their games but those were the first Rams games I'd been to. I was a big football fan in my younger years and it was so interesting to hear you talk about Ditka 'cause I knew him back in his real wild crazy Dallas Cowboy days. I had since heard a lot about how he had really turned his life over to the Lord and is witnessing to other players and I thought that was so great. At that time I was not the Christian I am today and it's neat to have the Lord say I have something for you now you just go with it. I hung out with their wives all the time. It was a neat fun experience. Ditka, Charlie Waters, Donny Talbert, Leroy Caffey, LeRoy Jordan, and Walt Garrison hung out a lot together, and I was always with them and went to all the games. I laugh now because it is so different now. Even though the Cowboys were really a great team at that time, it was still a whole different flavor from the way the players are today. The players didn't make millions of dollars. We went to the state fair together and people flogged us and asked for autographs but we could still have a personal life. But now they've turned the players into such gods of themselves that I think it really impedes the personal life of the players. It's a great blessing, don't take me wrong, but my husband was visiting with the Warners and went to church with them, which is probably the only safe haven they have in their life right now. When they go to dinner, people flog them, in the parking lot, people are after him. So really they don't do much of anything except go to games, interviews, and things like that. They don't have any personal life that people don't infringe on.

I have a twin sister. My twin and her husband and Don and all of us went to Redksins weekend – Redskins versus Cowboys. Back in Dallas years ago, Diron Talbert and some big Redskins guys, huge people, decide they'll join us for our birthday dinner. So it was a big deal. Diron and Don's team would play each other and so we go out to dinner with these four Redskins and three Cowboys, my sister and I and her husband and all their wives. We're at a table for twelve, fourteen people and they get to playing their Varmint act until the waitress was ready to wring our neck. Finally the manager said, "I'll pay you to leave." It was all in fun. They weren't bad boys. But they were Varmints, and my roommate couldn't stand it. They always had a practical joke to play on us every time they came around. It was too much fun. They were the bad boys and definitely knew how to get in trouble.

My sister told me about a year ago she ran into Leroy Caffey's wife and they stood and talked forever 'cause I had lost touch with all of them after I got married and moved away. She was just saying that all the guys have settled and have great home lives. Don married very late, has two beautiful children, then his wife had cancer and died while the children are still pretty young. So he's had that tragedy, but he's settled into being a real neat dad and a great family man and my sister said I can't imagine that. My roommates used to go, "Please get those guys out of here." They had all these little varmints, that's why they called them The Varmint Brothers. They always played tricks with these little pretend raccoons, rats, etc. They had these stuffed animals and they were always hiding them and my roommate would be screaming.

Like I said it was all in jest, it was never bad-boy stuff – like drinking and carousing. I rarely saw Don take a drink; he was really committed to being in shape – just craziness and pranks. They had an RV that we traveled around in and tried to promote Dolph Brisco for governor of Texas at the shopping centers and places like that. I'd get on the RV never knowing what to suspect that I was gonna sit on – there always had to be something if they were both on it. Now Don by himself wasn't nearly as rowdy as when Diron was in town. Their older brother, Charlie, who was never in pro football but he was a captain of the University of Texas team, was much calmer, but get the three of them together and he was one of the team.

We were at a Rams thing with Brenda and met a bunch of the players' wives and a bunch of the coaches and people, and I was going, "I know that person from the Varmint days." I said to Brenda, "Be glad that the football player you met was a really good one because there's some real varmints out there. But like I said, Don was one of the most sincere caring people you could ever have for a friend. He was a good man, just crazy. Don Meredith was already retired from the team, He came to some of the fund-raising stuff but I never got to know him well.

Some of the things that Kurt shared with us is what he really wanted was an opportunity to play football. The reason it's important to him to win is because it gives him a chance to be in front of the camera and tell people what it's about is God. That's what it's about to him. "I love playing ball and this is my avenue to witnessing to people." If anything, we feel he has held on tighter to the need to be Brenda's partner in life and to have a family first. The harder the media pushed, the harder the fame has gotten to handle personally, the more he's leaned on his family first.

This is such an awesome, incredible, amazing day for us, too. We just kinda came to work not expecting that our phone would ring off the wall. It's been great. If there's one thing I want to say, it's that Kurt's heart is totally in the right place. He loves God. He loves his family, and he loves football. He feels like the financial blessings God has given him, he wants to use to further the kingdom with it. I can't think of a better person to have on our team. He's such a mature man – not just spiritually mature, but like when he met Brenda he understood that loving her kids was the important thing. There aren't many men, who have not had their own child, he was like 20 years old, who could go there that could even entertain that responsibility and it didn't scare him at all.

Another benefit of his character, yes he had some hardships growing up but it developed him into such a neat man.

FINAL PAGE

There are some enduring mysteries of life:
What exactly does George Hamilton do for a living,
why is Peter Gammons' picture on the twenty dollar bill,
where do they find artificial lawn mowers for artificial turf,
why do sky divers wear helmets,
and why can't every man conduct his affairs
like Kurt Warner?

Go now.

APPENDIX

Kurt Warner had his appendix removed on May 16, 2000 at
Missouri Baptist Medical Center in St. Louis, MO.